The Complete Idiot's Mac Ref

Command-Key Roundup

Here's a handy-dandy table of the command-key combinations. Learn them when you have a chance—they'll save you time.

Action	Key Combination
Open any icon	Double-click on the icon, or select the icon, and then press ⌘-↓.
Copy an icon into another folder (without moving original)	Hold down the **Option** key while dragging the icon.
Clean up selected icons in a window	Hold down the **Shift** key while selecting **Clean Up** from the **Special** menu.
Clean up and sort icons alphabetically	Hold down the **Option** key while selecting **Clean Up** from the **Special** menu.
Select an icon by name	Type the first few letters of the name.
Select the next icon, alphabetically	Press the **Tab** key.
Select the previous icon, alphabetically	Press the **Shift** and **Tab** keys.
Select an icon to the left or right (in Icon views)	Press → or ←.
Select an icon above or below (any view)	Press ↑ or ↓.
Select multiple icons	Shift-click on the icons, or drag-select to enclose icons.
To make desktop active	Press ⌘-**Shift**-↑.
Close all windows	Press **Option** key while selecting **Close** under **File** menu, or press **Option** key while clicking on **Close** box.
Move a window without making it active	Hold down ⌘ key while dragging the window's title bar.
Display a window's lineage	Hold down ⌘ key while clicking the window title.
Open a window's parent window	Press ⌘-↑.
Close a window after opening an icon in it	Hold down the **Option** key while selecting **Open** from the **File** menu, or hold down the **Option** key while double-clicking on the icon.
Zoom a window to full screen size	Hold down **Option** key while clicking its Zoom Box.

ZIP!

There are also shortcuts for certain commands. Use these to perform Macintosh actions in a flash.

New Folder (file)	⌘-N	Paste	⌘-V
Open	⌘-O	Select All	⌘-A
Close Window	⌘-W	Print	⌘-P
Save	⌘-S	Find	⌘-F
Cut	⌘-X	Undo	⌘-Z
Copy	⌘-C	Duplicate (file)	⌘-D
Make Alias	⌘-M		

Mouse Movements

Point   Move the mouse pointer so that it rests on a specific screen location.

Click   Quickly press and release the left mouse button.

Double-click   Quickly press and release the left mouse button twice in succession.

Drag   Press and hold down the mouse button, and then move the mouse.

When Things Go Flaky

If you have any trouble with your Mac, the first thing you should do is check the obvious:

- Is everything plugged in and turned on?
- Are cables connected securely to your Mac and the peripherals?
- Are the correct cables plugged into the correct peripherals?
- If it's a monitor problem (say, no picture), check the contrast and brightness controls.
- Are you using the right software for the hardware (the correct printer driver in the Chooser, the right telecommunications software for the service, and so on)?
- What's the dumbest thing you could have forgotten to do? Check that, too—check it twice.

Cool Tip #1

You can take a picture (a screenshot) of your Mac's screen just like those used in this book: just press the ⌘-**Shift-3** combination. The picture will be saved on your hard drive; you can view it or print it out with SimpleText.

Cool Tip #2

That little box in the upper left-hand corner of a window is the **Close Box**. When you click on it, the window closes.

Cool Tip #3

If you want to see every item in a window, you can quickly size the window to fit exactly around everything by clicking on the **Zoom Box**. It's in the upper right-hand corner of the window.

alpha
books

The

COMPLETE

IDIOT'S

GUIDE TO

the Mac,
Second Edition

by John Pivovarnick

**alpha
books**

A Division of Macmillan Computer Publishing
A Prentice Hall Macmillan Company
201 W. 103rd Street, Indianapolis, IN 46290 USA

International Standard Book Number:1-56761-534-1
Library of Congress Catalog Card Number: 94-78339

96 95 94   8 7 6 5 4 3 2

Interpretation of the printing code: the rightmost number of the first series of numbers is the year of the book's printing; the rightmost number of the second series of numbers is the number of the book's printing. For example, a printing code of 94-2 shows that the second printing of the book occurred in 1994.

Screen reproductions in this book were created by means of the program Collage Complete from Inner Media, Inc., Hollis, NH.

Printed in the United States of America

Publisher
Marie Butler-Knight

Managing Editor
Elizabeth Keaffaber

Acquisitions Editor
Barry Pruett

Product Development Manager
Faithe Wempen

Development Editor
Heather Stith

Production Editor
Mark Enochs

Copy Editor
San Dee Phillips

Cover Designer
Scott Cook

Designer
Barbara Kordesh

Illustrations
Judd Winick

Indexer
Bront Davis

Production Team
Gary Adair, Dan Caparo, Brad Chinn, Kim Cofer, Lisa Daugherty, David Dean, Cynthia Drouin, Jennifer Eberhardt, David Garratt, Erika Millen, Beth Rago, Bobbi Satterfield, Karen Walsh, Robert Wolf

Special thanks to Bob Zigon for ensuring the technical accuracy of this book.

Contents at a Glance

Contents

Introduction

The Complete Idiot

The following is an excerpt from the transcript of the December 1, 1989 meeting of the CIA: *Complete Idiot's Anonymous*. The names have been changed to protect the guilty.

J: Hi. My name's John... no, really, it *is*... and I'm an idiot.

CIA: Hi, John!

J: I didn't realize until a couple years ago how big an idiot I really am.

CIA: How many years ago was that?

J: (mutters something)

CIA: How many years?

J: Ten years, all right? Ten. Are you happy?

CIA: Calm down. No one's trying to embarrass you. Admitting your idiocy is an important first step.

J: I'm sorry... it's just (whimpers)...

CIA: It's okay. What made you think you had a problem?

J: That darn computer.

CIA: Oooooooh. Computer.

J: I wouldn't read manuals, or ask questions. I'd just try to figure things out on my own. You know, by trial and error. Mostly error.

CIA: And?

J: And when I hit a problem I couldn't fake my way through, I'd read the manual, but I could barely understand them (sobbing). After ten years, I still can't get my first printer to underline or do boldface!

CIA: (nods and murmurs of agreement) So what happened?

J: I did what any self-respecting idiot would do. I bought another printer.

CIA: Tsk-tsk. You've got it bad.

J: Gosh, I feel better just admitting that.

CIA: Thanks for sharing, John.

It Takes One to Know One

I don't know how often I've said, "I feel like such an idiot." At least a dozen times a day—more if I was heavily into some project or another. But that was before I got help, before I admitted I was an idiot and started on the road to recovery.

When a computer, even a plug-and-play Macintosh, smells fear on you, it pushes at it and pushes at it until you're ready to snap, or until you show it who's boss. I know. I've been there. That story about the printer was true. I had that sucker for almost six years, and I couldn't get the bloody thing to do what I wanted. If I got it to underline, I couldn't get it to stop. If I got it to do letter-quality printing, I couldn't get it to do italics. I was ready to take a baseball bat to it.

Instead, I bought a new printer, and things have gone swimmingly. However, buying new equipment is not a practical solution for most problems. I learned that the hard way, too. I've learned many things on my personal road to recovery. I fell into a lot of traps and pitfalls I'd like to see you avoid. If I could, I'd include a big picture of me from my brazen idiot days, with bags under my eyes and cowlicked hair. There would be three-inch-tall red letters stamped over my face, warning everyone: **DON'T LET THIS HAPPEN TO YOU!**

Instead, let me pass on the tips and tricks I've learned about dealing with computers in general and Macs in particular. Here comes the first tip, and it's a biggie. Keep it in mind as you go through the rest of the book: *You* **are not the idiot. The** *Macintosh* **is the idiot.**

Much as it pains me to say this about a machine I dearly love, Macs are stupid. *Stoo*-pid! As simple and elegant as they are, they are still only machines. They do exactly what they're told to do. If you tell your Mac to do two conflicting things at once, that dopey little machine will try its best to do both, even if it blows up in the process. If there is any problem you or I have in dealing with our Macs, it's that we're too smart. We know what we want to do and how we want to do it. If we happen to forget an important step, well, that's okay. We can improvise and make it up as we go along.

If you try to get a Mac to keep step with the way your mind leaps around, it goes nuts. Why? Because they can't figure things out. Macs don't think, "Oh, he must have meant this," and then just do it. They can only do exactly what you tell them to do, with the tools (software) you give them to do it. If the information or the tools aren't appropriate to the job, Macs (or any computer) will crash. When they crash, we feel like idiots. That's not the way it should be. Remember:

➤ Macs take everything literally.

➤ You have to learn to think like a Mac.

➤ Therefore, you have to take everything literally.

How's that for logic? Sister Margo (my high school geometry teacher) would be so proud.

The aim of this book, aside from enlightening and entertaining you, is to show you how your Mac works, thinks, and does things. You will learn how to tell it exactly what you want it to do, without giving it (or you) a nervous breakdown.

How to Use This Book

If I were you (which I'm not), I'd read or skim the book once straight through, and then I'd put it beside my Mac where it is within easy reach for questions or problems when they crop up.

The book is organized (I hope) logically. Part I shows you how to unpack and assemble your Mac. If your Mac is already up and running, you can probably skip Part I or skim ahead to Part II.

Part II deals exclusively with Mac basics: using System 7.5's spiffy new features, formatting disks, copying files and folders, moving things around, throwing junk away, and keeping things clean and safe. All this good stuff lays the groundwork for Part III.

Part III covers Mac *applications* (or programs). You'll find the scoop on the stuff that came with your Mac (those Desk Accessories, SimpleText, and such), everything from starting them up and using them to shutting them down. It also explains the ins and outs of fonts and printing.

Part IV is a mixed bag. It gives you advice on where you can go with your Mac in the future, how to shop for more stuff, and how to deal with the peculiarities of PowerBooks. It also rounds up and reviews all the major application and hardware types that didn't come with your Mac; the stuff that, if you want it, you have to go out and buy. Most importantly, it gives you a big, fat section on troubleshooting some of the most common problems that crop up in Macintosh computing. There's also a section on installing System software. Sure, your Mac came with it installed, but as my white-haired mom is so fond of saying: *poop happens*. Usually she says it with a grandson's diaper in her hand, but I think it applies to both Macs and life. Bringing up the rear is a glossary of sorts, with a plethora of the computer-ese terms in one easy section. Be warned: these are not definitions according to Mr. Webster—these are my definitions.

Let's move on. Everyone, stay together, and remember where you parked your car.

Convenient Conventions

The thing I like most about writing this stuff is I get to tell people what to do. To make it easier for you to follow what I want you to do, there are several conventions used throughout the book.

If I want you to type something, I'll say something clever, like:

Type **Poop Happens**.

And I'll expect you to type whatever comes after "Type." I'll put it in **boldface** so it's easy to spot. In this example, for some reason, I want you to type "Poop Happens." I don't know why I'd want you to type that; it's just an example.

If I want you to press a couple of keys on your keyboard at the same time, I'll say:

Press ⌘-**W**

That means press and hold down the ⌘ key (also known as the Command key or the key with the little squiggle that looks like a four-petaled flower on it—it all depends on what keyboard you have). While you're holding that key down, press the second key. In this example, it's the **W**. These key-combinations are very handy. The ⌘-W combination will close a window in almost any Mac application. You'll be hearing more about key combinations later.

You should know that the first key of most key combinations will invariably be one of three: either the ⌘/Command/ Flower-thingy key, the Control key, or the Option key. They're usually located at the right or left of the Spacebar. Find them now; I'll wait.

When it comes to mousing around, I'll ask you to click, double-click, or even triple-click on things. That means I'll want you to move the mouse pointer to something, then click once, twice, or three times on it. If it's an icon, I'll say, "Double-click on the **System Folder** (or whatever) icon." If it's a menu item, I'll say, "Click on the **File** (or whatever) menu." If it's a button in a dialog box, I'll say "Click on the **Cancel** (or whatever) button." Notice how I cleverly made the words **File** and **Cancel** bold? That's a clue that I'm expecting you to *do* something with that menu item or button.

Finally, I may give you a list of several things to do. They'll show up in a numbered list like this:

1. Click on the **Special** menu, and hold down the mouse button.

2. With mouse button still pressed, move the pointer down the menu until you highlight the **Empty Trash** item.

3. Release the mouse button.

If none of this pointing, clicking, and selecting means anything to you, don't worry. I'll go over every excruciating detail in Chapter 4, before you need to do any of it. Don't panic.

Geekazoid Stuff You Can Ignore

As if actually expecting you to do stuff wasn't bad enough, I'm also going to give you the opportunity to learn things that go above and beyond the call of duty. None of it is absolutely, positively essential. The world will not end if you ignore it, but it can make your computing life a little easier, maybe even more fun. If you're interested, you'll find the scoop in boxes like these:

These explain some of the more technical information on the Macintosh. You'll find some behind-the-scenes information about the working of Macs and applications presented in a painless way. It may interest you; it may not. If it does interest you, you may be a potential propeller-head.

These define some of the more technical terms in ways a non-propeller-head can understand. If nothing else, you'll be able to work words like **propeller-head** into any conversation.

These contain quick tips and work-arounds that save you time and keep you from tearing your hair out. That ⌘-W key combination that closes a window would fit in well here.

These contain warnings and other helpful information for when things go worng… er, *wrong*.

On Your Mark

This is the newly revised edition of this book. The old saying, "The more things change, the more they stay the same" is in full force. Even though the last time we were here, the Power Macintosh was just hype and talk, now it's real. System 7 just turned 7.1; now it's 7.5 (don't ask what happened to points 2, 3, and 4). CD-ROM drives are now pretty common options. In spite of all the changes and new junk hitting the stores, it still seems like it was all designed to make us feel… well, idiotic (I've been fighting with a goofy little hand scanner for a week, trying to keep it from turning my SCSI chain into chopped liver—baseball bats were reached for).

Rest assured, if you're coming to this from the first edition (thanks, by the way), it's still the same pain-free, slightly loopy approach to Macintosh. There are no monsters in here. If you're coming at this fresh, you'll see.

Part I
Some Assembly Required

The phrase "Plug and Play" was coined for the original Mac. All you had to do then was plug the keyboard into the computer, the mouse into the keyboard, and the whole thing into a power outlet. You were ready to play.

Naturally, things are a little more complicated now. You can't even buy a new compact-style Mac in the U.S. anymore (like the old Volkswagen Beetle, you have to leave the country to get one), but the main difference is that there's a little more plugging to do. Big deal. (In an effort to promote peace, the obligatory IBM-compatible computer insult is herewith deleted. Other forms of pointless intolerance and violence should be so easily dispensed with.)

Before you get to the actual assembly stuff, there's a list of the top ten things you should know about your Mac before you use it. If your Macintosh is already together and humming on your desk, you may talk quietly among yourselves and skim Part I or skip to Part II (after you check out the top ten).

SKIP HAD SOME TROUBLE WITH THE NEW SOFTWARE

Chapter 1

The Least You Need to Know

Most folks don't pick up a *Complete Idiot's Guide* unless the idea of dealing with a computer makes them a little queasy—even the folks who chose a Mac because it's "the easy one" may be feeling a *little* nauseous. Let me set your mind (and possibly your stomach) at ease: You were right; Macs are easy.

Even though there are a little over 300 pages of tips, tricks, and information here, there are ten really simple concepts that will calm you down and get you into the spirit of Macintosh. Take a couple of deep breaths and plunge ahead.

Ready? Here they come:

1. Easy-to-use is easy to say, but the Mac truly is easy to use.

From dealing with files and folders to adding hardware and software, the Mac remains the plug-and-play beauty it was when it first appeared in 1984. Don't panic; you picked the right machine.

2. You can have your Macintosh up and running in very little time.

If it takes you more than 20–40 minutes to hook up your Mac, I'll be very surprised. I know people who are *such* idiots I wonder how they find their way home at night, but I've seen these same people set up their Macs in 30 minutes or less.

The little pictures on the ports and plugs *really* help. If you can figure out what those international traffic signs mean (you know, the ones with the little stick figures on them rather than words), you can put a Mac together (see Chapter 3 for more information).

3. No matter what DOS-aficionados say, the Mac is not a toy.

The fact that even children can master the basics of a Mac in no time just annoys DOS users (see Chapter 5). Macs are serious, capable machines that can handle just about any task you can throw at them (given the right hardware and software tools). They're appropriate for personal, educational, home, business, and even personal home-business use. If a DOS user tries to give you grief over your computer preference, just agree to disagree.

Although Macs are serious machines, they should not be taken seriously. They're easy and fun to use. You shouldn't get gray hair trying to type up a report or a shopping list—or anything else for that matter.

4. You have to format floppy disks before you can use them to store junk.

Chapter 9 goes over this stuff in excruciating detail—well, I hope it isn't excruciating, but it is, shall we say, *complete.*

The beauty of Macintosh is that since you *shouldn't* use a disk that hasn't been formatted, you *can't* use a disk that hasn't been formatted. If you happen to forget that little fact, your Mac will politely remind you.

5. You can customize the way your Mac works and looks.

My Mac has custom icons all over the place, custom startup screens (to replace that boring "Welcome to Macintosh"), and a fleet of funky sounds. I have other customizing doodads (extensions and control panels) out the wazoo. I rotate the custom features in and out of use to suit my mood—and I'll be the first one to tell you, I can be pretty moody.

My favorites include: a startup screen featuring Michaelangelo's Creation of Man scene from the Sistine Chapel; Ren & Stimpy disk icons, and a pile of sounds from the *Wizard of Oz* ("Are you a good witch, or a bad witch?").

The inclusion of AppleScript in System 7.5 (see Chapter 12) lets you customize and automate things you do every day with the Finder and with applications that are *scriptable*—many are, and many more will be.

6. You can work with your Mac right out of the box: you already have some software!

You may not have enough software to write the Great American Novel, but you certainly have enough to tackle the Great American Memo or Thank-You Note (see Chapter 12).

If you were lucky (or smart), you bought a Mac that came bundled with some additional software to get you started (one of the integrated Works packages), in which case, you probably *can* tackle the Great American Novel. I'd like an autographed copy, please.

7. There's a full range of software available for your Mac, suitable for home, business, or educational uses.

Chapter 16 gives you the lowdown on what's out there.

8. You can easily add accessories, such as CD-ROM drives, scanners, and other exciting equipment, to Macs.

In addition to the software and hardware roundups in Chapters 16 and 17, Chapter 15 gives you some pointers on how to shop. (How's that old adage go: *The best revenge is shopping well…*) For the terminally curious, there are even parts of Chapter 15 devoted to the hardware and software *I* own, and what I'd spring for if someone else was footing the bill (like that would happen).

9. Once you learn a standard command in one application, you'll know it for all Mac applications (see Chapter 6).

10. Lighten up! This is Macintosh. It's supposed to be the fun one.

Computing can be a scary and very serious business, especially if your livelihood or sanity depends upon it. That's a given. However, you shouldn't have to fight with your computer to get your very important work done. You'll find a lot of space and words in this book devoted to what to do when things go wrong. It doesn't mean that because I spend a lot of time talking about bad things that can happen, you'll be spending a lot of time dealing with them (boy, it's hard to find real wood to knock on, these days). Call it an ounce of prevention, and stop worrying. This stuff is easy, once you get the hang of it.

Chapter 2

A Field Guide to Macintosh Computers

In This Chapter

➤ CPU chips and quips

➤ Rachel Hunter... or the current models

➤ Models coming down the pike

You may want to think of this chapter as a humongous Techno Nerd Teaches. It's just dripping with technical information (wait, I'll get the mop) about the current crop of Macintosh computers. If you're thinking about buying a Mac, you may want to read or skim through all of it in order to put the various models' power and features into perspective. If you already have a Mac, you may want to see whether I included your model, so you can have the *Reader's Digest* condensed scoop on yours without having to slog through the technical specifications section of the manual, armed with a Geek-to-English dictionary. If you don't give a rat's hindquarters, just skip it. It will still be here if you change your mind.

But first...

A Word of Warning

Every month, when the new crop of Mac magazines lands with a thud on my coffee table, I feel like Dorothy in the land of Oz, whining, "Macs come and go so quickly here," with Toto piddling on my shoes. That's the danger of including information like this in a book.

Between the time I write this, and the time you read it, the Mac landscape may have changed completely—if not the Mac models, the prices, and sometimes both. So, a warning: this guide will be useful, if not 100% accurate by the time you read it. Take the information here with a grain or two of your favorite salt-substitute, and do some additional checking if you're in the process of buying a Mac. (And take a look at Chapter 15 before you whip out your credit card or checkbook.)

CPU Chips and Dips

In spite of whatever advertising hype you may hear or have heard about the various features of various Macs, the thing that separates Mac models is the CPU chip involved.

CPU stands for **Central Processing Unit**, and it's the chip that does most or all of the work inside of your Mac. It's also referred to as the computer's **microprocessor**.

The current line of Macs use either Motorola or IBM processor chips. The chips are identified by a number. Macs use 68000 numbered chips, either 68030 or 68040 (older models also use 68020). Power Macs use the IBM-designed PowerPC chip, numbered in the 600s (601, and so on). Since the introduction of the Power Mac, Macs using the Motorola chips have become generically known as "68K Macs," as a shorthand way of referring to all Macs with a 680X0 processor.

When people refer to chips in conversation, they usually shorten the number to the last three digits: 030 ("oh-thirty") or 040 ("oh-forty"). Power Mac chips are only three digits, so just say it (don't spray it). Real propeller-heads, when pontificating or bragging, also include the clock speed of the chip (how fast the chip works) by adding the clock speed to the abbreviated chip number: "I've got an 040/33." Translated, that means this particular propeller-head has a 68040-based Mac with a clock speed of 33 megahertz.

There's plenty to know and learn about these chips, but the only things that come in handy for regular folks like you and me are these:

> ➤ The higher the chip's number, the faster and more powerful the chip.

> ➤ The higher the clock speed, the faster the chip.

> ➤ The faster the chip, the more it costs.

The **clock speed** is a measurement of how many instructions the chip can carry out in one second. A microprocessor that runs at 1 megahertz (MHz) can carry out one million instructions per second, so a chip that runs at 33 MHz can do 33 million things in that same second.

While geeks may drool over an 80 or 100 MHz clock speed, it is not the be-all and end-all of microprocessors. Just because a chip *can* do 100 million things per second doesn't mean it will. The rest of the computer's gizzards, the *architecture,* can have positive and negative effects on the chip's capability. If you test two different computers with identical microprocessors running at, say, 20 MHz, one can seem noticeably zippier than the other. The rest of the computer's design may make more efficient use of every last MHz.

Actually trying out two computers (Macs, or anything else) with the same microprocessor, doing the same operation (opening a large graphics file, for example) will give you a better idea of the machine's overall speed than that little /33 tacked onto the chip number in the advertising material. Likewise, between two similar processor chips with different clock speeds (say 040/25 MHz vs. 040/33 MHz), the 25 MHz machine may seem faster than the one rated at 33 MHz because it makes better use of the speed available. This is one of the reasons why shopping for a computer system takes so much legwork— for me at least.

Slot Machines

Another major variation between Mac models, even between similar models, is the number and kind of expansion slots that are available inside the system unit.

Expansion slots allow you to add cards to your Mac that increase its power, or range of functions. For example, an internal modem is an expansion card, as are video and accelerator cards (discussed in Chapter 17). Macs come with two kinds of expansion slots: NuBus or PDS.

NuBus slots are high-speed connections that allow you to install a card that works alongside your Mac's central processor. The information the card processes or creates travels along a data path (called a *bus*) to the CPU, which then deals with it. PDS slots (which is redundant, because PDS stands for Processor Direct Slot) accept expansion cards that feed their information directly into the Mac's processor, without making it travel by bus.

Some Macs only come with one PDS, which may limit your expansion capability down the road. Others come with several NuBus slots—you can add doodads for days. Still others come with one or more of each. The number of slots (of either type) will affect the price of the Mac. Most high-end, big money machines have an assortment of slots. The lower-priced models tend to have one PDS (though the Quadra 660AV, on the pricey side, has only one PDS—but most of the funky gew-gaws you'd want to add are already built-in).

When considering which Mac to buy, it's important to think about how many additional features and functions you may want to add in the future, so you can buy a Mac with enough slots to meet your needs, or with built-in options (like the video features of the AV Macs) so you won't need as many slots. If you already have a one-slot Mac, you have to think very hard before you invest in a card that will fill it up for good: is that the best use of that slot?

The Current Line: An Overview

At this point in Mac history, there are four (sort of) distinct lines of Macintosh: Quadra, PowerBook, LC, and Performa. They're only "sort of" distinct, because the Performa line consists of minor variations of other Mac models with a different distribution channel—in English, that means you buy them in generic stores, rather than "computer" stores.

Purists may quibble with only four classifications, wanting a fifth category for Power Macs. You may be right; I may be crazy. However, for now, I've grouped the Power Macs with their immediate ancestors, the Quadras, even if they are mutant children—that's mutant as in genetic mutation, not an offhand science fiction-type slam. I'm being clinical, not insulting.

The Quadras and Power Macs

These are the machines that Apple used to insinuate themselves in the business world. They're fast, powerful, and flexible. Those were Quadras you saw in the control room of *Jurassic Park*.

The machines that actually wear the name Quadra all use the Motorola 68040 chips, the four being the reason they were called Quadras (if your Latin is rusty, *quad* means four, as in *quadrangle* (a four-sided shape) and *quadrant* (a quarter of an area)—sorry, I'm channeling Sister Margo again).

Quadras have three different clock speed variations, 25, 33, and 40 MHz, and most come with an *FPU* chip as part of the package, or an optional accessory. FPU chips speed up many graphics programs, especially those (like 3-D rendering programs) that are math-intensive.

Power Macs, as mentioned earlier, use the IBM PowerPC chips—currently the 601, but I'm sure we'll see that number creep higher soon enough. Power Macs come in three clock speeds, right now: 60, 66, and 80 MHz. That clock speed, however, goes right out the window if you run them in *emulation mode* to make use of non-Power Mac software. All Power Macs have FPU chips built-in. When running Power Mac software in native mode, these babies can run rings around even the latest Pentium-based, DOS-compatible computers, making Power Macs even more attractive to business users.

FPU (Floating Point Unit) chip A chip that relieves the CPU of the burden of doing mathematical calculations, thereby giving the Mac some added speed. They're sometimes called math chips, or math co-processors. Believe it or not, many spreadsheets and other applications that you think of as obviously math-related (calculators, and so on) don't make use of an FPU. Go figure. (There's more about FPUs in Chapter 17.)

Also falling under the Quadra/Power Mac banner are Apple's Workgroup Servers. Definitely aimed at the business market, a server is a central computer that holds and passes off information and applications to satellite computers on a network. By their nature (being at the beck-and-call of everyone on a network), servers have to be powerful and zippy machines. The older 040-based servers have been repackaged as regular Quadras, and servers using the PowerPC chip are the current models.

All of the above (Quadras, Power Macs, and Workgroup Servers) are modular Macs. You buy the CPU, and then accessorize with the monitor, keyboard, and any other peripherals you care to add.

The PowerBooks

PowerBooks are the laptops of the Macintosh world and may be run off of a battery or plugged into an electrical outlet. They're for anyone who needs computing power to go. The current line of PowerBooks is split into two subgroups: regular PowerBooks and the PowerBook Duos.

Duos are portables with a split personality: on the road, they're small, lightweight computers with few frills. Get them home, or back in your office, and Duos slip like a video cassette into a desktop *docking station* that adds the features (big monitor, keyboard, mouse, and more) of a desktop computer. For those who don't need a full-blown docking station, there are scaled-down versions available as well.

PowerBooks all have built-in liquid crystal displays (LCD)—like a digital watch's display, as opposed to a television-like monitor. Most are in grayscale with a few in color. At the moment, the PowerBook line uses 040 chips, except for one model in each subgroup that still uses 030 CPUs (this is a trend we'll look at again, shortly). They all run at either 25 or 33 MHz.

The most-offered option for a PowerBook is a modem (covered in detail in Chapters 17 and 18), which makes it easier to stay in touch with your home-base while on the road. You'll find a pile of PowerBook tips in Chapter 19.

The LC Family

The original Macintosh LC was an immediate hit. It cost less than most modular Macs, had built-in color video support, and could be decked out with an Apple IIe emulator card (which made it very attractive to schools because the Apple II family of computers was and is a mainstay of education). The LC's appeal to schools was so great that Apple cut the LC from the rest of the herd of Macs and made it available only to the educational market. You'll find them in classrooms, college book and computer stores, and the homes of students and education professionals.

The LC family has models with 030 and 040 CPUs, running at either 25 or 33 MHz. This is also the line (along with their Performa cousins) where you'll find all-in-one models with the monitor welded to the system unit. If you are a student or education professional, you may want to check out your LC-buying options before you consider other Mac models. Educational pricing is heavily discounted, and the machines are very nice. (I may be biased, though—I had an original LC for years and just put it up for adoption... sniff.)

The Performas

Sounding more like a new line of cars than computers (but there's a lot of that going around these days), Performas are Macs aimed at the home computer market. To that end, they're sold in places you don't normally think of as selling computers: department stores, office supply stores, electronics stores that sell TVs and VCRs, and discount chains, such as Wal-Mart.

The main difference between Performas and other Macs are few. Basically, they *are* the other Macs, with new names tacked on. There are some changes, though. Most Performas aren't as expandable as their cousins (generally coming with one PDS slot), which keeps their prices down. Most don't come with an FPU, though some will let you add one should the need arise. Finally, most come complete with monitor, keyboard, and mouse, so technically timid folks don't have to match up any other accessories themselves.

Many Performas are more than completely decked out. Very often they come bundled with an assortment of software already installed on the hard drive (even with CD software for CD-ROM equipped models), and additional hardware (such as a printer or modem). The bulk of the Performa line are renamed LC models, so most of the information above applies.

The Current Line: Details, Details

The following table lists all of the Macintosh models that are shipping as of this writing. Be aware that Apple tends to announce and/or release new models around August and January each year to coincide with the two largest Macworld Expos in Boston and San Francisco, respectively.

There are a few technoid-type things you'll notice as you scrutinize the table. First, Macs that have a 68LC040 CPU don't have an FPU chip. That's because the FPU chip is built into the regular 68040, and the LC in the middle means the FPU was left out. Maybe LC stands for "Lacks Chip?" If not, it's an easy way to remember that it doesn't have an FPU. You'll also notice that there's a fleet of Performas numbered similarly (575, 577, 578). They're the same machine, except higher numbers have more RAM and a larger hard drive than lower numbered models.

All Macs come with the standard 3.5-inch, high-density SuperDrive, as well as all the ports that are the Mac standard. AV models have the additional video-in and -out ports. You can find most Mac models, these days, with a built-in CD-ROM drive (except the PowerBooks, of course). Performas that have the word "included" in the Monitor column come with a 14-inch Performa color monitor. N/A, in the same column, means you have to buy a monitor separately.

Table 2.1 Current Mac Models

Model	CPU/Speed (MHz)	FPU (Y, N, or Opt.)	Monitor Variations	Performance
LC Family				
475	68LC040/25	N	N/A	475, 476
550	68030/33	Optional	Built-in	550
575	68LC040/33	N	Built-in	575
630	68LC040/33	N	N/A	630
Performas				
410	68030/16	N	Included	
460	68030/33	Optional	Included	
466	68030/33	Optional	Included	
467	68030/33	Optional	Included	
475	68LC040/25	N	Included	

Model	CPU/Speed (MHz)	FPU (Y, N, or Opt.)	Monitor Variations	Performance
475	68LC040/25	N	Included	
550	68030/33	Optional	Built-in	
560	68030/33	Optional	Built-in	
575	68LC040/33	N	Built-in	
577	68LC040/33	N	Built-in	
578	68LC040/33	N	Built-in	
630	68LC040/33	N	N/A	
635	68LC040/33	N	N/A	
636	68LC040/33	N	N/A	
638	68LC040/33	N	N/A	
Quadras				
605	68LC040/25	N	N/A	475, 476
630	68040/33	Y	N/A	630
650	68040/33	Y	N/A	
660AV	68040/25	Y	N/A	
950	68040/33	Y	N/A	
Power Macs				
6100/60	601/60	Y	N/A	
6100/60AV	601/60	Y	N/A	
7100/66	601/66	Y	N/A	
7100/66AV	601/66	Y	N/A	
8100/80	601/80	Y	N/A	
8100/80AV	601/80	Y	N/A	

continues

Table 2.1 Continued

Model	CPU/Speed (MHz)	FPU (Y, N, or Opt.)	Monitor Variations	Performance
PowerBooks				
150	68030/33	N	9.5-inch	
520	68LC040/25	N	9.5-inch	
520c	68LC040/25	N	9.5-inch Color	
540	68LC040/33	N	9.5-inch	
540c	68LC040/33	N	9.5-inch Color	
Duo 280	68LC040/33	N	9.0-inch	
Duo 280c	68LC040/33	N	8.4-inch Color	

The Shape of Macs to Come

In 1994, three big changes hit the world of Macintosh computing. The first was the introduction of the Power Macintosh. The second was the introduction of System 7.5, now generically known as the Mac OS. The third was Apple's decision to (finally) license the Mac OS to other computer manufacturers.

The Power Mac Paradigm

The Power Mac was an important change because it moved Macs away from the old 68000 family of microprocessors. These were known as CISC chips, for Complex Instruction Set Chip (another redundancy). The new PowerPC chips are RISC chips, for Reduced Instruction Set Chip, and they're wicked fast in comparison.

The Power Mac spurred two changes: first and less important to this discussion, it scared the bejabbers out of IBM-compatible manufacturers; second, Apple started letting older 68030-based Macs either die off, or upgraded them to new 040 architecture. The reason is simple: you can't turn an 030-based Mac into a Power Mac. Soon, in the next year or so, 030 Macs will disappear from the scene. There will only be Power Macs, and Macs that can be turned into Power Macs. That's to give hesitant types (like yours truly) who don't want to plunge into a new type of Mac, a chance to sit back and let the eager beavers work the kinks out of the new CPU. After that, the family of 040-based Macs will dwindle as Apple releases more Power Mac models and discontinues their earlier 040 incarnations.

System 7.5: Survival of the Fattest

System 7.5 is important because it's the first time since the introduction of System 7.0 that all of the Macintosh variations have been able to run exactly the same version of the Mac OS . When the Performas were introduced, they ran their own variation of System 7, specifically 7.0.1P (for Performa). New, regular Macs were lumbered with a Byzantine set of *system enablers* that tinkered with System 7 so they could run it. Power Macs had their own enabler variation, too.

System 7.5 runs on *all* Macs with enough RAM and hard drive space to install it. Call 7.5 a synthesis of existing versions, with some other new features thrown in for kicks. This is possible because System 7.5 is written in Fat Binary. System 7.5 assesses your system when you begin the installation and then installs the 7.5 variation appropriate to your machine. That's an important step, because Fat Binary assures that, regardless of what the "current" Macintosh line may be and what Mac you own, you should be able to keep upgrading your operating system, at least until Apple tires of keeping you in the System software loop.

"Do You Have a License for That Mac?"

The reason there are so many manufacturers of IBM-compatible computers is that, early on in the personal computer game, IBM *licensed* their operating system to other manufacturers, giving these smaller companies a chance to build computers compatible with IBM's. Macs, save for the short-lived Outbound portable line, have always been made by Apple, and only Apple. By and large, that's the reason that, until recently, IBM-compatible (clone) computers have been less expensive than Macs. Competition almost always lowers prices.

Apple broke that trend by cutting their prices to be competitive with the clone makers (sounds like the name of a trashy horror movie: *The Clone Makers*, in 3-D!). Now, the buzz is that Apple will license the

Mac OS, so that third-party companies can manufacture Mac clones of their own. If and when this happens, it will mean three things: lower prices, more options for Mac buyers, and more Macs and compatibles.

So What's It to You?

Overall, this is all marketing strategy. Apple has a foothold in the very lucrative, and formerly IBM-compatible dominated, business market, and Apple wants to expand that foothold into a fortress. It's all about sales, market share, and profits.

For Apple, it means big bucks. Phasing out the 68K Macs over the next few years means Power Mac and Power Mac upgrade sales. Even if the Power Mac you buy is from a company other than Apple, Apple's coffers will still clank with coin from the licensing fees. For the Mac that sits on your desk right now, it means that (unless it's 040-based, or a Power Mac already) an upgrade is just around the corner, or it will become a digital outcast as older models fall out of favor both with Apple and software/hardware developers.

If you decide to upgrade, you may have a wider variety of Macs to choose from (some from vendors other than Apple) with all the perils and pitfalls that implies. Apple makes solid computers. My very first (an Apple IIe) is still in service and running well at the ripe old age of 11—that's 77 in dog years, and a couple thousand in computer years. The same is true of my old LC (pushing 5 now). That reliability may not be the same for all the companies that license and build clone Macs. You often hear horror stories from DOS users who bought terribly made computers from fly-by-night companies (I have one or two stories of my own—I tell them on Halloween). For you and me, it means shopping carefully, more than ever before.

The long and short of it is, your Mac may become obsolete faster than you think. You may be able to buy a cheap Mac clone, made by one of a hundred manufacturers. It may be a piece of crap; it may not. There are other, stranger rumors flying around about the future of the Mac OS, but that's too far in the future to bother worrying about now. Of course, this is all sheer speculation. Only time will tell.

The Least You Need to Know

Well, the absolute least you need to know is that all of the information in this chapter is subject to change without notice. Just to underline that fact: between the time I wrote this and the time I reviewed it before publication, Apple released new Performa models based on Power Mac technology. I wish I could stop my head from spinning; I feel like Linda Blair in *The Exorcist.* (Mommy, make it stop! Make it stop!)

➤ All Macs are based on either Motorola 68000-series or IBM-designed 600-series CPU chips.

➤ Macs based on Motorola 68000 chips are now known collectively as 68K Macs.

➤ Macs can have PDS or NuBus expansion slots. Some models even come with both.

➤ The type of CPU chip and the number or kind of expansion slots will limit your ability to expand your Mac.

ON YER' MARK!

MAC

THIS SIDE UP

MAC

MAC

MAC

Getting Ready and Setting Up Your Mac

In This Chapter

➤ Deciding where to put the darn thing

➤ Planning for future expansion

➤ Unpacking the little rascal

➤ Getting set up and hooking everything together

There you stand in a pile of Apple's environmentally correct, natural-brown cardboard boxes. The credit card in your wallet is still tingling from charging your Mac, and now you want to put this puppy together.

Before you do anything else, *walk away from the boxes*. Don't even look at them. Don't cut the packing tape, don't jiggle the funny little box to see what's inside. Instead, go to the room where you're going to set up your computer, and check it out.

Where to Set Up

Ideally—and I do mean ideally, as "in the best of all possible worlds"—the room you set up your Mac in should be an official-type office. A place where you can work or play in peace and quiet, with a door that closes and a window that opens. Because that's not always possible or practical, here are some simple guidelines for deciding where to set up.

First, be sure your little corner of the world is out of a high-traffic area. A bedroom would be ideal if no one shares your bedroom or your Mac. A dining room table would be good, too, if you never actually use it for dining. This brings us to the second consideration: be sure it's a space where the Mac can stay put. Unless you managed to snag a Classic or one of the other compact models (such as the Color Classic) before they were discontinued in the U.S., your Mac isn't designed to be moved around. Regular assembling and reassembling can cause wear and tear on your connectors, cables, and your nerves, too. Plus, the more you move something heavy, the more chances you have to drop something heavy.

Third is the whole table issue. You just spent a big chunk of change on a Mac; why would you want to set it up on a cheapo card table? It isn't the price of the card table, but the design. The legs fold; the top is cardboard. Card tables are made to stand up to such vigorous uses as holding playing cards, maybe some chips (poker and/or potato), beverages, some dip, and that's about it. Don't trust your Macintosh to pressed cardboard and folding legs. Use a real table. You don't have to spend a bazillion dollars on a computer table. If you can sit on the table or desk without making it wobble, it's probably sturdy enough to hold your Mac—as long as you weigh more than 100 pounds. If you don't, I hate you. Eat something.

If you're thinking of using a sturdy table or desk that you already own, go for it. Set up the space with a chair, even unpack the Mac's keyboard, set it on top, and try sitting and typing for a while. If it's comfortable for twenty minutes or so, you're probably safe setting your Mac up for keeps. If you're going to buy a desk or table, be sure to try it on for size before you buy it. Nothing can kill productivity like an uncomfortable, or downright painful, desk or chair.

Good Light, Comfy Chair

While we're on the subject of comfort, you'll need good light and a comfy chair. Work light is a very personal issue, like how you make peanut butter and jelly sandwiches. Fights have broken out over it. Some folks I know like to work under the glare of a fluorescent desk lamp suitable for sweating confessions out of suspects. Others can work with a naked ten-watt bulb. Both of these give me headaches. I prefer a nice, bright halogen lamp, far enough away that the light doesn't glare off of my monitor, but close enough that it lights up all the things I need to see.

Pundits and office designers, sharing their conventional wisdom, have written volumes about the kind and placement of lights in a work space (ways to light your work to avoid eyestrain and headaches). If you're creating an office from the ground up, you may want to consult one of their books. If you're cobbling together an office or work area from stuff you already have, well, you may still want to consult the experts—but remember, *your* comfort is the final consideration.

> **Ergonomics** is the science of designing things to accommodate the natural shape and motion of the human body. The bridge of the Starship Enterprise is very ergonomically designed. Its root is the Greek word *erg*, meaning a unit of work. It may also be a cross between "ergo" and "economics" because any product that boasts "ergonomic styling" will, ergo, cost 50% more than its nonergonomic competitor.

The same goes for comfy chairs. The experts suggest lower back support, arm rests, and adjustability, among other things. Me, I slouch; I spin. I don't keep my feet flat on the floor. I often work with a cat in my lap. I crack my knuckles and do other things the experts don't approve of, such as smoke and drink lots of coffee. Comfort is always the final consideration. *Your* behind will be in that chair, not some ergonomics specialist's.

Reliable Power and the Urge to Surge

There are a few other things you need to have handy in order to run a Mac, or any computer for that matter. One is a convenient electrical outlet. Convenient as in close to your Mac, so you don't have to snake dangerous extension cords all over the place. Convenient also as in an outlet with good wiring and reliable power.

Urban areas tend to have a couple of common power problems, the most common of which is *spiking*. Spiking (also called a *surge*) happens when the flow of electricity is uneven, sometimes a little less than normal, and then (suddenly) more than normal. If you've ever seen a light bulb dim for no good reason, and then suddenly flare up brighter than ever, you have actually seen a power spike, or surge. If you've also seen that same bulb just die suddenly after a spike, you've seen the damage spikes can do.

One of the goodies invented to protect expensive electronics from the perils of power surges is called (oddly enough) a *surge protector*. Surge protectors are handy for two reasons. The obvious one is that they protect your equipment from surges and spikes. There's a small fuse inside designed to blow out before a dangerous amount of power can zap your Mac (or whatever you have plugged into it). The second reason is a special added bonus: surge protectors come in multiple-outlet designs; I've seen them with as many as ten outlets. You can plug in all your high-tech toys and turn them on with a flip of the surge protector's on-switch. Very convenient.

Being able to turn on all of your Mac's peripherals (the monitor, printer, CPU, and so on) is the overriding reason for buying a surge protector. Fact is, your Mac already has a built-in surge protector, so buying another one is really not *mandatory*. Surge protectors range in price from about $10 to $100. The $100 jobbies have all the bells and whistles; some even have an outlet for a phone line to pass through the protector to keep your modem from being fried. However, I haven't talked about modems yet, so forget I mentioned it.

Another problem is that electricity can be completely unreliable. If you live in a big metropolitan area that's subject to brown-outs—especially during air conditioner season—or in a rural area where storms and other hazards knock out your power regularly, you could be traumatized by the sudden loss of unsaved work. There you are in the middle of writing the great American novel when *bam!* The power goes out. There goes all of your unsaved work, and **THERE'S NO WAY TO GET IT BACK** except to recreate it from scratch. Trust me; this is traumatic. And I have the emotional scars and therapy bills to prove it.

If you live in an area subject to frequent power losses, you may want to consider getting a UPS—an uninterruptable power supply. A UPS does two things for your Mac. It filters out the irregularities of your power supply (brown-outs and spikes) and provides your Mac with a consistent level of power. A UPS also acts as a storage battery—if the power goes out, your Mac won't notice. The UPS will keep feeding it power, giving you enough time to save whatever you're working on, exit your applications, and shut down your Mac properly.

Does everybody need one? No, unless your work is constantly in danger of loss from power problems, or your paranoia level is so high you won't be able to sleep at night unless you have one.

If you decide you do want a UPS, you need to add up the power requirements of all your computer equipment (it will be in the technical specifications section at the back of all your manuals) and make sure you get a UPS that provides more than enough power to meet your system's needs, plus a little more for whatever hardware you buy down the road a piece.

UPSs are reasonably priced, considering the amount of anguish they can spare you, but $200 to $500 is not to be spent on a whim (at least that's what I keep telling myself). Unless your area has regular electrical problems, you'll probably be happy with an inexpensive multi-outlet surge protector.

Planning Ahead

Before getting down to the nitty-gritty of assembling your Mac, there's one last thing to take into consideration: room to grow. Right now, at the very least, you have a Mac that takes up a few square feet of desk space. You also have a keyboard, mouse, and mouse pad all fighting for desktop real estate. You probably have (or will want soon) a printer of some kind. That's just to *start*.

Down the road, you may want to add an external hard drive, a CD-ROM drive, a scanner, a different printer, big disk storage boxes, plus stuff that hasn't even been invented yet. If you start out all cramped, you'll have nowhere to go, without moving everything to a larger desk.

A **modem** is an electronic device that allows your Mac to interact with a distant computer over phone lines. More about modems in Chapters 17 and 18.

Give yourself some room to grow—try to anticipate your future needs. Set up your Mac on a clear desk with room to breathe. Locate your desk near a phone jack. At the very least, you'll be able to answer the phone without walking away from your desk. At most, you'll be able to painlessly add a modem (which requires a phone line) later in your computing career without having to move your desk or install another jack.

Insert Tab A into Slot B

Let's go over generic assembly instructions for a desktop Mac. Generic, because there's no way I can know exactly what you bought, just like there's no way you want to plow through instructions on how to assemble all the different Mac variations. Yawn. What a thrill. Consider yourself warned then. If what I'm saying here doesn't jive with the machine you have in front of your face, ignore me, and go along with the *Getting Started With Your Macintosh (insert your model name here)* manual that came with your machine.

First Things First

The first thing to do is unpack everything (you may want to put on some good, head-bopping, toe-tapping, good-to-work-by tunes before you start). Check all the Mac parts for obvious damage: cracks, dents, divots, dings, and other signs of broken-ness. If you find any damage, call the place where you purchased the Mac and tell them you want a replacement. You shelled out big bucks for a new machine; you deserve the privilege of dinging it up yourself.

A word about boxes: Save them. (Okay, that's two words; so sue me.) Save the foam protectors, too. Why should you save them when they'll take up so much of your valuable storage space? Well, if you move, you'll have protected packaging to save your Mac from the moving company (or your close, but clumsy, friends); if you need to ship your Mac somewhere, you'll have the proper packaging.

Next thing to do: gather up all the little plastic bags of paper (manuals, warranty, and registration cards), and put them all together in one place. Deal with them later.

Each box should also have a packing list right on top: if you bought a modular Mac, maybe an AV Quadra or Power Mac, you'll have several boxes and several lists. If you bought a Performa 575, or similar all-in-one model, everything will be in one big box, unless you bought a printer or other peripherals. The packing list tells you what's supposed to be inside. Use it to make sure you have everything you're supposed to have.

If everything is there, you're ready to move on. If something's missing, call the place where you bought the Mac and tell them what's missing. If you bought your Mac locally, you may be able to just pick up the missing piece(s). Otherwise, you may have to wait until your dealer ships out the missing parts.

The CPU

The *CPU* (central processing unit) is the part of your Mac that does all the work. In reality, the CPU is the main chip inside your Mac that does the work, but the term has come to mean the box that contains the CPU and all the other goodies that make computers compute. In an all-in-one Mac, such as the Performa 575 or the short-lived Mac TV, the box with the welded-on monitor and disk drive is the CPU. A modular Mac's CPU (any of the Quadras) is a fairly plain-looking box with the disk drive slot in front and the connector ports (more about these later) in the back.

A **peripheral** is an add-on piece of equipment, such as a printer, that's not essential to operate the computer—like extra options on a car. You don't need air conditioning to use the car, but it makes you more comfortable.

Set the CPU (whatever kind you have) backward on your desk with the connector ports facing you, and the disk drive slot facing away from you. (Of course, if there's nothing (like a wall) to keep you from working on the backside of your Mac in its final resting place, simply ignore all of this "set it up backward, then turn it around" junk.) The backside of your Mac will look something like this:

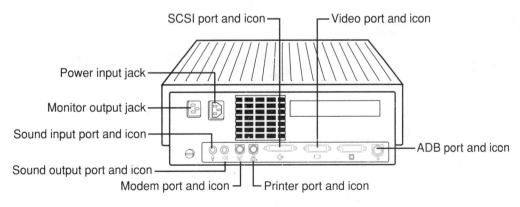

The back of a Mac.

27

 You never want to connect anything to your Mac while there's power running through it. You can short out both the Mac and whatever you're plugging into it. You can also give yourself a nasty shock. Always install stuff with the Mac turned off—you can leave it plugged in, but turn it off.

If you bought one of the AV (Audio-Visual) Macs, you'll also have two video-in and two video-out ports for hooking up video equipment (camcorder, VCR, and so on). A Mac with built-in networking will also have an Ethernet port. Right out of the box, you probably won't need to mess with any of these. If you do, check your manual for details.

Now go and find the Mac's power cord. It will have a standard, grounded (three-pronged) plug on one end and a three-prong socket on the other. Plug the socket end of the power cord into the power socket on the back of your Mac. DON'T plug the other end into a power outlet or surge protector yet. You won't be doing that until *everything* is together. Why? Just because I'm safety conscious.

The Mac's power socket.

Mission accomplished!

Keyboard and Mouse

The next thing you're going to want to do is grab the Mac's keyboard, keyboard cable, and the mouse (the mouse cable is part of the mouse). Take the keyboard cable, and plug it into the ADB port on the back of your Mac. It doesn't matter which end of the cable you plug into the ADB (both ends are the same).

The Mac's ADB port and icon.

Notice that the ADB icon below the ADB port is also stamped on the flat side of both ends of the keyboard cable and the plug end of the mouse cable. That's so you can easily figure out which cable to plug into which port, and it's true for all the cables that Apple supplies. Other manufacturers aren't so kind.

The ADB icon also appears on your keyboard, at the upper-right and upper-left corners. That's because the other end of the keyboard cable plugs into one of these ports, and the mouse into the other. Which plugs where is completely up to you. If you're right-handed, you'll probably want to plug the mouse into the ADB port on the right of your keyboard. If you're left-handed, you'll probably want the mouse on the left of the keyboard.

ADB stands for Apple Desktop Bus and you pronounce it by saying each letter ("A-D-B"). The Apple Desktop Bus is the standard way of connecting mice, keyboards, and a few other peripherals to the Mac.

The Desktop Bus has been standard since Apple introduced the Macintosh SE. (Before the SE, they used connectors that looked like the plugs that connect your telephone to the wall jack—in case the question ever comes up on *Jeopardy!* or something.)

Whichever port you plug the mouse into, you'll plug the keyboard cable into the other one, but don't do it yet. If you attach your keyboard now, you'll just have one more thing to juggle when you turn your Mac to face front. Set the keyboard and mouse aside, and let the keyboard cable attached to the back of your Mac dangle. We'll do a grand plug-in in a couple of minutes.

29

If you have an all-in-one Mac, you can skip the monitor section. Your monitor is permanently attached, and you don't have to bother with it.

The Monitor

If you bought a Mac model other than an all-in-one Performa or a PowerBook (also with a built-in monitor), you have to add a monitor so you can see what you're doing. Depending on the monitor, you may also need a video card. A video card is a circuit board that processes all of the video information that goes to the monitor.

Most Macs, these days, have built-in video; you do not need an extra video card unless you want to use a monitor larger than the built-in hardware supports. Older Macs (if you bought used), like the IIfx, don't have built-in video and need a video card installed to run any monitor. Check the manual called *Special Features of Your Macintosh (insert model name here)*, for a section called "Video Display Support." It will tell if you need a video card for the monitor you purchased.

Warranty Warning! If you do decide to install the video card yourself, be aware that opening the Mac's case can void Apple's warranty. If something goes wrong and you damage the Mac or the card, you may be out of luck. If you manage to install the card without a hitch and you don't tell anyone, then your warranty should still be intact. It's a question of how much you trust yourself.

If you need a video card, don't panic. If the company you purchased your Mac from is worth its salt, they told you that before they sold you the monitor. If they were really good, they installed the card for you, and you don't have to worry about it. If they were extra good, you knew all this already. One sure sign that you need a card, have the card, and the card is installed in your Mac is the packing list from the monitor box. If the packing slip specifies a video card, but there isn't one in the box, you can call the place where you bought your Mac to be sure they installed the video card.

If there is a video card in the box, then you either need to install it yourself (a potentially scary thing; follow the installation instructions carefully), or take your CPU and the video card back to the place of purchase, and let them install it like they should have done in the first place.

Now that you've figured out if you do or don't need a video card installed, and you (or your dealer) installed it, let's hook this baby up. Carefully now, pick up your monitor (it's heavy), and set it on the desk beside your Mac. Turn the monitor so the screen is facing away from you and you're looking at the back of it.

Your monitor has two cables coming from the back of it. One is the power cord. Let that one be for a minute. The other is the cable that attaches to the video port on the back of your Mac. The video port has an icon that looks like a TV picture tube. The end of the monitor's cable has the same icon if you have an *Apple* monitor (if you bought another brand, it's probably blank).

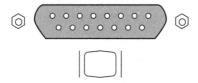

The video port on the back of a Mac.

Plug the video cable into the video port. Tighten the thumbscrews—*not* the Inquisition kind, but the kind that keeps the cable from flopping out of the port—so they're finger tight. You'll want to be able to loosen them with your fingers, too, so not too tight. Don't plug the monitor's power cord into anything yet. Save that for the grand plug-in.

At this point, you can set the monitor on top of the CPU or wherever you're going to place it. If you're putting your monitor on top of the CPU, keep the screen facing away from you, toward the disk drive end of your Mac. That way, when you're ready to turn it around, the monitor and CPU turn at once.

Peripheral Vision

We're almost at the end now; be brave. This is the point where you can plug in any of the other doodads you may have acquired when you bought your Mac. Let's get the little stuff out of the way first.

Microphone

You may have a microphone; you may not. If you have one, you either bought a Mac that was packaged before Apple decided to sell these little darlings as optional accessories, or you paid extra money for it. Or you got one of the Audio Vision monitors that has a built-in microphone.

If your microphone is built-in, just check your manual to make sure everything is connected properly. If it came as a separate piece, well, you have to do one or two things. One is to mount the little bracket on the side of your monitor, which involves pulling a piece of waxy paper off of the sticky part and (steady yourself) sticking it on the side of the monitor. Did you work up a sweat? If your Mac came with a PlainTalk microphone, you don't even have to do that—it just rests on top of your monitor.

Next, you have to plug the microphone jack (which looks suspiciously like the jack you'll find on a set of Walkman headphones) into the sound input port on the back of your Mac. It's the one with the microphone icon under it.

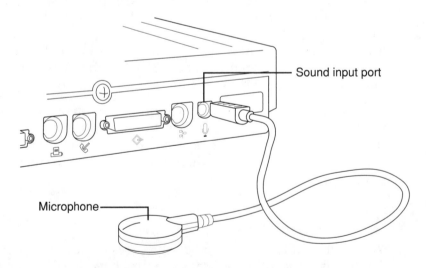

Mac with microphone installed.

Speakers

If your Mac came with a built-in CD-ROM drive, you may also have a separate set of speakers for dazzling stereophonic sound, or speakers built into the monitor (also for dazzling stereophonic sound). If the speakers are part of your monitor, check your manual to be sure all your connections are correct. If you have separate speakers, plug their jack into the sound output port on the back of your Mac. It's right next to the sound input jack and looks exactly like it, except there is an icon of (duh) a speaker under it.

You may want to wait to plug in your speakers until you turn your Mac around; the speakers may be a little awkward to drag around as you turn the CPU.

Printer

A printer is probably the last thing you'll have to hook up right now (unless you were inspired or bullied by a salesman and purchased a modem). Printers, except for those cute, little StyleWriters and other tiny inkjet printers, tend to be large, chunky-looking things, not unlike myself.

Set the printer on (or near) your desk, close enough to your Mac that the cable reaches both with enough slack in the cable so you can plug in both ends. Turn the printer so you can easily reach the port on its back. Take the cable and plug the small, round end (it should look like the end of your keyboard cable) into the port on the back of your Mac with the little printer icon under it. Leave the other end of the printer cable unplugged.

Find the printer's power cord (if it's not built into the printer), and plug the socket end of the cord into the power outlet on the back of the printer. Like every other power cord you've touched, don't plug the business end (the prong end) into your outlet or surge protector yet. That's coming up soon, but not yet.

The Grand Finale!

You survived! Congratulations! All that's left is so simple; just use this checklist:

1. Carefully lift and turn your Mac so the front is facing you again.

2. Position your Mac where you want it to stay, leaving room at the front for the keyboard and at the side for the mouse.

3. Plug the loose end of the keyboard cable into the right or left ADB port on the keyboard.

4. If you haven't already, plug the mouse cable into the other ADB port on the keyboard (the one you didn't use for the keyboard cable).

5. Now would be a good time to plug in your speakers, if you have them. Your microphone should already be plugged in (if you have one), so plug the speakers into the little port right beside the microphone.

6. Plug the loose end of your printer cable into the printer's port, and reposition the printer.

7. Take all the plug-ends of your power cords (the Mac's, the printer's), and plug them into the outlet or surge protector of your choice. Your monitor (depending on your Mac model) may not have a plug (all-in-one Mac), or may have a funky-looking plug that plugs into the back of your CPU—check your manual(s) for details.

8. Take a break, because you're done.

You'll fire this puppy up in the next chapter. While you take your break, now may be a good time to sort through all of those packs of paper that came with your Mac. Dig them out; sort them out (separate the manuals, the disks, and the warranty and registration cards). *Don't* fill out whatever needs filling out; wait until you've fired up your Mac and are sure that everything works. Missing or filled-in box litter (like the registration cards) can booger up the return process, should the need arise.

 Filling out and returning your registration cards is important. First, because Apple and the other hardware manufacturers need to know you bought their product. Second, it gives the manufacturers your address so they can let you know about cool stuff, such as new Mac models, upgrades (improvements made to stuff you already bought), or if there's ever a recall or repair (heaven forbid!) that needs to be done on a particular model.

Finally, you should fill out your registration cards because then you'll be in the company's computers, and you'll be able to get technical support by phone. That means you can call them if there's a problem you can't solve, and they'll help you solve it. (Before you call, read the "Okay, *Now* You Can Panic" section of Chapter 21, because there's a right way and a wrong way to get technical support.) However, wait until you're sure what you bought is working in the first place.

The Least You Need to Know

While you're taking your break, here are some essentials from this chapter for you to mull over:

➤ Choose a sturdy desk or table as your dedicated work space.

➤ Check out your power supply. If it's subject to brown- or black-outs, consider getting an uninterruptible power supply (UPS). Otherwise, maybe just a surge protector.

➤ Leave yourself room to grow.

➤ Never connect anything to your Mac while there's power running through it. Make sure it's turned off.

➤ Remember your port icons; they make life so much easier.

Power input jack: To connect the power cord.

Video port: To connect your monitor.

Printer port: For connecting your printer cable.

Modem port: For connecting a modem.

SCSI port: We'll talk more about this one later.

ADB connector: For connecting your keyboard to the Mac and a mouse to the keyboard.

Sound output port: For connecting speakers.

Sound input port: For connecting your microphone.

➤ Whenever you buy new stuff, remember to fill out and mail your product registration cards after you're satisfied that the product works and you want to keep it.

Get it? Got it. Good! Going on.

Chapter 4

Why Don't You Start Me Up?

In This Chapter

➤ Turning on everything in order

➤ What to do if it looks weird

➤ Shutting down

Okay! You've come very far very fast, and here comes the payoff: now you are ready to fire up your Mac and enter the wonderful world of computing. In this chapter, we'll go over all the basics of starting up and shutting down your Mac, and take the briefest of peeks at some of the magic of Macintosh.

This little taste is like the first taste of a new bottle of wine in a restaurant, except you don't have to sniff the cork. Right after this little snip of a chapter, we'll jump into your new Mac with both feet—try doing that with a glass of Chateau Marmoset.

Power On!

Before you turn *anything* on, make sure that you plug in everything, either into a live wall outlet, or into a multi-outlet power strip or surge protector that you plug into a wall outlet. If you're using a power strip or surge protector, make sure it's turned off, too.

Next, find all of the appropriate On/Off switches, both on your equipment and on your surge protector (if you have one). Your typical On/Off switch looks something like the one in the figure below. The side of the switch with the circle is the Off position. The side with the line is the On position. Why? I haven't a clue.

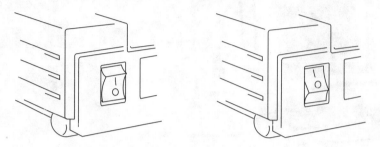

Your typical On/Off switch for the '90s.

Newer Macs have (*ta-da!*) the power switch on the front, and it's a simple push button below the floppy drive—much easier than reaching around to the back of your Mac and searching for the old-style switches.

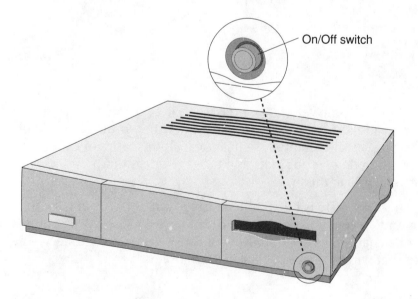

On/Off switch

A new-fangled power switch.

If you plug in everything and are ready to go, let's do it. Here's the order you should turn things on (turn them on one at a time):

1. External hard drive (if you have one) to get it up to speed before the Mac comes looking for it.

2. Printer, if you need it on.

3. External modem, if you have one and want it on.

4. The CPU.

5. The monitor.

6. The power strip/surge protector (if you have one).

Converts from the world of DOS should take special note that this is a *power switch*, not an eject button. Macs don't have an eject button, so put that thought right out of your head—it will only get you into trouble.

If you have a high-end Performa, Quadra, or Power Mac, you may be able to turn your Mac on from the keyboard. There's a button that floats all by its lonesome on the keyboard that has a little left-pointing arrow on it. That's your power switch. Press that, and your Mac should fire right up.

If you have any *other* model Mac, you'll *still* have that key, and you can punch it until you're black-and-blue in the finger, but it won't do anything. Like Eeyore says, "Some can and some can't—that's the way it is with buttons."

Some models of Macintosh monitors will also turn themselves on automatically when you fire up the CPU. Don't panic. It *means* to do that. Your Mac isn't possessed. Naturally, you'll know which kind you have the first time you power on the CPU.

What Happens Next

When the power reaches your Mac, you'll hear a variety of noises. Macs are like people in the morning—it takes a little grunting and groaning to get them out of bed. First you'll hear a little whine. That's your hard drive spinning up to speed and the Mac's internal fan starting up. Then you'll hear some ticka-ticka kind of noises; that's the startup information being read from the hard drive. Finally, you'll hear a musical tone. The sound varies from Mac model to Mac model. On mine, it's an operatic *bong*. Yours may be something different.

Put on a Happy Mac

If everything goes smoothly, a smiling Mac appears briefly on your screen, as shown in the figure below. A few seconds later, it disappears and a screen welcoming you to the wonderful world of Macintosh appears. What a polite machine!

The happy Mac.

After a few more seconds, you may or may not see some small icons appear at the bottom of your screen—either way, they're nothing to be alarmed about. They only appear if your Mac is loading teeny-tiny programs (called *Extensions*). If there aren't any installed on your Mac, you won't see them. I'll talk about Extensions in more detail in Chapter 11.

After a few more seconds, the startup screen and the tiny icons (if any) disappear, and you're at the desktop.

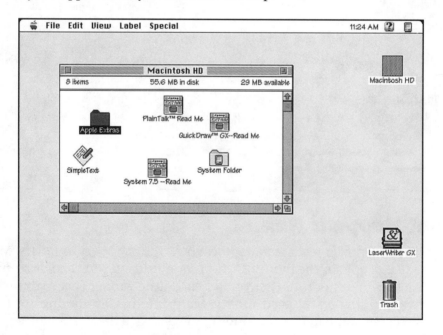

The desktop.

40

Questionable Disk

If you were greeted by a picture of a floppy disk with a question mark (like the one in the following figure) instead of a smiling Mac, you've gotten your hands on a Mac without its System software installed, and your Mac doesn't know what to do with itself.

Disk with question mark icon.

Don't worry; it's not a big deal. Turn your Mac off, either just the CPU with the switch on the front or back, or the whole system with the switch on the surge protector. Then locate your System Disks. They'll be in with the bags of paperwork and junk from the Mac's box. If your Mac has a built-in CD-ROM drive, you may have one floppy disk and a CD.

With the disks in hand, flip to Chapter 20 for the lowdown on installing System and other software.

Shutting Down

Well, I think that's quite enough excitement for one chapter. Let's shut this puppy down—but don't reach for those power switches yet. Because of the way Macs work, you should shut down everything the machine is doing before you actually shut off the machine.

If anything else (other than the two scenarios described earlier) happens when you power up your Mac, run—do not walk—to the "Startup Problems" section in Chapter 21. It explains, in gory detail, all of the bad things that can happen at startup and what you can do to fix them.

This is important because shutting down what your Mac is doing saves the *state* of your Mac. Remember the picture of the desktop shown earlier? When the Mac saves its state, that means that it saves all that stuff you see on the desktop (the Trash, the hard drive icon, plus funky stuff, such as windows, that we haven't talked about yet) just the way it appears. The next time you turn your Mac on, everything will be exactly the way you left it. How many other things can you say that about?

If your software is **corrupt**, that doesn't mean you will find it taking bribes or trying to lure school kids into the back seat of your car with candy. It means that the program information can become unreadable. If the Mac can't read the information, the Mac can't use the information, and that's a bad thing.

Just cutting off the power can do bad things to whatever programs you're running—especially the System software. The program information can become *corrupt*. (This doesn't mean that you can never turn off your Mac without shutting it down properly. You'll find examples in Chapter 21, the troubleshooting section, where just turning it off is *all* you can do.)

Shutting down is so important that in System 7.5, if you kill the power without shutting down, the next time you turn your Mac on you'll get a friendly reminder about shutting down properly, and a small pair of mechanical hands come out of your monitor and slap your wrists... okay, I made that last bit up, but you will get a warning.

The **cursor** is a mouse-controlled pointer (that can take many shapes). It indicates where you are on your Mac's screen. We'll talk more about the cursor in the next chapter.

In order for you to be able to shut down the Mac, you need to know a little bit about the mouse and cursor. Start by moving your mouse around randomly on your desk or tabletop, while watching the monitor. See how the arrow moves around the desktop the same way you move the mouse? Practice for a minute or two, until you can get the arrow cursor to point where you want. This is one of the few circumstances where it *is* polite to point.

When you feel comfortable moving the mouse and arrow cursor around, move the mouse so the arrow cursor points at the word **Special** in the menu bar at the top of your screen. With the cursor still touching the word **Special**, press and hold down the mouse button. *Voilà!* A menu drops down.

The extremely Special menu.

Still holding down the mouse button—don't worry, this gets easier with practice—slide the arrow cursor down the center of the menu. That's called *dragging*. As the cursor touches a word, you'll see it turn white with a black bar behind it. That word is now *selected*.

Move the arrow cursor down and select the phrase **Shut Down**, and then release the mouse button. The black bar blinks a few times, and your Mac shuts itself down. If it doesn't, your hand probably slipped and you missed the words **Shut Down**. Try, try again.

Now it's safe for you to turn off the power.

The Least You Need to Know

Okay, a short and sweet chapter, but very important. Here's the least you need to remember:

➤ Turn on your peripherals first, then your Mac and monitor (unless you're turning it all on from a surge protector or power strip).

➤ Don't just turn the power off when you finish. Use the **Shut Down** command under the **Special** menu before you turn off the power.

Part II
Getting Down to Brass Macs

Cool—you can turn your Mac on, wiggle the mouse, select a menu item, and turn it off again. Essentially, you can begin and end a session on your Mac. Now, what about that stuff in the middle?

This part of the book covers the essential things you really need to know to work your way around your Mac. It's basic stuff that you'll use day in and day out, every time you power up your Mac. Billy Joel may think it's "all about soul," but your Mac thinks it's all about pointing, clicking, selecting, dragging, keyboard shortcuts, and menus—menus for days.

If you're like me (and I know that you are), you're probably in a hurry to fire up that word processor, drawing program, game, or CD-ROM disc that came bundled with your Mac. Resist the urge, for a measly 60 pages or so, if you can. If you neglect the basics covered here, you'll miss out on many great tips and tricks, not to mention some other (always helpful) informa-tion that will make your life easier when you do finally fire up that word processor or game.

Fasten your seat belts. The captain has turned on the no skimming sign.

MUST YOU DO THIS EVERYTIME YOU TRY TO RETRIEVE A LOST FILE?!

Chapter 5

All Systems Go

In This Chapter

➤ The nickel tour of the desktop

➤ Manipulating your mouse

➤ Fun with windows

In this chapter and the next, I'll lay down the very basic concepts of the Macintosh, the ones that make Macs Macs. You'll start with the desktop, add the mouse, and then go over the windows. Chapter 6 discusses menus, icons, and other stuff you'll find littered all over the desktop.

This is all basic System information. You should read it, and where appropriate, follow along on your very own Mac. Pictures of my Mac's screen won't help much if you can't reproduce them on your own screen. If the writing gets dense (meaning if I get dense) and stops making sense to you, stop. Go back, reread it, and retry it until you get it. I can't stress enough that this stuff will come in handy *every time you turn on your Mac.*

A Tour of the Desktop

If your Mac is turned off, fire it up (unless you're reading this standing on a bus or in the bathtub, or something). The first place to start is the desktop. If you've forgotten what it looks like, here's a little refresher I like to call *the desktop* figure. (Actually, I like to call it "Nude Descending a Staircase," but that's just me.)

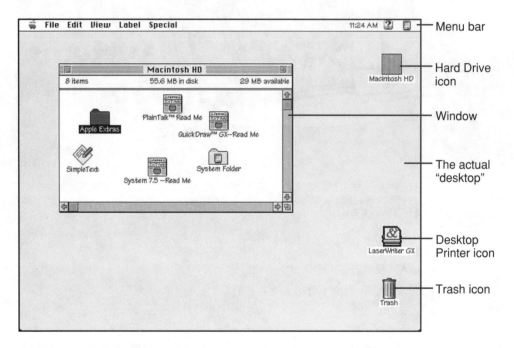

The desktop.

The Mac's desktop doesn't look or work like any desktop I've ever seen. Who keeps their garbage can on their desk? The Mac's desktop is a metaphor—the folks who named the desktop called it that to give you the idea that it's your home base, the place where you begin, tinker with, and complete all of your work on your Mac. A desktop is familiar—every desk you ever worked at had one. It's a known quantity, and the known is always more comfortable than the unknown.

To carry the idea of a real desktop through the whole Mac environment, you'll use folders that work like file folders, and throw stuff you don't want or need any more in the trash. That's about as far as the metaphor goes, though. (Unless you have a really funky desk that has windows you can open.) The part of the Mac's operating system (or OS, for the abbreviation dependent) that puts the desktop on your screen is called the *Finder*.

In computerese, the **environment** is much like the environment of the world at large, or your **work environment**. It's the atmosphere, surroundings, and even the decor of your computer. The Macintosh environment is graphical (sometimes called a graphical user interface or GUI—pronounced "GOO-ey") because it uses pictures (icons) to represent functions and operations.

You'll spend a lot of time flitting back and forth between the desktop and all the other things you do on your Mac. The secret little ways around, over, and through the desktop can make your computing life very simple and satisfying. Some of the more fundamental ways around the desktop are coming right up.

Click a Little, Drag a Little

Raise your right hand and repeat after me: "The mouse is my friend, I shall not fling it across the room in fits of irritation." Think of your mouse as a digital index finger. You'll use it to point at and select all kinds of doo-doo (I mean doo-doo in the kindest possible sense of the word) around the desktop—just like you did in the last chapter when you shut down your Mac.

If you actually pick up your mouse and turn it over, you'll see that the mouse moves the cursor (right now, the cursor is an arrow) by means of a small, hard rubber ball in the bottom. When you move the mouse, the ball rolls with the motion, and the mouse translates that motion and sends it to your Mac. Your Mac then moves the cursor accordingly. It all happens so quickly that you don't even notice the time it takes to relay the movement to the screen.

Click!

When I (or anyone) tell you to *click on* something, that's a shorthand way of saying move the mouse until the tip of the arrow cursor is touching the icon (or menu, or folder, or whatever), and then press the mouse button once. *Click!*

Whatever you were pointing at is now *selected*. When you select something on the desktop, the Mac lets you know it's been selected by changing how it looks. Because it's easier to show you than to explain how things look when they're selected, let's select something.

Move your mouse so the arrow pointer is pointing at your Hard Drive icon. The tip of the arrow should be touching either the picture of the hard drive, or the name below the picture. When it is, click once. If you point and click accurately, your Hard Drive icon is now selected. To give you a comparison, there's a before- and after-clicking picture shown in the following figure. You'll notice how the picture of the hard drive darkens, while the name of the drive goes from black-on-white to white-on-black.

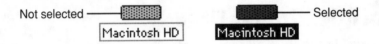

The Hard Drive icon before and after selecting.

If you accidentally select something you don't want selected, just click once somewhere else (preferably on the thing you do want selected).

To unselect (or deselect) the icon, just click anywhere else on the desktop. That works in most circumstances.

This is such a difficult concept (SARCASM ALERT! SARCASM ALERT!), I expect you to be wrapped up in its tacky rococo intricacies for all of five seconds. Once you feel comfortable selecting and deselecting the Hard Drive icon, why don't you try clicking once on some of the other things littered around the desktop, just for laughs.

Click and Hold

If you—in the course of your clicking experiments—happened to click on one of the words (menu names) or icons in the menu bar, you may have seen a menu drop down briefly and disappear. Getting the menu to stay around (so you can read it and do something with it) requires another step added to the basic click.

When you click on a menu heading in the menu bar, you need to click and hold; that is, don't release the mouse button. As long as you hold the mouse button down, the menu stays open, and you can select something from it (like when you selected **Shut Down** from the **Special** menu in the last chapter). We'll be doing a complete menu roundup in the next chapter. For the moment, just get used to clicking and holding open the menus without trying to select anything.

What a Drag!

Okay, so you've clicked and you've held. Next on your list of things to do is *drag*. Now, don't go running to your closet to pull out your stash of the opposite sex's clothing. It's not that kind of drag. I'm talking about drag as in, "Look what the cat dragged in." Only in this case, it's the mouse that does the dragging.

The principle is simple, and it proceeds from the mouse maneuvers you've already mastered. First, you click on something (let's say the Trash) to select it. When you've selected it (that is, it turned dark like the Hard Drive icon did earlier), click and hold on it. While you're holding down the mouse button, move the mouse around. The pointer drags the Trash can around the desktop—actually, the pointer drags just an outline of the Trash, as shown in the following figure—until you release the mouse button. When you release the button, the Trash drops wherever it is.

The Trash does drag.

The same thing happens with any icon on the desktop or in a window. Menus and windows themselves behave differently, but you'll learn all you need to know about them in later parts of this chapter and in the next chapter. Let's proceed with this click thing.

Click-Click!

Since we've pretty much exhausted the clicking, holding, and dragging options on the bare desktop, let's dig up some more stuff to fool around with. To do that, you're going to double-click on your Hard Drive icon to get at the goodies within.

A double-click (if you haven't guessed) is just two clicks in click... er, quick succession. Click, click. For some folks, double-clicking can take a little practice. If you click too slowly, the Mac treats your double-click as two single clicks. If you double-click too quickly, it treats it as just one single click.

Fortunately, the Mac's designers knew that everybody wouldn't double-click at the same speed. There is a way to adjust how your Mac receives and interprets your clicks (we'll cover that in Chapter 11 when we talk about your customizing options). For now, it will do you good to learn double-clicking at the preset speed; later, you'll know whether you want to change the mouse's response speed.

To try out this double-clicking thing, move your mouse so that the tip of the arrow pointer is touching the Hard Drive icon, just like you did when you first learned how to click. This time, instead of a single click, hit it with a double-click and watch what happens.

Windows and Icons and Bears (Oh, My!)

When you double-clicked on your Hard Drive icon, you should have seen the icon go very dark (darker than when only selected), and a little animation should have happened as the hard drive *window* opened.

If an icon is a picture that represents something else, like a hard drive, then the window is the way you get at the stuff inside the icon. In this case, the window holds the stuff that's stored on the hard drive.

With the window to your hard drive open, it should look something like the one shown in the figure of the desktop at the beginning of this chapter. It will look only something like it because while the window itself (the box or frame) will be the same, I probably have more junk stored on my hard drive than you do on yours.

To level the playing field a little bit, let's take a look at a window full of completely made up stuff, just so you get to know the parts of the window before you start worrying about what's inside.

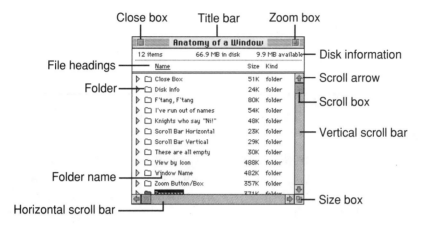

Anatomy of a window.

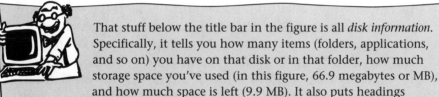

That stuff below the title bar in the figure is all *disk information*. Specifically, it tells you how many items (folders, applications, and so on) you have on that disk or in that folder, how much storage space you've used (in this figure, 66.9 megabytes or MB), and how much space is left (9.9 MB). It also puts headings above the information, so you know what you're looking at in each column. All of these are important bits of information and will be covered in detail later. The column headings appear automatically. To get the disk information to show up, you have to ask for it—I'll tell you how when you look at the Views control panel in Chapter 11.

Breaking (Down) Windows

As long as you're staring at a window, let's break it down into its component parts. You can refer to the one in the preceding figure, or you can look at one on your own Mac. It makes me no nevermind. (That's hillbilly for "I don't care.")

Close Box

In the upper left-hand corner of the window, you'll see a small box. That's the *Close box*. When you click on it, the window closes. If you're at your Mac, try it with your hard drive window, and then just double-click on the Hard Drive icon to reopen it.

Title Bar

That striped bar that the Close box sits on is called the title bar because it contains the title of the window (which is the same as the name of the hard drive or folder the window belongs to).

The title bar can do a couple of cool things. First, it acts as a handle to make moving windows around easier. If you click and hold on the window name (in the last figure, that would be **Anatomy of a Window**), you can drag the window around the desktop. Try it, you'll like it.

If you press and hold the ⌘ key (a.k.a. the **Command** key beside the Spacebar on your keyboard) before you click on the name in the title bar, and then click and hold on the name, you'll see a listing of the window's *lineage*. We talk about the lineage (especially of several windows) as *parents* and *children*. Continuing with the example, my **Anatomy of a Window** window is the child of **Macintosh HD** because the **Anatomy of a Window** folder is on the **Macintosh HD**. I have to open the **Macintosh HD** window to get to its child, the **Anatomy of a Window** window.

If I opened a folder (say the one called **Knights who say "Ni!"**) from the **Anatomy of a Window** window and held the ⌘ key while clicking on its name, the pop-up list would show:

➤ The folder **Knights who say "Ni!"**

➤ Its parent folder, **Anatomy of a Window**.

➤ Its *grandparent* (the parent of the parent of the child) folder, **Macintosh HD**.

I'll talk about this feature in more detail later because it's one of those truly helpful features that many folks seem to forget about (me included). I thought a little extra exposure to it would help you re-member it. It can be as confusing as all those "begats" in the Bible, but you'll get the hang of it.

Zoom Box

In the right-hand corner of the window is a small box with a smaller box inside. That's the *Zoom box*. It's called that because when you click on it, the window zooms out to a larger size, or (if it's already large) zooms down to a smaller size.

Try it now. Try it twice.

This kind of function is called a *toggle*. Think of a toggle like an On/Off switch. If you hit the switch, it does one thing (in this case, zooms the window to a larger size); when you hit the switch again, it does the opposite (zooms the window small again). You'll run into a lot of toggles, not only on the desktop, but in other applications: to turn features on and off, to do and undo certain actions, and so on. They're handy because you can do two functions by remembering just one action. What a bargain!

Hey, Scroll Me Over

On the right and bottom sides of the window are what I call the "scroll assemblies." I call them that because I haven't heard an official term for them. They are generally talked about by their component parts. *Scrolling* is another important concept that you'll use all the time.

Your Mac's screen is only so big. Any window you open is always somewhat smaller than the monitor. What you're looking at, or working on, in the window may be longer or wider than the window displaying it. With a real window (the kind built into walls), you can mash your nose against the glass to see something outside, or just open the window and stick your head out. That doesn't work on a computer. Scrolling lets you look at everything that's hiding beyond the edges of the windows.

Clicking once on one of the scroll arrows rolls the window's contents one line in the direction the arrow is pointing. Clicking once in the scroll bar rolls the window's contents several lines towards the side of the scroll bar where you clicked.

With the scroll box, you can click-hold and drag the box to the exact position you want. The window's contents move accordingly.

55

You know what I'm going to say now: try it. So what am I saying it for? If the window's scroll bar (either horizontal or vertical) is completely gray (without the usual dot pattern inside), that means there's nowhere to scroll—everything there is to see is displayed.

Does Size Count?

Yeah, size counts. If it didn't, why would your Mac windows have a second sizing option built into it? It's right down there at the lower right hand corner of the window: a box with overlapping boxes inside. It's cleverly called the *Size box*. You use it to manually resize the window to the exact size you'd like.

To use the Size box, click-hold on it, and drag the corner down and/or to the right to enlarge the window, or up and/or to the left to make it smaller. The window won't resize as you drag the Size box, instead you'll see an outline of the window moving as you resize. (See what I mean in the following figure.) When you release the mouse button, the window itself changes size.

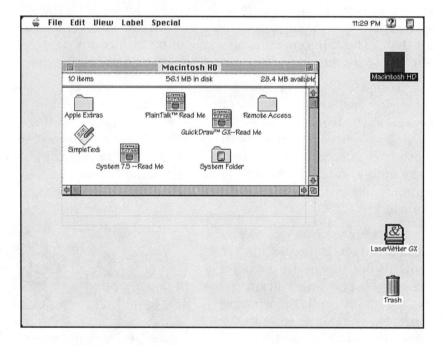

Resizing a window manually.

Try it on for size. (Ouch! Sorry.)

Window Management Tips

Don't waste your money buying expensive window cleaners and paper towels. Instead, use a little vinegar in warm water and old newspapers to clean your windows. Oh, wait. This is a computer book, not a *Hints from Heloise* column. Seriously, just like there are tips to make cleaning the windows in your home easier, there are tips to make managing windows on your Mac easier. Here are a few of them.

Which Window Is Which?

That's not as silly a question as it sounds. Not that you wouldn't be able to tell which window is which by name, because the name is right up there in the title bar. The annoying question is which window is the *active* one.

To figure this out, you'll need more than one window open on your desktop, so double-click on the **Trash** icon. Unless you threw something away when I wasn't looking, you should now have an empty window named **Trash** on your desktop, in addition to the one called **Macintosh HD**.

With windows (and applications), **active** and **inactive** mean pretty much what you'd expect. You can work in or with active windows. You can't do anything with an inactive window unless you make it active first.

You'll notice when the Trash window opened, it opened on top of the one called **Macintosh HD**. The one called **Macintosh HD** also kind of faded into obscurity: the stripes disappeared from the title bar; the scroll bars turned white and lost all detail. That color change is a visual clue to tell you that the window in the background that turned white is *inactive*. You can't do anything with it, unless you click on it to make it *active* again. Go ahead and click on its title bar or any portion of it that's showing.

You'll notice that the two windows have traded places: the Trash window has moved behind the Macintosh HD window; the Trash window also lost all of its details, while the Macintosh HD window has earned back its stripes. The Macintosh HD window is now the active one (the one you can work with), and the Trash is inactive. You can click on each of them in turn, switching them from active to inactive until you're bored senseless, which takes about 10 seconds.

Working with Multiple Windows

Window management gets a little complicated when you have a pile of overlapping windows open on the desktop. Usually, some are completely hidden so you can't even find a corner to click on. That can get ugly.

Click on the desktop, and all of the open windows become inactive.

There are three ways to avoid that. The first is annoying: keep all of your windows small and arrange them so the title bars are all showing so you can click on the one you want to bring to the front as the active window. I've never been able to orchestrate it without losing track of what I was really trying to do. That brings us to way number two.

The second way you already know. Remember when I told you about holding down the ⌘ key when clicking on the window's name? That list of the window's parents and grandparents that popped up can cut through a lot of the confusion surrounding a lot of open windows. Many of the windows and folders you'll work with on a single project (if you're organized) will be parents, grandparents, or children of the same folder or two. So if you need to pull a related window to the front, you can select it from this pop-up list rather than clicking and dragging a bazillion windows around on your desktop.

You select the name of the window you want from the list by dragging the pointer down the list of names until you select the one you want. Select the same way you selected the **Shut Down** option from the **Special** menu back in Chapter 4. The selected window will leap to the front and become active. Very handy.

Finally, if you turn on the **WindowShade** control panel (covered in Chapter 11), you can use the title bar as a window management tool. WindowShade, when turned on, will "roll up" everything below a window's title bar (like a window shade, if you haven't figured that out yet). With WindowShade, open windows hardly take up any room at all and are easier to manage. When you click on a window's title bar, the shade "rolls down" so you can see everything in the window.

We'll talk about other organizational strategies in Chapter 10. Be warned that organizing your hard drive, and therefore your work, is a highly personal thing. If you're sloppy away from your desk, you'll probably be a slob at your desk (I know I am).

With time, your Mac skills will develop, as will your personal computing style. Managing your windows will become second nature to you, and your management style will reflect your personality. I'm all for personality and style, so while I'll give advice and tips, I don't expect you to swallow it all hook, line, and sinker. I expect you to develop your own. My feelings won't be hurt if you try my advice and then chuck it in the Trash—hey, I won't even know that you did it.

Closing Windows

That's about it for windows, for now. Let's clean up your desktop so we can move on. You'll recall from the section on the anatomy of windows that you can close a window by clicking on the **Close** box in the upper left-hand corner. That works.

You can also (if you remember how from the Introduction) use the key combination ⌘-**W**. That means that you press the **Command** (⌘) key and hold it down. While still holding that down, press the **W** key. The active window closes.

Or you can hold down the **Option** key while you click on the **Close** box (or press ⌘-**W**), and all of the open windows on your desktop close.

You'll find that you can do many things on the Mac in about three different ways: via the mouse by clicking or double-clicking on a box or something; via the keyboard by using a command-key combination; or via a menu by selecting a command from a list of related functions.

The Least You Need to Know

This is a deceptively simple chapter (covering some basic, important ideas). You've probably already absorbed everything you need to start. However, for the few, the proud, and the not very absorbent, here are some highlights for further pondering:

➤ The Mac's desktop is a metaphor to make it easier for you to get a handle on what it does. File folders are for putting junk in; the trash is for throwing stuff away.

➤ Your mouse makes manipulating things on the desktop easy. You'll use it to click, double-click, click-hold, and drag various things, and to select commands from menus.

➤ You access all of your files and folders via windows that you can make bigger, smaller, or scroll through to view everything inside.

➤ You can only work in the active (foremost) window on the desktop. To work in any inactive window, click on it to make it the active one.

Chapter 6

Menus in the Macintosh Café

In This Chapter

➤ What's on the menu?

➤ Chopping up the menu bar

➤ Throwing it all away

Why don't we take a quick spin through the menus: see what they are, what they do, and why they don't do everything all of the time.

A Word about the Menus

If you look at your Mac's menu bar, you'll notice that there are two kinds of menus on a Mac. The first is an *icon* or *picture* menu. Instead of a descriptive word heading, there's a picture of Apple's seven-color apple logo. At the other end of the menu bar, there's the Apple Guide menu (the one with the... hey, what is that? A light bulb? The thingy with a question mark inside.), and the Application menu (the one with the little picture of a Mac). These *icon menus* let you do specific things all the time, regardless of what application you are using.

Between the icons on the menu bar are five menus with *word* headings. Unlike the icon menus, the word menus do specific things under certain conditions. Working with the word menus on your Mac is like ordering from a menu in any restaurant. Because I love it and because I'm craving some, let's say it's like ordering food in your favorite Chinese restaurant.

Let's be even more specific and say that you're ordering from the family special page. You know the page I mean, the one where you choose a soup for everyone, an appetizer (I'll have the Pu-Pu platter, thank you), and then two or more entrées: one from column A and one from column B. With the Mac's word-headed menus, you need to choose *two* things. The first is the thing (a folder, document, line of text, or whatever) you'd like to do something to; the second is what you want done.

Because many of the operations chosen through the word menus depend on you selecting something for them to work on, the menus or items in the menu are sometimes unavailable. They won't become available until you select something they can work with. When they're unavailable, the word heading or an individual menu item will turn from black to gray. For example, if you don't have any open windows, your View and Label menus will be gray because they both require an open window on the desktop to be active. The Label menu also requires that you select an icon in that window (a folder, document, or application) before it will become active.

Okay, if you're not totally confused, let's look at the menus one at a time (in order of appearance). I'll try to refresh you on the difference between menus with icon headings and those with word headings.

The Apple Menu

Since it is an icon-headed menu, the Menu (shown in the following figure) does only specific things, but it does them all the time, no matter what application you're using. It is the home of your Desk Accessories (DAs) which we'll go over in Chapter 12. For now, you should know that Desk Accessories, such as Stickies or the Calculator, are available to you whenever you're at your Mac.

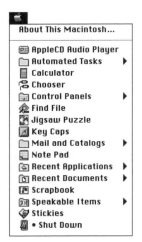

The Apple (🍎) Menu.

The *folders* that appear in the 🍎 menu give you quick access to stuff that may be buried deep within your System folder. The right-pointing arrows beside the folder names indicate that there are *sub-* or secondary menus that will pop-up when the cursor touches these items, allowing you to select particular items in the folder without having to open yet another window on the desktop. Here's what each of the folders contains:

Automated Tasks Gives you access to predefined AppleScripts (also known as *macros* or just *scripts*) that automate certain functions in the Finder. More about that (are you tired of hearing this?) in Chapter 12.

Control Panels Lets you access any or all of the control panels installed on your Mac without having to go rooting around in your System Folder.

Desk Accessories (DAs) are mini-applications that let you do a variety of things. Why call them Desk Accessories instead of little applications? Because you can call them up and use them no matter where you are or what you're doing on your Mac. Instead of being full-featured applications, most Desk Accessories will help you do one or two little things (jot a note, add a couple of numbers, and so on). Desk Accessories include Apple CD Audio Player (if you have an Apple CD-ROM drive), Calculator, the Chooser, Find File, Jigsaw Puzzle, Key Caps, Note Pad, Scrapbook, Stickies, and Shut Down.

Mail and Catalogs   Part of PowerTalk. If you didn't install it, this item won't be there. If you're not on a network (a couple of computers hooked together) you don't need it.

Recent Applications   Contains a list of the last five applications you used. You can select one from the list and relaunch it without having to look for it on your hard drive.

Recent Documents   A list of the last 10 documents (files) you worked with. Selecting one from the list will open both the document and the application you used to create it.

Speakable Items   Lets you open a folder of *speech macros* if you have PlainTalk installed (more about that in Chapter 12).

The most informative item in the ♥ menu is the first one. It's called **About This Macintosh...** , and it gives you information about your Macintosh. Go figure. Just for the heck of it, click-hold on the ♥ menu, and drag the mouse pointer down a little bit, until you select **About This Macintosh...** . Release the mouse button. After your Mac churns for a second, you'll see a window something like the following figure.

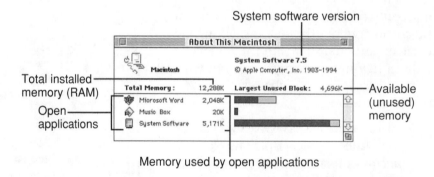

About This Macintosh.

The About This Macintosh window is chock-full of useful information. It tells you the version of the System Software installed (which is good if you're looking at an unfamiliar Mac). The rest of the information shows you how much memory your Mac has and how much memory is used by each application.

The About This Macintosh window shows you how much random-access memory (or *RAM*) is installed in your Mac. You can think about RAM like your own memory: all the things you can remember off the top of your head. RAM is volatile. It doesn't have a temper, but any information in your Mac's RAM disappears when you turn your Mac off. We'll talk more about memory a little later. For right now, you should know that the About This Macintosh item in the menu can display how much RAM you have and how it's being used.

The lower half of the window shows you all the applications you have running (including your System Software) and how much RAM each is eating up. The display changes as you open and close applications. This information comes in handy if you find yourself getting a lot of **Out of Memory** messages in the middle of important projects. Out of Memory messages are discussed in the "Digital Amnesia" section in Chapter 21.

Applications have their own menus, with their very own "About *Application...* " item. You can use it to find out a little bit more about the application you're using.

Computer programmers are an interesting bunch. They like to sign their work by hiding their names in funny, little animations in their programs. These hidden gems are called *Easter Eggs*, because you have to hunt for them.

Usually, finding an Easter Egg involves using an extra key while clicking on something in a program. One Easter Egg is on your desktop right now. Press and hold the **Option** key before clicking on the menu. When the menu drops down, instead of About This Macintosh, you'll see **About The Finder**. (The *Finder* is the part of the System Software that gives you the desktop and the menu bar, and so on.) When you select **About The Finder**, you'll get a black-and-white drawing of the sun rising (setting?) over a mountain range. That's what the first Mac owners saw. Wait a few seconds and a scroll of programmers' names will run across the bottom of the picture. It's a real history of the Macintosh.

That's just one of the dozens of Easter Eggs salted around your Mac's System Software. Try and find others. Happy hunting!

The File Menu

The **File** menu is one of those word-headed menus that usually requires you to select or open something on the desktop before you can use it. The **File** menu (shown in the following figure) has several active functions and several that are inactive (grayed-out).

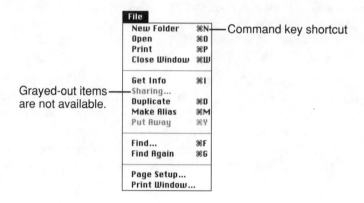

The File menu. Oooh. Ahh.

After some of the menu items, you'll see a command-key equivalent or keyboard shortcut. You use these by pressing and holding down the command key and pressing the indicated letter key (such as ⌘-**W**, to close a window). You'll find keyboard shortcuts in most Mac menus. You'll also find most of the same shortcuts in most Mac applications, which means you only have to learn them once. They're very good to know.

Though the specific functions of each menu (or even the number of menus) change in each program you use, the basic commands remain the same. That's a good thing. When you know how these work, you'll pretty much know how they work in almost any application you use. To spare you any more confusion, I'll just run down the list of commands in the **File** menu, in order:

New Folder Creates a new, empty, untitled folder on the desktop or in the active window.

Open Opens the selected item, if appropriate.

Print Sends a selected file to the printer for printing.

Close Window Closes the currently active window, as we discussed earlier.

Get Info   Gives you information on the item you select on the desktop or in a window.

Sharing   Applies only to Macs on a network. If your Mac isn't on a network, ignore it. If your Mac is on a network, then you probably have a network administrator to manage this stuff. Don't sweat it.

Duplicate   Makes a copy of the selected item.

Make Alias   Makes a little clone of the selected item. It's a handy feature we'll talk about in Chapter 7.

Put Away   Ejects a selected disk from the disk drive and removes its icon from the desktop.

Find   Helps you find a misplaced file on your hard drive or a disk.

Find Again   Lets you search more or widen the search for the thing you were trying to find with the **Find** command.

Page Setup   Tells your printer what size paper you're using, as well as other special printer commands. More on this in Chapter 13.

Print Window   Prints the contents of the currently active window. If there is no window open on the desktop, this item reads **Print Desktop**.

Many of these menu items will be covered in upcoming sections, but it never hurts to see them before you need to use them.

The Edit Menu

The **Edit** menu (as shown in the following figure) deals almost exclusively with text and graphic information. On the desktop, you'll use the **Edit** menu mainly for changing the names of folders and icons.

The Edit menu.

Again, I'll briefly describe the **Edit** menu's functions, but we'll explore them in detail in an upcoming section:

Undo   Restores the very last thing you did to the way it was before you did it. If you accidentally delete a paragraph of text, Undo will bring it back.

The **Clipboard** is a bit of reserved memory that holds a limited amount of information, both text and graphics. It's handy to cut or copy stuff from what you are doing, and then paste it back in at one or more locations. What you store there stays put until you cut or copy something else, or until you turn off your Mac. The bad thing is that the Clipboard can hold only one thing at a time. You can't add to the Clipboard; you can only replace its contents.

Warning! Undo is a great command, but some things simply cannot be undone. In the Finder, Undo only works on the very last action you took. Selecting Undo won't fix what you did three commands ago, and it won't recover a file you accidentally deleted. Don't get the idea that you can do no wrong as long as the Undo item exists. You can—so be careful.

Cut   Removes the selected text or graphic from wherever it is and places it in the *Clipboard* for later use, or until you cut or copy (see below) something else.

Copy   Similar to **Cut**, except that it leaves the selected text or graphic in its original position and places a copy (duh) in the Clipboard.

Paste   Takes whatever you store in the Clipboard and places it where the insertion point (or cursor) is.

Clear   Works like **Cut**, except the selected text or graphic does not go to the Clipboard. It goes bye-bye.

Select All   Selects anything and everything selectable in the currently active window.

Show Clipboard   Displays the contents of the Clipboard in case you forgot what's in there.

The View Menu

The **View** menu (shown in the following figure) lets you control how you want information displayed in your windows. How you want to look at stuff is strictly up to you and your eyesight.

```
View
  by Small Icon
  by Icon
✓ by Name
  by Size
  by Kind
  by Label
  by Date
  by Version
```

The striking, yet handsome, View menu.

View by Small Icon Gives you the smallest icons for your folders and so on, with no other information to get in your way.

View by Icon Gives you the largest icons for your folders and so on, also with no other information to get in your way.

View by Name The display option I personally prefer. It gives you a tiny icon for folders and so on, in alphabetical order by name, but follows each up with more information. *Kind* tells you if it's a folder, application, or document. *Size* tells you how much room it takes up.

> There are a variety of cursors you will use on your Mac. One is the arrow you've seen so far, another is the **insertion point**. It's a vertical line that moves ahead of your typing to show you where the next thing you type will land. Another is the ubiquitous stop watch cursor that lets you know when your Mac is doing something that's taking its full attention, so don't try to do anything else.

View by Size Only works when you display by Name. If you select **View by Size** while displaying either of the icon views, the display will automatically switch to Name view. Instead of alphabetical order by name, View by Size sorts from the largest to the smallest items in your window.

View by Kind Like View by Size, View by Kind only works when you display by Name. If you select **View by Kind** while displaying either of the icon views, the display will automatically switch to Name view. Instead of alphabetical order, View by Kind sorts your window by putting applications first, then documents, and then folders.

The **View** menu only affects the active window. You may want to have different windows show different views. Only time and experience will tell you what works best for you. With the window of your hard drive open, why don't you try each option and see which you like best. I'll wait.

The companion piece to the View menu is the Views control panel, which lets you tinker further with how (and what) information you display in your windows. We'll look at that in Chapter 12.

The Label Menu

The **Label** menu is a handy way of color coding the stuff on your Mac. Simply select an icon, and click-drag on the **Label Menu** (shown in the following figure) until you select the label you want. When you release the mouse button, the selected icon turns the color of the label you choose. The label word (like *Essential* or *Hot*) appears in the Label column when you view by Name, Size, or Kind.

When viewing by name, the arrows in front of the folder icons let you look at what's in each folder without opening another window. Just click on an arrow, and the folder's contents will drop down from the folder (indented a few spaces). Clicking on the same arrow will hide the folder's innards again. It's a great feature that spares you window clutter.

When you view by name and have labels applied to stuff in a window, you can also sort the window by labels by clicking on the word **Label** beneath the title bar as described in the sidebar on the following page. It's convenient for pulling related files (for a project like this book) together without having to hurt yourself coming up with an alphabetical naming scheme for each project. If you don't have any labels applied, then there's nothing to sort by, so nothing happens.

You can customize the labels shown in the last figure to suit your needs. I'll show you how later when we go through the Control Panels in Chapter 12. Be patient.

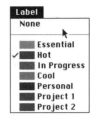

The Label menu.

The Special Menu

We already looked at the **Special** menu back in Part I when I showed you how to shut down your Mac. Of course, it does other things, or it wouldn't be special, now would it? The following figure shows the **Special** menu in all its glory.

The very Special menu.

Clean Up Window Sometimes, the icons in a window just get to be a mess. They fall all over each other so you can't read their names or see how many folders are piled up on each other. Select **Clean Up Window** to make your Mac try to straighten things out for you.

Empty Trash Empties the Trash after you've chucked something into it. We'll do an exercise with this one at the end of the chapter.

Eject Disk Gets your Mac to spit out the floppy disk in your disk drive. You must select a diskette icon

> You can also sort a window in Name view by simply clicking on the word (Size or Kind) below the title bar. The window contents sorts by the word you click, and that word appears underlined to remind you of how you sorted things.

If you like to view your files by icon in your windows (like we discussed when we talked about the **View** menu), but you like the convenience of having them in alphabetical order, do this:

With the window you want to alphabetize active (open it, or click on it to make it active), hold down the **Option** key while you select the **Special** menu. When the **Special** menu drops down, the **Clean Up Window** option will have changed to **Clean Up By Name**. Select **Clean Up By Name**, and watch as your window throws itself into alphabetical order.

for this option to work. Unlike **Put Away** (under the **File** menu), the disk's icon remains on the desktop. This is good for copying disks or working with files from several disks at one time.

Erase Disk   Completely erases the contents of the selected disk, even your hard drive. Don't use it unless you really, really mean it.

Luckily, the ellipsis (…) after the name means that selecting this menu item (or any menu item with "… " after it) will bring up a *dialog box* before it actually does anything. It gives you a chance to chicken out if you've selected it accidentally. Erasing disks and all sorts of other disk tips will be covered in Chapter 9. It's required reading—no excuses.

Restart   Puts your Mac through its startup routine without having to turn the power off. When you install software, you are sometimes required to restart your Mac before you can use the new software.

Did you ever accidentally (or on purpose) stick your finger into an electrical socket? (If you were ever a three-year-old, you must have.) It wasn't very pleasant, was it? Well, something similar happens to your Mac every time you turn on the power. Some compare it to pouring hot water into a cold glass, or constantly revving the engine on your car. It isn't necessarily a bad thing to do; you have to turn your Mac on to use it. However, overusing it can put unnecessary strain on the electronic components. That's why there's a **Restart** option in the **Special** menu. Using **Restart** puts your Mac through its startup sequence without applying a shock (literally) to its System.

It is better for your machine if you leave it running, rather than turning it on and off two or three times a day. If you need to restart it because of a problem or because of new software you've installed, use **Restart**. Your Mac will be much happier.

Shut Down Shuts off all the applications (even the System software) running on your Mac before you turn the power off. On some Mac models (such as some of the Quadras—check your manual), it even turns the power off, too.

The Apple Guide Menu

Apple Guide marks the return to those icon-headed menus that perform specific functions almost all of the time. The following figure shows the menu when pulled down.

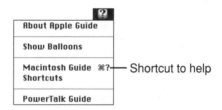

The Apple Guide menu.

The Apple Guide menu is the source of two (count 'em: two) levels of help for you and your Mac. The first, Apple Guide, is a new feature of System 7.5. Apple Guide is an online help system that will literally walk you through an operation that is giving you a case of the heebie-jeebies. At the moment, Apple Guide is available for your Mac itself, and some of the extras that come with System 7.5 (QuickDraw GX and PowerTalk). Other software companies will probably add it to most applications when they release new versions.

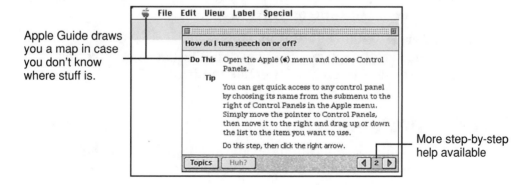

Apple Guide in action—it literally draws you a picture.

The second help feature is Balloon Help which, when turned on, displays little speech balloons with short explanations when you point at various things around the desktop. Keep in mind that it only works in applications written to include help balloons (most do). You'll probably find Balloon Help really cool—for about a hot minute. It is handy for folks just starting out with Macs; there's no denying it. There is, however, also no denying that it slows you down: every time the arrow cursor touches something that has a help balloon attached, you get to see it whether you want to or not. After a while, once you have the basics down, you'll probably want to keep it turned off until you have a new program to learn, need a refresher on some basics, or forget just what that odd-looking button does in Microsoft Word, or something.

Here's the menu summary:

About Apple Guide   Tells you about Apple Guide.

Show Balloons   Turns Balloon Help on. If Balloon Help is already on, this item becomes **Hide Balloons**, and selecting it turns Balloon Help off. (This is known as a what, class? A *toggle*, like we talked about in "Anatomy of a Window" in Chapter 5.)

Macintosh Guide   Opens up the set of Apple Guides for your Mac and System 7.5. This option disappears when you open an application (when applications include their own guides, it will let you access that guide).

Shortcuts   Brings up a set of cards that summarize the assortment of keyboard shortcuts that you can use at the desktop. When you're using an application that includes Balloon Help, this item turns into that application's access to help (in Microsoft Word, for instance, it reads **Microsoft Word Help**).

PowerTalk Guide   Opens the Apple Guides for PowerTalk, included with System 7.5. If you didn't install PowerTalk, this won't be here (more on PowerTalk in Chapter 12).

The Application Menu

Right now, with no applications open, your Application menu isn't very helpful. However, the Application menu does come in handy when you have one or more applications running at once (that's called *multitasking*). As you open applications, your Mac adds their names to the list at the bottom of the menu. The next figure shows the Application menu with some of the programs I used while putting together the screen shots you'll see throughout the book.

Multitasking is a geeky way of saying "doing more than one thing at a time." In computing, it generally means running more than one program simultaneously.

The Application menu with stuff in it.

I'm going to run through the menu based on the figure above, the one with other applications showing, because the menu really only works when you have other stuff running. When you go to use it yourself later, just substitute your own application names for the ones shown here, okay?

The Menu Icon While it isn't really a selectable menu item, the menu's icon lets you know what application is active in the foreground. Like an active window, an active application is the one up front on the desktop (the one you can actually do stuff with). In the preceding figure, the active application is the Finder (the desktop). You can tell, first, by the little Mac icon that heads the menu, and second, because there is a check mark next to the Finder in the bottom half of the menu. If Microsoft Word were the active application, it would be checked in the bottom half of the menu, and its icon (to the left of its name) would be the one that appears in the menu bar.

Hide Finder Hides all of the windows on the desktop associated with the Finder. If Microsoft Word were the active application, this item would read **Hide Microsoft Word**.

Hide Others   Hides all of the windows associated with applications other than the active application. This is handy for reducing desktop clutter when working on a complicated project.

Show All   Shows all the windows associated with all of the open applications. This is handy if you're lost and don't know where you want to go or what you want to do. (Needless to say, I use this feature a lot.) **Show All** only becomes an active (not grayed-out) choice when you use **Hide Others** to hide other windows and applications.

The Applications List   You can select the name of any application in this list to make it the active application (that is, the one in the front that you can do something with). I think it's easier to select an application from this list than to **Show All** of your application windows and then click on a window associated with the project you want. Both ways work, though, and you may find it easier the other way.

The benefits of the Application menu and System 7.5's capability for multitasking become more apparent if you've ever worked on an involved project and only been able to use one application at a time. With the Application menu, you can burn up the desktop, flipping between applications, and as Ray Bradbury says, "It [is] a pleasure to burn."

Taking Out the Trash: An Exorcise

By the way, the above isn't a typographical error, it's a joke, and we haven't quite gotten to the punch line yet. (I hope it'll still be funny when we get to it.)

We certainly covered a lot of stuff in this chapter. I think you should probably take a break right about now—unless you snuck out while I was babbling away. Before you run off for a cup of coffee or some other beverage, let's run through a quick exercise to pull some of this huge amount of boring, yet factual, information together so it sticks in your mind a little better.

If you're not at your Mac, get to it. If it isn't turned on, fire it up. You'll need your hard drive window open on the desktop, so if it isn't, double-click on your **Hard Drive** icon to get it there. Okay. We're going to create and dispose of a little trash that will let you use some of the menu and window features we've been talking about without running the risk of accidentally throwing out something you need. Follow these steps:

1. Select **New Folder** under the **File** menu. That creates an *untitled folder* in your hard drive's window.

    > If the folder name doesn't get high- lighted (it should, but just in case), hit the **Enter** key. That should do it.

2. When the untitled folder appears, its name is first black (new folders are automatically selected) and then turns a different color (probably gray, unless you've been playing with the Color Control Panel behind my back). That's the *highlight color*, and the name is *highlighted.* That means you can change the folder's name.

    > Your Mac **highlights** an item to show you that you've selected it. Icons go dark. Text, including the names of files and folders, gets washed with a color (I'll show you how to change the highlight color when we talk about **Control Panels** in Chapter 12). To remember the high- lighting term, think of the colored, highlighting markers you buy to mark important phrases in a textbook.

3. While the folder name is still highlighted, type its new name. For the sake of my pathetic joke, type: **Demon Folder** (if you don't want to play along, call it anything— up to 27 characters, numbers, and spaces). The first character you type replaces the old name. Press **Enter** again. The folder is renamed, re- alphabetized by its new name, and still selected.

4. Now, while the renamed folder is still selected, pull down the **File** menu again, and select **Duplicate**.

5. A folder called **Demon Folder copy** (if you called it Demon Folder like I asked you to) appears in the window after the original. It's a carbon copy of the original, except for the name: you can't have

two files with exactly the same name in any window or folder—your Mac won't let you, so don't even try.

6. Rename the copy as you did the original. Name it **Beelzububba**.

7. Click and drag the folder Beelzububba until it is on top of the original Demon Folder. The Demon Folder turns dark, as if selected, when the arrow pointer touches it. Let go of the mouse button. The folder Beelzububba is now inside the Demon Folder (you can double-click on the Demon Folder icon and see, if you don't believe me).

8. If you care to, you can repeat the process (creating new or duplicate folders, renaming them, and dropping them into the Demon Folder) to your heart's content, or at least until you run out of demon names. Or you can just move on to the next step.

9. Now click the **Demon Folder** and drag it onto the **Trash** icon. The Trash behaves like any other folder; when the pointer dragging the folder touches the Trash, the Trash turns dark. When you drop (release the mouse button) the Demon Folder into the Trash, the Trash icon changes to show you there's something inside. Neat, huh?

10. Now that the Trash is full, you may as well empty it. Select **Empty Trash** from the **Special** menu.

11. You'll receive a warning that you're about to throw away something that may be important. Since we want to get rid of these Demons (exorcise them, as it were), click in the circle that says **OK**. That's called a *button*, and they work like, well, buttons that you push (as opposed to buttons on clothes).

If you find that warning annoying each and every time you want to throw something away, you can turn it off. Click on the **Trash** icon to select it. Then select **Get Info** from the **File** menu. You'll see the Info window. Click on the check mark in front of **Warn Before Emptying** so the check mark goes away. Congratulations, your Trash Warning is disabled. Now be careful that you don't throw anything important away.

That wasn't too difficult, was it? And you even picked up a few bonus bits of information along the way.

The Least You Need to Know

I don't expect all of this menu stuff to stick. It gets easier with practice and patience. The essential thing to remember is where this chapter is for easy reference as you explore your new Mac. If you must have something to remember from this chapter, remember:

➤ The menu bar is your friend. It gives you speedy access to nearly every single function your Mac can perform.

➤ You'll also find *keyboard shortcuts* for the most frequently used commands right after their menu entries (like ⌘-S for Save). They give you even speedier access to often-used commands.

➤ The View and Label menus offer great organizational tools, if you're inclined to use them.

➤ The icon-headed menus (the and Application menus) give your Mac an incredible amount of flexibility: the menu for enabling you to use DAs any time, and the Application menu for enabling you to switch between any and all open applications without having to quit or restart any of them.

➤ The Apple Guide menu is a source of help, whenever you need it.

Programs, Aliases, and Other Hocus-Pocus

In This Chapter

➤ Launching programs (3, 2, 1... we have lift-off!)

➤ The alias relocation program

➤ Automated aliases

➤ One-click launching with the Launcher

Welcome to Chapter 7. In this chapter, we'll look at all the different ways there are to launch (that is, *start*) applications, and how to simplify that process with spiffy little things called *aliases*.

Believe it or not, there's a method to my madness (people don't usually question the *madness* part, just the method). What I'm trying to do is build up your Mac skills gradually, layer upon layer, so that by the time we're done, you'll be ready to take on any application or problem the Mac throws at you. You may not learn exactly what you need for every situation, but I hope to give you the power to know where to look and how to look for solutions on your own.

The Face That Launched 1,OOO Applications

Actually, I don't think Helen of Troy owned a Mac, but if she had, she'd have launched *billions* of applications by now. *Launching*, or starting, an application is something you're going to do often. As cool as the desktop is, there aren't many productive things you can do with it. You have to start up another program. So, let's see how to do it.

As I mentioned earlier (and will mention again) there are usually several ways to accomplish the same task on a Mac. Launching an application is no different. Here are five methods you can use to *directly* launch a program. (I stress *directly* because there is a way to launch a program *indirectly*. We'll be talking about that later on.) We'll go over each of these ways in the next few sections.

Click on an Icon and Use a Menu

A common way to launch a program is to select the program's icon, and then use the **Open** command. To select an icon, simply click on it. When it's highlighted, pull down the **File** menu, and choose the **Open** command.

For example, look in your hard drive's window for the **SimpleText** icon. It should be right out there in the open. When you find it, click on it to select it. While it's selected, go to the **File** menu, and select **Open**. Then, jump back. (James Brown noises are optional.)

Click on an Icon and Use a Shortcut Key

A careful observer may have noticed that the **Open** command on the **File** menu has a keyboard shortcut: ⌘-**O**. Surprisingly enough, that shortcut key is the second way to launch a program. To use it, you select the program's icon, and then press the ⌘ and O keys simultaneously.

Simon Says Click Twice

Here is an excruciatingly simple way to start a program: **just double-click on the application's icon**. This is probably the fastest way to launch an application. Just point right at the program's icon with the mouse pointer, and click twice on it. It'll start right up, easy as pie.

The Sneaky Back-Door Method: Double-Clicking on a Document

Did you notice that in the preceding sections I kept telling you to select a *program* or *application* icon? I had to be specific because there are different types of files. There are also *document* files, the files you create when you use a program. Your Mac calls these files *documents* to easily distinguish them from applications and folders. (You can see what your Mac calls each type of file by reading down the **Kind** column when you view a window by name.)

Double-clicking on a document file works because every document you produce with a program is tagged with *File Type* and *Creator* information. The File Type tells whether a file is a word processing document, picture file, or something else entirely. The Creator is a coded version of the name of the program that produced the file. Both are stored in a little snip of information called a *File Header*, the first place your Mac looks when you double-click on a document.

You can launch a program through one of its documents just by double-clicking on the document's icon. For example, if you double-clicked on a **Read Me** file, the SimpleText program would start, and the Read Me document would immediately appear on-screen.

If you get a disk of software with a **Read Me** or **Read Me First** file on it, you really should read it first. They generally contain late-breaking news about the software that didn't make the printed manual. The information is often very helpful and can spare you a lot of grief.

So, you've just learned another way to launch a program. Believe it or not, there is still another way. Keep reading.

Drag 'N' Drop

The last way you can open an application directly is by dragging a document icon and dropping it right on the application you want to use to open it. I say the application you *want* to use because sometimes you have a mystery file and you don't know (or don't own) the program that created it. You can try to open it with an application you do own by dragging and dropping the document on that application. Sometimes it works and sometimes it doesn't, but it doesn't hurt to try.

You drag and drop a document onto an application the same way you dragged and dropped a folder onto the Trash: click-hold and drag the document to the application's icon. The application icon will darken, as if it's selected; then let go of the mouse button. The application will launch and try to open the document you dropped on it.

Get Me Outta Here! Quitting an Application

Now that you've launched the program, you're going to need to know how to get out of it. That's called *quitting*. Quitting an application is just a fancy-shmancy way of saying "shutting it off." To quit, select **Quit** from the program's **File** menu. Or you can use the key combination ⌘-Q to quit.

Alias Smith and Jones

I mentioned *aliases* earlier when we looked at the **Make Alias** command in the **File** menu. You were probably scratching your head over that one. Rest assured, they have nothing to do with the Witness (or in my case, Witless) Relocation Program. Aliases are *so cool*. They are little clones of anything you care to clone: applications, documents, file folders, even of your hard drive or the Trash. They take up very little disk space—only 1–3K each—*gobs* less than if you dropped actual copies of things all over the place.

Aliases act like a trail of bread crumbs leading back to the original application (or whatever). When you double-click on an alias, the double-click follows the trail back to the original application (or whatever) and reacts as if you'd double-clicked on it. It's like you're creating little Brothers Karamazov: poke one, the other says *"ouch!"*

You leave your frequently used items (applications or folders, and so on) wherever they are on your hard drive, and scatter their aliases where you can get at them easily (on the desktop, in the menu, anywhere convenient for you).

Let's make an alias. In this example, you'll make an alias of SimpleText and put it on the desktop, and then move it into the menu. Although this example uses SimpleText, keep in mind that the procedure is the same for everything you want an alias of.

Start by clicking on the **SimpleText** icon to select it. While SimpleText is selected, click on the **File** menu, and select the **Make Alias** option (or use the shortcut ⌘-**M**). When you see the SimpleText icon again, you'll be surprised to find its alias lying right beside it in the window (as shown in the following figure). That's all there is to it.

Aliases are a smart idea. Your Mac, however, is still an idiot. If you move (or remove) the original application (or whatever), the alias' trail of bread crumbs won't follow along. The double-click follows the trail back to where the application used to be, and you get a cranky screen message about being unable to locate the original. When you move an original, you have to delete the old alias and make a new one. If you delete an original, delete the alias.

SimpleText and its alias.

You'll notice two things about the alias. First, your Mac added the word *alias* to the end of the file's name. This is partially to identify it as the alias, but your Mac added *alias* to the name mostly because you can't have two files with exactly the same name in the same place. Second, you'll notice that an alias' name appears in *italics*; even if you change the alias' name (and we will), it will always be in italics.

The Alias Relocation Program

One of the handier places to put an alias of a frequently used item is right on the desktop. As long as it doesn't get buried behind a dozen windows, it's always right there where you can see it and get to it. Another good place to put an alias is on the menu, so you have access to it from any application.

To the Desktop

To put your SimpleText alias on the desktop, just drag it from your hard drive's window, and drop it wherever you like on your desktop. You can form a conga-line of aliases across the bottom or down the left side of your screen—whatever works for you.

Now that it's out of the same window as its original, you can rename the SimpleText alias, if you care to. Personally, I just delete the word "alias" and shorten the name: I shortened my **Microsoft Word alias** to just **Word**. (If you don't remember how to rename a file, look back in the last section of Chapter 6, where you renamed the untitled folders for the Trash exercise.)

With the alias settled in its new home on the desktop, you can use it to open SimpleText without having to root around for the original. The SimpleText alias responds exactly the same way the original SimpleText icon responds to any of the launching techniques you've already learned. Try some now.

When you've finished amusing yourself with opening the alias, let's move it into the Menu.

To the Menu

Putting an alias into the menu is easier than you think. To begin, look for the folder named **System Folder** in your hard drive's window. Double-click on it when you've found it. This is the granddaddy of all folders.

Look around inside the System Folder for the folder named **Apple Menu Items**, and double-click on that. You'll recognize it by the Apple logo on the folder. When the Apple Menu Items window opens, you'll find everything that shows up in your menu (except **About This Macintosh...**). If you look closely, you'll see you already have an alias in there: the *Control Panels* folder. You can tell it's an alias because its name is in *italics*, even though the word "alias" was edited out.

Drag the SimpleText alias from the desktop, and drop it in the Apple Menu Items window. Your Mac will churn for a second or two (you'll know it's working because the pointer icon will turn briefly into an animated ticking watch). Now, select the ⌘ menu, and scroll down the list. You'll see your SimpleText alias listed there, right after the Scrapbook DA. To launch SimpleText from the alias in the ⌘ menu, just select it like you would any other menu item. SimpleText will launch.

With System 7.5's scriptable Finder (if you have AppleScript installed), there is a script called **Add Alias to Apple Menu** under the **Automated Tasks** entry in the ⌘ menu. Just click on the item you want to make an alias of and select **Add Alias to Apple Menu** from the **Automated Tasks** list. A little hocus-pocus, and there's a new alias in your ⌘ menu.

Sorting Aliases in the ⌘ Menu

Things in the ⌘ menu are sorted alphabetically. If I'm remembering the alphabet correctly, that's why SimpleText shows up after the Scrapbook. You can't change how the ⌘ menu sorts things, so if you want menu items to show up in a different order, you have to change their names so they fall where you'd like alphabetically. The easiest way to do that is to add a space in front of the name(s) you want at the top of your list, because blank spaces come before everything else in the alphabet.

To add a space, click on the **SimpleText alias** icon to select it. When the name is highlighted, position the I-beam cursor over the beginning of the name, and click so that the insertion point appears before the **S** in **Simple** (as shown in the next figure). Press the **Spacebar** once, and then press **Enter**.

Editing an alias' name.

If you want to get fancy, you can use two spaces for some menu items, and they'll float to the very top of the list. Use one space for the ones you want below those. Leave the names of the ones you want below those alone; don't add anything. You now have three levels of importance in the ⌘ menu. Slick.

Woomp! Here it is.

SimpleText alias on top of the ᯓ menu.

If you want to add another level to your ᯓ menu, you can add a *special character* called a *bullet* (•) to the beginning of the alias' name by pressing the **Option-8** key combination instead of the Spacebar. Special characters, like the bullet, sink to the bottom of the list alphabetically. I'll talk more about customizing the ᯓ menu when we talk about customizing options on your Mac in Chapter 10.

Special characters, such as the bullet (•), are part of the character sets of most of the *fonts* (typefaces, such as Times and Helvetica) on your Mac. You can access special characters by using the **Option key** plus a **character key** (like the Option-8 combination for the bullet), or the **Option key** plus the **Shift key** plus a **character key** (Option-Shift-8 gives you the symbol for degrees Fahrenheit, as in 451°). We'll talk more about these special characters in Chapters 12 and 14, when we talk about the *Key Caps* Desk Accessory *and fonts*. (You can make the ᯓ symbol by pressing **Option-Shift-K**, by the way.)

As you get more experience and rely heavily on more programs and folders on your Mac, you may wind up with a very full ᯓ menu. You can avoid that, if you're using System 7.5, by leaving the ᯓ menu alone—at least as far as *application* aliases are concerned. Save the

⌘ menu for aliases of frequently accessed folders, desk accessories, and so on. Throw all of your program aliases into the Launcher.

The One Click Launcher

The Launcher (shown in the following figure) used to only be available to Performa users—now it's available to all Mac users with System 7.5. The Launcher gives you a palette of icons that you simply click on to launch the associated application, hence the name.

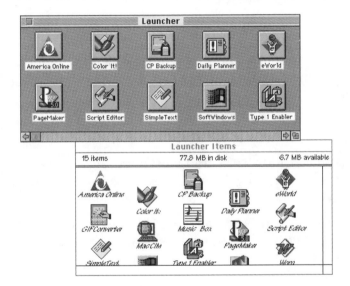

The Launcher (top) and Launcher Items folder (bottom).

When you first install System 7.5, there are only two items in the Launcher: SimpleText, and the AppleScript Script Editor (the program you use to write scripts like those in the Automated Tasks folder—it's discussed in Chapter 12). To add more, simply make aliases of your favorite/most used applications, and drag those aliases into the **Launcher Items folder** located inside your System folder.

When you next open the Launcher (by selecting it from the **Control Panels**

By the way, items in the Launcher are also sorted alphabetically, so you can tinker with the alias names (as we did with those in the Apple Menu Items folder) to move the applications you use most to the front of the line.

submenu under the menu) all of your newly created aliases will show up—in alphabetical order—in the Launcher palette. To launch an application on the Launcher, just click on its icon, and it will fire right up.

The Least You Need to Know

Now that you know how to launch applications, you're probably going to want to actually do something with them once you start them up. Before you skip to the next chapter and start learning, refresh your memory by perusing these important concepts:

➤ You can launch (*start*) an application with its icon, or with a document's icon, by selecting it and choosing **Open** from the **File** menu, or pressing ⌘-O. Double-clicking on either kind of icon also works.

➤ Aliases are simple to make: click on an application (or whatever) icon, and select **Make Alias** from the **File** menu (or press ⌘-M). They simplify your life.

➤ You can add aliases (and most anything you like) to the menu, just by dragging them into the Apple Menu Items folder inside the System Folder.

➤ Using System 7.5's Launcher will keep your menu from getting choked with too many application aliases.

Chapter 8

Your Basic, Everyday Mac Duties

In This Chapter

➤ Chatting with dialog boxes

➤ Opening, saving, and closing files

➤ S.C.R.A.P.: selecting, copying, replacing, and pasting

➤ Clipping without penalties

I'm almost ashamed to admit it, but I am a "Talk Soup" junkie. If you don't know what it is, "Talk Soup" is a show on the E! cable channel that features clips of daytime talk shows, and it's hosted by Greg Kinnear. It's funny, sarcastic, and just a little bit cranky—much like yours truly. I can't start my day without it. I'm hooked because it spares me the greater embarrassment of having to watch a full-length talk show, while still fulfilling my need for trash TV. Because it only shows clips of the talk shows, I think of "Talk Soup" as a trash compactor—all the trash with less time wasted.

It's an appropriate lead-in for this chapter because *clips* feature prominently in both. "Talk Soup" is all about talk show clips. This chapter is all about the most commonly used Mac commands, including: Copy (⌘-C), Cut (⌘-X), and Paste (⌘-V), which allow you to work with clips from your own documents. It's also about the new (and very handy) *clipping* feature that has been built into System 7.5. (Hey, it's hard to work a "Talk Soup" mention into a computer book.)

These everyday functions are located in your File and Edit menus (except for clipping, which is so simple, there isn't even a menu command for it). How common are they? Well, try not using at least one of them in any session on your Mac—it can't be done. You'll wind up just sitting there, staring at your desktop. That's how common these beauties are.

Open Sez-Me

Say you're using SimpleText and you want to *open* a file (that is, load it into memory so you can tinker with it). When you select **Open** from the **File** menu, SimpleText presents the Open dialog box shown in the next figure. This dialog box is necessary because the Mac needs to know which file you'd like to open.

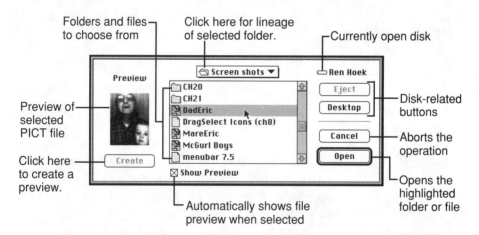

SimpleText's Open dialog box.

Using the Open dialog box, you can navigate to the exact file in the exact folder you want opened. Clicking on the name of the currently displayed folder (**Screen shots** in the figure) brings up the folder's lineage (just like you did in Chapter 5 with a regular window by ⌘-clicking on its title). You can search all the way back to the desktop to locate the file.

> Use the shortcut key ⌘-O to open a file. It will work in any Mac application worth its salt... in short, it's standard.

On the right is a little picture of a hard drive (named **Ren Hoek**—of "Ren and Stimpy" fame—in the figure) showing the name of the currently open disk or drive. If it's a disk you're looking at, the picture of the hard drive is replaced by a picture of a diskette. If you're looking for a file on a disk and the disk doesn't contain the file you want, clicking once on the **Eject** button (grayed out in the figure) ejects that disk from the drive.

> Sometimes, when you give your Mac a command (like to *open* or *save* a file), your Mac requests more information to complete the task. Macs get this information by using **dialog boxes**. They're called dialog boxes because the Mac asks you a question and you answer it. That's a dialog—short and sweet.

Clicking on the **Desktop** button changes the file display to show all of the items, such as hard drives, disks, or files (even the Trash), actually stored on the desktop. This is a speedy way of digging yourself out of a folder buried deep within other folders.

The **Cancel** button lets you stop the process (if you clicked **Open** by mistake or change your mind). Your Mac always gives you a chance to change your mind, especially before you do something destructive, such as erase a disk. I'll talk about destructive things in detail in Chapter 9. Just call me Uncle Fester.

When you locate the file you want to open, click on it to select it. In the previous figure, the selected file is a PICT file (short for PICTure). With PICT files and QuickTime movies, SimpleText's Open dialog lets you take a peek at the file without actually opening it: notice the small picture at the left of the dialog. It's a great time-saver if you can't remember which picture file is which—I never can.

The **Open** button opens the selected file or folder in the List box. Imagine that. (*Pssst!* If you're following along on your own Mac and can't find a document to open, you can create a brand-spanking-new one by selecting the **New** command from SimpleText's **File** menu. You can also use the ⌘-N key combination. Any application that lets you create a document of any kind will respond to the New command.)

Save Me!

Do you remember reading about *RAM* (random-access memory) in Chapter 6? Whenever you work with a document in an application, the document is held in your Mac's RAM. It's the kind of memory that goes away when you switch off your Mac. As you add or remove stuff from the document, the changes are also stored only in RAM.

If you switch off your Mac, the document goes away forever unless you first save it to your hard drive or a diskette. You save a document by selecting **Save** from the **File** Menu. When you use the **Save** command in SimpleText, you'll see the Save dialog box shown in the following figure. Other programs use variations of this dialog box. Some are more complicated, others are less complicated. Through them all, these features remain standard.

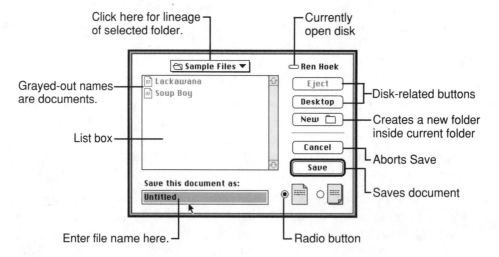

SimpleText's Save dialog box.

The Save dialog box is a kissing-cousin, as it were, to the Open dialog box. Let's take the nickel tour of it, my treat.

The *folder name* (which pops up with the folder's lineage) and the *current disk name*, **Eject**, and **Desktop** buttons function exactly the same way as they do in the Open dialog box (or any dialog box, for that matter). You can use them to navigate to the exact disk or folder where you want to save your file.

> To quickly save a file, use the key combination ⌘-S. This shortcut works in any Mac application.

Here's a helpful hint: If you want to save your file to a disk that isn't in your disk drive, save the file normally (with ⌘-S), and when the dialog box appears, pop in the disk. The disk will automatically become the selected disk, and you won't have to navigate to it.

The **New Folder** button creates a new folder in the currently open disk or folder. If you click on it, a smaller dialog box appears asking you to enter a name for the new folder. Type in a name and press **Enter**.

The **Cancel** button aborts the Save operation and returns you to the application.

The **Save** button saves your document in the currently open folder or disk. Because it has that thick, black border, you can simply press your **Enter** key, rather than clicking on it to save. You can, of course, click on it, too. By the way, if you select a *folder* in the list box, the **Save** button changes to **Open**, so you can open that folder. (You can also open a folder by double-clicking on its name in the list box.)

> A **Stationery Pad** behaves like its real-world counterpart. A document saved as stationery, when opened in an application, appears as a new, untitled document, so the original file is never altered. This format is ideal for letterheads, form letters, or any other kind of file or information you use frequently with only minor changes.

Below the Save button, you see two document icons with *radio buttons* beside them. The filled (selected) radio button indicates that the current document will be saved as a regular document. The icon beside it, with the bottom right corner folded up, will save the current document as a *Stationery Pad* when selected (just click on the radio button to select).

Finally, below the **Save this document as:** is an edit box where you can enter a name for the file you are saving. The name should be something obvious and under 32 characters. A letter to your parole board might be named ParoleBoard Memo (or ParoleBoard Memo10, if you write to them frequently). When you have the List box displaying the folder you want to save the file in and you've entered the file's name, just click on the **Save** button (or press **Enter**), and the file will be saved with that name in that folder.

You'll only be confronted with the Save dialog the first time you save a file, or when you use the **Save As** command to save a copy of the file with a different name. Every time you save a file after that, the changed copy will automatically replace the old copy on your disk or hard drive.

Closing Time

So, you've saved your file, and you're ready to work on something else. Before you open another file, you should close the one you're working on. You could leave it open, but if you leave all your files open, you'll wind up with a bunch of open windows scattered all over. They'll hog your system's resources and slow down your Mac. Bad news. It's best to close documents if you know you're done with them.

An **Alert Box** will warn you that you're about to do something you may not want to do. If you close a file without saving any changes you made, you'll lose those changes. The Alert Box just wants to be sure you really, really want to do whatever you just told your Mac to do. You can tell it to carry out your order, or you can cancel the order.

To close a file, select **Close** from the **File** menu (or use ⌘-**W**, or click in the document window's **Close Box**). If you've saved your document, the window will close without a fuss, and you'll be able to open an existing file or create a new one. If you made changes to your file since the last time you saved it, an alert box will ask if you want to save the latest changes. I suggest saving your changes. When the Mac finishes updating the file, the window closes.

Now that you know how to get in and out of documents, let's move on to something meatier.

Selecting Stuff

Probably the most-used operations on the Mac are copying, replacing, and pasting. In order to do those actions, you have to first learn how to select the things that you want to copy, replace, or paste. You've already done some selecting when you clicked on an icon to select it, but there are many other ways to select things. Let's go over a few.

Icon Selection

You already know how to select a single icon, but if you have a few you want to do something to (like make a pile of aliases all at once), it's easiest to select them altogether. If you selected them singly (clicking on one, making an alias, clicking on the next, and so on), it can get pretty tedious. Don't worry; you're covered.

Try these handy selection methods:

➤ If you hold down the **Shift** key, you can click on several icons, and you can select them all. Strangely enough, this maneuver is a *shift-click*.

If you select an icon in a group that you don't really want selected, you can hold down the **Shift** key and click on the selected icon to deselect it.

➤ You can also select a whole slew of icons: Click in the window *near* the first icon, and drag the mouse toward the other icons you want to select. You see a dotted-line box start at the point where you clicked. When you drag, as the box touches icons, you will select them (as shown in the next figure). That's a *drag-select*.

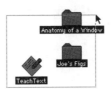

Drag-selecting icons.

➤ If you want to select everything in a window you can use the key combination ⌘-A (A is for All). ⌘-A is another of the key combinations that works in most applications.

Text Selection

You have a few more options when you select text, depending on the complexity of the word processor you're using. SimpleText, which we'll use for the examples here, has very few text selecting options. Microsoft Word, on the other hand, has gazillions of them.

We'll look at the basic ones that are available in SimpleText. When you move up to a more comprehensive word processor, make sure you check out your text selecting options in the manual.

To start, launch SimpleText by whatever method you prefer. When it opens, an *untitled* text window appears. In order to select some text, you're going to need some text to select. Type in a paragraph or so of anything you care to enter.

After you've entered text, you may as well save it, just for the practice. Select **Save** from the **File** Menu, or press ⌘-S. When you see the Save dialog box, type in an appropriate name and press **Enter**, or click on the **Save** button. After you save the text, the **Untitled1** in the title bar changes to whatever you've named your document.

Move the cursor around your screen: you'll see when the cursor is over the text window; it's the I-beam cursor. When it strays to the scroll, title, or menu bars, it turns back into the arrow cursor. That's because your Mac only lets you do what's appropriate at the point the cursor is touching. It's not appropriate to enter text directly on the title bar, so you don't even have that option.

Position the I-beam cursor so it's touching one word, and double-click. Boom, that word is highlighted/selected. To select more than one word, position the I-beam cursor at the beginning of the first word you want to select, and then click-drag until you highlight all the words you want selected. In this manner, you can select two words, a sentence, a whole paragraph, or more.

To select all of your sample text, you can click-drag over the whole paragraph. Or you can simply use the **Select All** command under the **Edit** menu, or press the ⌘-A combination.

Copy, Cut, and Paste

Sister Mary Mayonnaise was a terror when it came to her students' copying. I guess this is the best revenge: teaching a lot of people how to copy all at once. I'll try not to be smug.

Copy

Copying text comes in handy when you find yourself typing the same word or phrase over and over in a document. Say, you were writing a paper about Joseph Conrad's *Heart of Darkness*. You'd get tired of typing "Belgian Congo" and "whited sepulchers" over and over (especially "sepulchers" because its hard to spell).

By using the **Copy** command, you can copy the ticklish word or phrase to the Clipboard (discussed back in Chapter 4), and then just **Paste** it into your document wherever you need it. Here's how: pick a word, any word, from your sample text. Double-click on it to select it. While the word is highlighted, select **Copy** from the **Edit** menu (or press the ⌘-C combination). That word is now in your Clipboard. If you don't believe me, you can select the **Show Clipboard** command, also under the **Edit** menu.

Paste

Now that the tricky word (or phrase, or paragraph) is right where you want it, you can **Paste** it anywhere you care to. To Paste anything from the Clipboard, simply move the I-beam cursor to the spot where you want to paste, and click once to put the insertion point on that spot. Select **Paste** from the **Edit** menu (or press ⌘-V). Your Mac drops the word, words, or whatever from the Clipboard at the insertion point.

Remember that the Clipboard can only hold *one thing at a time*. If you copy another word or phrase to the Clipboard, it replaces whatever was there before. If there's something you want available for pasting all of the time (like your name and address), you may want to add it to your Scrapbook. I'll show you how in Chapter 12 in the "Night of the Living DAs" section.

Cut and Paste

Cut and Paste is a similar operation to Copy and Paste, except for one big difference. When you copy text, the original word or phrase you selected stays right where it was in your document. When you cut text, you remove the original word or phrase from the document.

Cut and Paste comes in handy if you find yourself juggling paragraphs. If you find a paragraph at the end of your *Heart of Darkness* report that should have been at the beginning, you can click-drag to select it, and choose **Cut** from the **Edit** menu (or press the ⌘-X combination). Then **Paste** (⌘-V) it where it belongs. Cut and Paste can save you a lot of tedious retyping.

Replacing Text

Sometimes, when you're writing (at least when I'm writing), you find that a word or phrase is completely wrong. You want to replace it with something else—preferably something better. There are several ways to do that:

If you accidentally start to type while you have a word or phrase selected, stop. Select **Undo** from the **Edit** menu (or use ⌘-Z), and cross your fingers. That should restore the text you accidentally replaced.

➤ You can position the insertion point after the offending word or phrase, and use the **Delete** key to delete it one letter at a time, and then type in a new word or phrase.

➤ You can select the offending word or phrase and **Cut** it, and then type in the new one.

➤ You can select the word or phrase, and then just start to type. Whenever you select a letter, word, line, or paragraph of text, it is replaced by whatever you type next. Take this as a warning as well as a hint: Whenever you select a letter, word, line, or paragraph of text, whatever you type next will replace it.

Clipping!

The biggest limitation of using Cut and Copy to move stuff around in a document (or between several documents) is that if you want to paste more than one thing, you wind up copying each item to the Clipboard over and over, because the Clipboard only holds one thing at a time.

In order to remedy that situation, System 7.5 has built in a no-fuss, no-muss, no-bother clipping creator that lets you select text (or a picture, QuickTime movie, or sound), drag it to another location (in the same document, another document, or even to your desktop), and drop it right into place. Strangely enough, it's called Macintosh drag and drop.

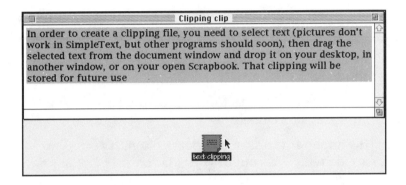

Creating a text clipping.

In the figure above, I dragged the selected text to my Mac's desktop, where it became a *text clipping.* I could then drag that clipping from the desktop into any application that supports Macintosh drag and drop.

At this writing, the only applications that do support Macintosh drag and drop are the applications that came with System 7.5 (that is, Note Pad, SimpleText, Scrapbook, and Stickies—all covered in Chapter 12). However, by the time you read this, many more applications will support it—probably with their next upgrades. You can practice clipping and get used to the idea, but it won't be the great nifto-swifto solution it could be until major applications start to support it.

It's a very handy feature for stuff you use often. Instead of having to retype your name and address, paste in your favorite piece of clip art, or whatever, you can simply save it as a clipping file, and drag and drop it wherever you want, whenever you want.

Of course, it also helps if the application you're dragging a clipping to supports the kind of clipping you're trying to drop on it; not all applications can accept all kinds of clippings (especially sounds and QuickTime). Look in your manual before you drop on a document.

The Least You Need to Know

Whew! A lot of major concepts with everyday uses. Let's review:

➤ Use the **File** menu to Open, Save, and Close documents. Of course, you can also use the command-key shortcuts.

➤ Use the **Edit** menu to Copy, Cut, and Paste (or the keyboard shortcuts).

➤ It's important to save your work often. If your power accidentally goes out or your Mac crashes, you'll lose everything you haven't saved. Save early, and save often.

➤ Your Mac hits you with a dialog box when it needs more information from you to do its job.

➤ Before you can copy, replace, or paste anything, you have to select it.

➤ The Clipboard is the temporary holding area for all the things you cut and copy. Just remember, it can only hold one thing at a time.

➤ Clipping files, through Macintosh drag and drop, will be handy when popular applications support them.

Chapter 9

Floppies Don't Flop and Other Floppy Facts

In This Chapter

➤ Floppy flavors

➤ Inserting and formatting disks

➤ Care and feeding of your floppies

Once upon a time, there was a boy who didn't believe in floppy disks. Oh, he believed they existed; he just didn't use them. He was a diskless wonder. Sure, he used his original disks to install programs, but then he never touched them again. He saved all his work to his hard drive and thought it was good enough. Even though the Village Geek had warned him that not keeping backup copies of his programs and data was a big, BIG mistake, nothing swayed this diskless wonder. He was a very foolish boy.

Then one day, from out of the silicon jungle, a troll appeared. Not just any old troll, but a Technical Troll, wielding the awful power of magnets, dust, and other assorted airborne stuff. The troll saw the boy's hard drive and thought it a tasty-looking morsel. He let loose all his might upon it: magnetic fields to scramble the data; a fistful of poisonous dust and goat hair shoved right into the computer's case; and he even gave it a severe thwacking to jiggle the heads until they cracked and crashed.

The diskless wonder begged for mercy. "No, please, Mr. Troll, sir!" he cried, "My life is on that thing. How will I survive?" The troll finally went away, and the boy saw the state of his hard drive. He went wildly insane and disappeared into the silicon jungle. He was never heard from again. The end.

You may now hiss the villains: dust, magnetic fields, and other assorted shmootz. They're real bad guys. This chapter is your number one defense against these creeping horrors. In it, you'll learn all you need to know about floppy disks, and how they can save you and your valuable data from Techno Trolls and their nasty bags of tricks.

Floppies Are Your Friends

Next to your Mac, your best friend is your floppy drive—okay, people come first, then your Mac, then your floppy drive. In addition to being a way to get junk onto your Mac's hard drive, your floppy drive is a way to get your valuable data and programs out of your Mac onto floppy disks that you can keep somewhere safe in the event that disaster strikes your hard drive or disk files.

Floppy disks (otherwise known as floppies) are a storage medium (such as your hard drive). They hold data that you can read and load into your Mac's RAM, work with, and then save again to the storage disk. Storage, like RAM, is measured in bytes. Standard floppies hold either kilobytes (K or KB) or megabytes (M or MB) of information.

The first floppies were big, 8-inch monsters with a shell of a soft plastic that sort of flopped—well, wiggled, anyhow. Then came those 5.25-inch disks you'll see some DOS users using. When 3.5-inch disks were introduced (since they're so small and cute), they called them *diskettes*. But you can still call them disks if you want.

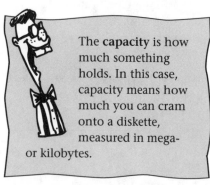

The **capacity** is how much something holds. In this case, capacity means how much you can cram onto a diskette, measured in mega- or kilobytes.

If you bought any model from the current Mac line (or a Mac made in the last couple of years), your Mac has a *SuperDrive*. It doesn't have a big S on its chest, but it *is* able to read and write to just about any capacity Mac-formatted 3.5-inch disk. With the PC Exchange Control Panel (I'll talk more about that a little later and in Chapter 11), it can even read, write to, and format DOS disks. (Maybe it *should* have a big S on its chest.)

Did all that read like a treatise on the laws of supply-side economics? Don't sweat it: here come the details.

Anatomy of a Floppy

From the outside, all 3.5-inch disks look kind of the same (if you scrunch up your eyes and ignore the little details). From the front, they're 3.5-inch × 3.5-inch squares of colored plastic with a shallow area for a label. A sliding metal shutter protects the disk's gizzards while it's out of a disk drive. A couple of holes and notches let your Mac know what kind of disk it is, and usually, some writing helps you identify the manufacturer and the disk's capacity.

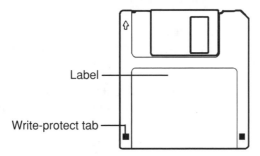

Here's your basic, run-of-the-mill 3.5-inch floppy disk.

On the backside of the disk, there's the back of the protective shutter, a metal circle that lets your drive spin the disk of magnetic media inside the plastic shell, and a couple more holes and notches. The magnetic disk inside is kind of shiny, and it's the same sort of stuff that video and audio cassettes are made of. You can look at it by carefully sliding the metal shutter back. Dust and grit can easily scratch the magnetic media, and the natural oils from your skin can easily clog your data—so you can look, but you'd better not touch.

On the back, in the upper left corner (with the shutter at the bottom) is a hole with a sliding tab. That's the *write-protect tab*, and it lets you *lock* the disk. When you lock the disk, you can't accidentally write to or erase anything from the disk. When the plastic tab covers the hole, the disk is unlocked (you can save to, and erase from the disk). When you can see through the hole (the tab is up) the disk is locked, and you can't do anything except read data from the disk. If

105

you forget which is which (I always have to look), the kinder diskette manufacturers put a little diagram on their labels to remind you how to lock and unlock the disk.

Floppy Flavors

While all 3.5-inch disks look kind of the same, they aren't: the main difference is how much they hold. Right now, 3.5-inch floppy disks come in three different capacities: 1.4 megabytes (*DSHD*), 800 kilobytes (*DSDD*), and 400 kilobytes (*SSDD*). Sound like more gibberish? Wait a sec; I'll explain everything.

SSDD: Single-Sided, Double-Density

Originally, 3.5-inch disks held about 400K of data written on only one-sided magnetic media. The "double-density" refers to how tightly spaced information can be written on the disk, not its stupidity.

Because "Single-sided, double-density disks" is a mouthful, the name is abbreviated to SSDD, or even 1S2D. (Don't you love how easy that makes remembering this stuff?) SSDD disks are pretty much obsolete. You can use them (if you can find them), but they don't hold much data. It's more economical (that is, cheaper) to use higher capacity disks.

DSDD: Double-Sided, Double-Density

Double-sided, double-density disks (also called DSDD, or 2S2D) have double the capacity of the older disks, about 800K. They added extra storage space by putting magnetic media on both sides of the disk (double-sided—get it?). These are the best disks to use for exchanging data with your fellow computer users, especially if you aren't sure the recipient has a high-density disk drive.

When you buy a box of DSDD diskettes, don't be shocked to see that the box claims that each disk holds 1.0 MB. A double-sided, high-density disk (DSHD) holds 2.0 MB of data. Brand new, right-out-of-the-box, they do hold that much, but you can't use it all. Here's the catch: you have to *format* or *initialize* a disk before you can use it. I'll tell you how in a minute. For now, just remember that formatting a disk uses up some of the available space.

DSHD: Double-Sided, High-Density

Double-sided, high-density disks (DSHD, 2SHD, or even just HD) hold twice the amount of data that DSDD disks hold, about 1.4 megabytes. The capacity was increased by decreasing the amount of space data takes up; data can be written smaller, fitting more information in the same amount of space.

High-density disks are workhorses; you can cram a lot of data on them. They're great for big data files and *backup* copies of your important data, and for programs from your hard drive. You do, however, need a drive designed to use them, like the SuperDrive.

You can spot a high-density 3.5-inch diskette by two easy means:

A **backup** is a spare, or emergency, copy of something. You can back up your hard drive, make a backup copy of a program or data disk, or even a single file. Although everybody should back up their data on a regular basis, the only folks who actually do it are the ones who have been traumatized by the loss of an important file. I have been traumatized by severe data losses. I'll explain how to make a backup shortly.

➤ Where 800K (DSDD) disks have only one hole (the write-protect notch), high-density disks have two, one on the right and left sides of the label. See the following figure.

➤ While not all DSDD disks have any writing on them to identify them as DSDD disks, all high-density disks have a stylized HD near the shutter (it looks like a mutant **CH** if you look at it upside down).

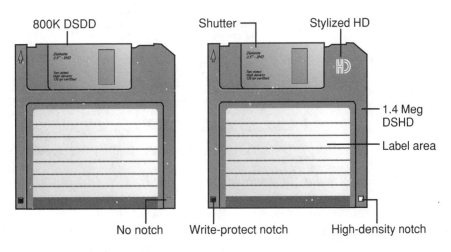

Floppy disks by formatted capacity.

Inserting, Formatting, and Other ING Words

Your disk drive is pretty smart. You can't insert a disk incorrectly (unless you take a hammer and force it), but just so we can say we've been through it, here's how disks go into your drive.

Formatting a disk is like cutting up a pizza into easy-to-manage, easy-to-eat slices. A whole blank disk is just too hard for a Mac to eat in one quick sitting, so it cuts it up into smaller, easier-to-read sections. It then writes a map of the different areas so it can keep track of where it puts things (this map is the *Desktop file*). That makes it easy for the Mac to find things quickly when you ask for them.

Holding your disk, label side up, between thumb and forefinger (the extended pinkie is optional), insert the shutter-end of the disk into the drive. It's like inserting a cassette into a VCR. After a certain point, you can feel the mechanism catch on and take the disk the rest of the way.

When you insert a disk, the drive whirs for a second trying to read whatever is on the disk. If it's a brand-spanking-new one, just out of the box, your Mac won't know what to make of it. Disks are meaningless to your Mac until they've been *formatted* (or *initialized*).

When you insert a disk that hasn't been formatted, your Mac tries to read it but can't. You'll get a message on your screen saying, **This disk is unreadable by this Macintosh. Do you want to initialize the disk?** with a pop-up menu beneath it, as shown here.

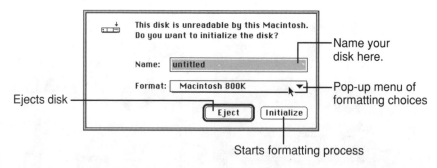

The ever-popular "unreadable disk" dialog box.

If you don't want to initialize the disk, click on the **Eject** button and your Mac will give it back to you. If you want to initialize the disk, select one of the formatting choices from the installed pop-up menu (where it says "Macintosh 800K" in the figure). With the PC Exchange

Control Panel, you'll be able to format disks not only for Macintosh, but also for MS-DOS (the dominant operating system for IBM and compatible computers) and PRODOS (the operating system for Apple II-family computers). Type in a name for your new disk (something obvious, so you can remember what's on it, or just let your Mac call it "Untitled") and click on the **Initialize** button.

When you tell it to initialize the disk, your Mac (kind and concerned as always) reminds you that formatting the disk erases any data that may be on it—are you sure you want to do this? If you suspect there's information on the disk that may have been damaged somehow (it can happen), you can click on the **Cancel** button and abort the operation. Formatting a disk destroys any files on it forever. Think before you click!

If you decide you want to proceed, click on **Continue**, or press the **Enter** key. Your disk drive churns away, formatting it. When it's done, the disk is ready to store your valuable data and program files.

> When I get a new box of disks, I format the whole thing at one sitting. I call them all **untitled** (which is the name your Mac automatically gives a disk) if I'm too lazy to type the word **blank** ten times. I slap a blank label on the formatted disks, so I know I formatted them. When I use them, I give them real names. When all my labeled, blank disks are gone, I know it's time to buy or format more.

Erasing a Disk

Eventually, you're going to find a mystery disk full of stuff. You don't remember what it is, or why you've kept it for so many years. If you have no further need for those cob-webby files on the disk, you can erase it and give yourself a new(ish) blank disk for other important data. There's two ways to do it.

First, you can double-click on the disk's icon to open its window, and then select everything in the disk's window with the **Select All** command under the **Edit** menu (or press ⌘-A). Drag everything into the Trash, and empty the Trash. The disk is empty.

The second way is easy too: insert the disk. When its icon appears on the desktop, click on it to be sure it's selected. Then select the **Erase Disk** option under the **Special** menu. The Erase Disk command works just the same as formatting, except the word "erase" is substituted for the word "initialize" in all of the dialog boxes.

The difference between the two methods is that using the Erase Disk command renders everything that was on the disk irretrievable— it's gone forever. Just throwing the files in the Trash and emptying it doesn't delete the files forever if (and only if) you have a file recovery utility, like those discussed in Chapter 16. Even then, you may not be able to recover the file, so delete files and erase disks only when you really, really mean it.

Ejecting a Disk

There are a few ways to eject a disk. First, you can drag the disk's icon onto the **Trash** icon to eject it. New Mac users are almost always scared of dragging a disk into the Trash. It just ejects the disk and removes its icon from the desktop. Really. It doesn't erase it. Scout's honor.

The Put Away command (⌘-Y) under the File menu does the same thing. After you select the disk icon and choose the command, it ejects the disk and removes its icon from the desktop. That's called *dis-* or *unmounting* a disk. It's the opposite of when you insert a disk and its icon appears on the desktop—that's called *mounting* a disk.

The Eject Disk command (⌘-E) under the Special menu ejects the disk but leaves its icon on the desktop. You'll see why in a minute. These disk commands work all the time you're at the desktop.

Storing Diskettes

The best way to store disks for easy access is in a disk-file that you keep near your Mac. The 3.5-inch disks aren't really fragile, but you can ruin them. Moisture, dust, too much heat, and too much cold aren't good for disks. Moisture mucks them up; dust (including cigarette smoke, pet hairs, food crumbs) clogs them up and scratches the media; and heat or cold melts or cracks them.

Magnets are a major no-no. The disks store your data magnetically. If another magnetic field (like a magnet's) gets near a disk, the disk's magnetic charges (your data) can get all scrambled. Bad, bad news. (By the way: all the things that are bad for your disks are also bad for your disk drive and computer. Go figure.)

You should duplicate important disks (original System disks, expensive applications, important documents), even before you use them. Keep the copies around to actually use, but put the originals somewhere safe. Some people go so far as to put their backup copies in a safe, a safe-deposit box, or even a fireproof box (but plastic melts before paper burns, so it really isn't that much protection). Other people put a rubber band around them and stack them on a shelf in the closet. Other people don't do diddly.

It's hard to say, "Do this; don't do that." It all depends on you and what you're like. How safety-conscious are you? How important is your data to you? Let your paranoia be your guide.

Stuff to Store

Once you have a stack of formatted disks, you can use them to hold anything you'd normally throw onto your hard drive. You can save your work to them directly (with the **Save** command), or copy files from your hard drive to a disk.

To copy data files from your hard drive (or from another disk), just drag the file's icon from your hard drive's window onto the disk's icon (or into its open window as shown in the following figure). Your Mac copies the file onto the disk. For multiple files, repeat the process for each, or just **shift-click** to select all of the files you want to move, and drag them onto the disk's icon. To copy files from a disk to your hard drive, just reverse the process.

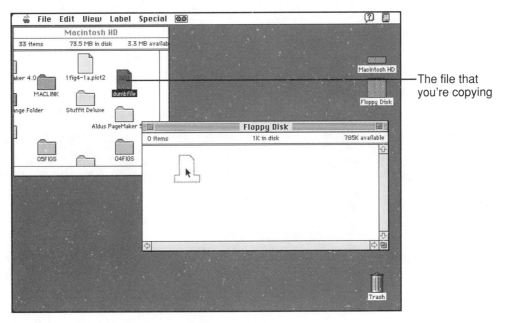

The file that you're copying

Copying a single file to a floppy disk.

111

A **compressed file** is a file that has been mashed down with a **file compression utility** to take up less disk space. Files get "mashed down," by replacing repetitive data in a file (like all the E's and I's in a text document) with teeny-tiny place-holders that take up less space than the original data. You must **decompress** compressed files before you can work with them.

If you have a Mac (like a Performa) that had all the System software and (maybe) some applications already installed on the hard drive and no actual disks included, you should run, not walk, to the nearest computer store, buy a couple of boxes of disks, and copy everything on your hard drive for safe-keeping, even if it means dragging each file or folder individually onto disks. If something nasty happens to that software while you're learning your way around, you're out of luck. Back it up now!

When you copy applications, you can also drag the application's icon onto the disk's icon. Be warned, though: most applications, these days, take up more than 1.4 megabytes of disk space. If something won't fit on your disk, you'll get a warning that says: **There is not enough room on the disk *"Name"* to copy *"File Name"* (an additional 00 KB is needed)**. You may be better off copying the original disk(s) the application came on (which are probably *compressed*) rather than the full-sized version from your hard drive.

You can copy an entire disk for backup purposes or to share files with a friend or co-worker. Follow these instructions (this is where the Eject Disk command comes in):

1. Insert the disk you want to copy (the original) into your disk drive.

2. When its icon appears on the desktop, select **Eject Disk** from the **Special** menu (or press ⌘-**E**). The disk ejects, but its grayed-out icon stays on the desktop.

3. Insert the disk you want to copy to (sometimes called the *destination disk*).

4. When its icon appears on the desktop, drag the grayed-out icon of the *original disk*, and drop it onto the new disk's icon.

5. Your Mac churns. It ejects the blank disk, and asks you to insert the original disk. Do what it says—it does this for what seems like forever. Keep swapping disks until the deed is done.

6. Pat yourself on the back. You've made yourself a backup copy.

The Least You Need to Know

As I said at the beginning of this chapter, floppy disks are your friends. They give you virtually unlimited storage capacity (as long as you have the space to store all those floppies), and they act as a safety net (when you back up your files) to keep you from losing your valuable data and applications should anything untoward happen.

➤ 3.5-inch floppy disks come in different capacities: 400K, 800K, and 1.4 MB. The 400K disks are pretty much obsolete. 800K disks are good. 1.4 MB disks are real workhorses.

➤ You have to *format*, or *initialize*, disks before you can use them.

➤ You should make *backup copies* of all your important data and application files just in case something bad happens.

➤ You can lock disks that contain important data, using the sliding tab on the back. If the tab is *open*, the disk is locked. When the tab is *closed*, the disk is unlocked.

➤ Disks should be stored carefully, away from moisture, dust, heat, and extreme cold. Be especially careful to keep disks away from magnets.

Chapter 10

Hard Drive Facts

In This Chapter

➤ Formatting and partitioning

➤ Making backups

➤ In case of emergency...

This chapter is all about intentionally destroying and preventing the unintentional destruction of your hard drive's data. Now, I'm not a violent person by nature (and I'll beat the crap out of anyone who disagrees—*kidding! I'm kidding!*), but I do get a certain grim satisfaction out of destroying things when it becomes necessary. I also feel smarter than all get-out when I accidentally trash some data but have a spare copy of it lying around—at least I don't feel like a total fool, anyhow. You may feel that way, too, but...

WARNING: DON'T do anything I talk about in this chapter while you're reading it. I don't want you accidentally erasing your hard drive. When you've read it all, you may want to try some of it; you may not. This chapter is mainly for future reference.

Formatting and Partitioning

The big truth about hard drives is that they're just like really big floppy disks to your Mac: they have to be formatted before your Mac can do anything with them. Don't panic! The hard drive that came installed in your Mac was already formatted. You don't have to do it. Later, if you get a new one or you decide to reorganize your old one, you may need to format or reformat.

Using the **Erase Disk** command under the **Special** menu is kind of slow for a 1.4 MB floppy. It could take hundreds of times as long to format a hard drive (depending on its size), so there's special software for it. One piece of hard drive formatting software came with your Mac: *Apple HD SC Setup*. You'll find it on the *Disk Tools* disk from your set of original System disks, or the *only* floppy disk that came with your System software CD-ROM disc. You'd launch it like any Mac application. When it starts up, you'll see the screen shown here.

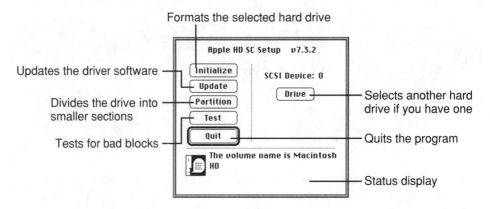

The Apple HD SC Setup utility.

By clicking on the **Initialize** button, you format your hard disk (and erase *everything* you had stored on it). Clicking on the **Update** button updates the software your Mac uses to control and read the hard drive. You use this if your drive starts behaving badly (the driver software may have developed a problem) or if you upgrade your System software (from 7.1, to 7.5, perhaps) and want to be sure the driver software is compatible—otherwise, you don't really have to worry about it.

Clicking on the **Partition** button brings up a new dialog box. The Partitions dialog box lets you drag the existing partitions (if any) on your hard drive to make them bigger or smaller, or add new ones.

Clicking on the **Test** button gets the utility to check your hard drive for *bad blocks* (tiny segments that can't be used because they are damaged somehow).

Clicking on the **Drive** button won't do anything unless you have more than one Apple hard drive connected to your Mac. If you do have two or more Apple hard drives, you can select which one you want to mess around with. If you want to partition or reformat another brand of hard drive, you need a different utility.

A **partition** on a hard drive is like a partition in a house. It's a wall that divides one section of your hard drive from another. Creating a partition is destructive: you'll erase everything from your hard drive. You need to copy *everything* onto floppies before you try this, so you can copy it all back when you're done.

Why would you want to partition your hard drive? Well, for a couple of reasons:

➤ Partitioning can speed up your Mac. If you have a big hard drive (over 100 megabytes) that isn't partitioned, your Mac has to look through every file on the drive until it finds what you're looking for.

➤ It can give you privacy if you password-protect it (more on passwords later).

➤ It can help keep you organized (more on that later, too).

Look Out, I'm Backing Up

Unlike floppy disks, you can't just drag your hard drive's icon onto the icon of a blank disk. All that stuff that's built up (or will build up) on your hard drive just won't fit on a floppy. You can, if you had a free day or two, just sit there dragging icon after icon onto disk after disk and back up the files manually. Talk about tedious!

There are such beasties as *backup utilities* (Central Point MacTools or The Norton Utilities for Macintosh to name two). In addition to other useful things, they take care of the annoying task of figuring out how much junk fits on how many disks. All you really have to do, besides remembering to do it, is sit there and feed disks into the floppy drive. It's still kind of tedious, but much less so than doing it all yourself.

There are less painful ways to back up your hard drive, but they require more hardware. You can (with the same backup utility) back up onto another hard drive, a *removable-media drive* (such as a SyQuest or Bernoulli drive, where the hard drive media pops out like a video tape), or *tape drive* that uses data cassettes to record huge amounts of data. Adding hardware to make backups isn't really practical unless you have a huge hard drive chock full o' data or you're backing up a lot of hard drives. I'll talk more about these hardware add-ons in Chapter 18.

Keeping House

You can keep your backup and maintenance chores down to a minimum if you start out with some good habits. The first way to keep your computing life simple is to start out organized—because it's easier to *stay* organized than it is to *get* organized.

I know Mac users whose hard drives are a mess: everything is everywhere and all higgeldy-piggeldy. There isn't a folder on the drive that doesn't have at least one more folder inside it. There's stuff buried so deep on their drives that it squints when they call it up into the light of day. That's not good. It's really easy to lose stuff that way. You don't have to be as picky as I am about it, but there are some easy things you can do to keep your act together:

➤ **Keep application-related stuff in one folder.** Most programs, when you install them, neatly put all the junk they need (and lots more) into one folder on your hard drive. Leave it there. If you want to move the application around, do it with aliases.

➤ **Keep project folders.** Letters, business, accounting, and homework folders— whatever is appropriate for whatever you do.

If you want to be really obsessive, you can group related applications, like those for word processing, into one folder, graphics into another, and games into another.

While revising this book, I had one **Idiot Mac 2e** folder, with everything I needed inside: a folder each for letters, original chapters, revised chapters, screen shots, notes, and sample files. The screen shot folder had a folder for each chapter inside. That way, the project never went more than three folders deep: The Idiot folder, the component folders, and chapter folders inside those. I didn't have to search far for anything.

➤ **Throw out old crap.** When you finish with a project, throw it away. If you think you may need it again, move it onto a floppy (or floppies) and file them somewhere safe, and trash the originals from your hard drive. It keeps you from building up too much folder fodder and from running out of space.

➤ **Make up your own mind; make your own style.** If this isn't your style, cross out this section with a thick magic marker and ignore it. I've been told I'm just the tiniest bit compulsive. My way may not be your way.

Save Early; Save Often

Whether you save your work to a hard drive or to a diskette, one of the best (and safest) habits you can develop is to *save often*. When you work on a file, it only exists as electronic impulses stored in your Mac's RAM until you save it. RAM is not permanent. If you turn off your Mac, the file goes away. If the power goes out, the file goes away. When you save a file, your Mac copies those electronic impulses in RAM and transcribes them to the disk of your choice. The file, written to a *storage* medium, stays exactly the way you saved it until you save it again.

You save a file, in any application, by selecting the **Save** command from the **File** menu. For a new file, one you haven't saved before, your Mac asks you to enter a name for a file, and tells it where to store it, just like it did back in Chapter 8 when you saved the sample SimpleText file.

Save a file quickly with ⌘-S.

After you save a file for the first time, you can simply use the **Save** command, and the new copy of the file replaces the old one. If you want to save another copy of the file, while you're working on it, you can use the **Save As** command, also under the **File** menu. **Save As** creates a whole new file on your disk. Your Mac asks you to give this new file a name (it can't be the same as the original; no two files can have exactly the same name in the same folder). You can add a number to the original name: save your file **Mom.letter** as **Mom.letter2**. Or add **copy** or **backup** to the original name (**Mom.letter copy**). If you're saving the copy to a different folder or disk, you can leave the name the same (as long as that won't confuse you—me it confuses, so I still change the name).

Saving costs you only a little effort and can save you some heartache. Here's a couple of good times to stop and save the file you're working with:

➤ Save your work before you walk away from your Mac.

➤ Save your work whenever you reach a point where you wouldn't want to go back and recreate it: after a page of text or a couple rows of a spreadsheet. Save it, and then continue working.

➤ Save your work when you stop to make changes and before you actually make them. That way, if you don't like the revisions, you still have the unaltered file on disk so you haven't actually changed the original file.

➤ Save your work whenever you stop to answer the phone, the door, the kids, the call of nature, the dog's call of nature—in other words, whenever you stop working and definitely before you walk away from your Mac.

Some programs give you the option of setting *automatic saves*. My copy of Microsoft Word is set to prompt me to save what I'm working on every 15 minutes. All I have to do is press **Enter** when it beeps, and Microsoft Word saves a copy of my current document. If I don't want to save it, I just click on the **Cancel** button. This is a great feature. More programs should offer it. I mean, I know how stupid I can be. That's why one of my mottos is this: *save early; save often.*

Safety First!

While saving your work often and backing up your hard drive regularly go a long way toward protecting your valuable work from disaster, there's more you can do. If you're the only one who uses (or is supposed to use) your Mac, you can install security software (such as NightWatch II) that requires a password before allowing access to the desktop. Theoretically, only you should be able to use your Mac. However, if you have to share your Mac with others, you can still protect your files.

You can (insert appropriate adjective here)-proof your Mac: If you have children using it, kid-proof it; nosy co-workers, snoop-proof it; and if your mom uses it, Mom-proof your Mac. There are a couple of ways you can do it. Start by doing a safety check: power up your Mac and look at everything that's accessible at startup. If there's anything there that you can't live without, or that you don't want just anyone looking at, protect it.

You can protect your data files easily: copy them onto disks and delete the originals from your hard drive. Put the disks with your sensitive files into a file box that locks. Keep the key with you. No one but you can get at the disks. If it's just a question of keeping the file safe (you don't care if someone looks at it), you can leave them on your hard drive and lock them.

To lock a file (only *files*, you can't lock folders this way), click on its icon to select it. Choose **Get Info** from the **File** menu (or press ⌘-**I**). You'll get a dialog box like the one shown in the following figure.

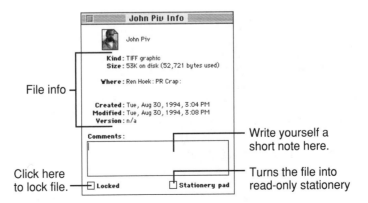

The File Info window.

If you have or plan to get a screen saver, such as Berkeley System's After Dark, you already have minimal password protection. When the screen saver kicks in, you can set it so no one can access the work you were doing without entering a password. There are ways to get around it, of course, but if you have minimal needs, it's a relatively inexpensive and entertaining option to consider. There's more about After Dark and screen savers in Chapter 16.

You can use the **Get Info** command to get some general information about the file. You can also click inside the Comments box and write yourself a note to remind you about the file. Most importantly, you can click in the check box at the bottom left corner of the dialog box to lock the file. A locked file, like a locked disk, cannot be altered or deleted without being unlocked first. Naturally, this is no protection if the tampering person knows how to unlock a file. It should, however, prevent the file from being accidentally deleted or altered.

You can add file protection software, such as FolderBolt, which password-protects certain folders and locks everything inside so it cannot be altered or deleted without the password. If you feel you need even more security for your data files and applications, you can create a separate partition on your hard drive (as discussed in a previous section) and password protect it with security software, such as NightWatch II.

Keep everything that's personal and confidential in that partition. Your Mac starts normally, and unprotected files are fully accessible to average users, but the things in that partition are unavailable unless the user knows the password. Some security programs even make that partition *invisible* (literally) so average users won't even know it's there.

Atten-shun! AtEase!

If your main concern is keeping kids and other Mac novices from accessing or deleting your important files, you can use Apple's own Finder replacement, AtEase 2.0, to restrict their access. As you can see in the following figure, AtEase allows limited access to the functions of the Finder. Instead of the desktop you're used to seeing, when you start up your Mac with AtEase installed, you get a different, simpler desktop. You can look at it as a restrictive security measure, or a simplification for youngsters and other Mac novices.

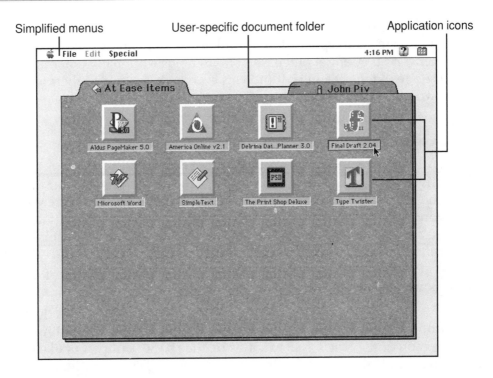

Simplified menus   User-specific document folder   Application icons

The AtEase 2.0 screen.

Users can only use the applications and documents set from the AtEase Control Panel or documents created while AtEase is running. You can also specify that files created in the AtEase environment must be saved to a floppy disk or the user's document folder, instead of just anywhere on your hard drive. You can also specify that documents can only be opened from that location as well. Users can't peek into your sensitive files, nor can they delete or accidentally alter them.

The AtEase Setup application lets you specify which users can access which advanced features (like getting at the full power of the Finder), and each users' settings (therefore their document folder) are also password-protected, keeping their data safe as well. The advantages of AtEase are: simpler interface, ease of use for kids and Mac novices of any age; password protection for the Finder and more powerful applications; and the *save only to disk* option.

The drawback of AtEase is that it's work (not a lot of work, but work nonetheless), both setting it up and maintaining it (people forget passwords, want you to add new applications, and so on). However, the value of protecting your data is well worth the occasional session with the AtEase Setup application. I think AtEase (or another Finder replacement) is an essential purchase in households with many potential Mac users, children or adults: it protects everybody's data and their privacy. Two important concerns.

Rescue Me

Okay, we've formatted disks and backed up everything on your hard drive. We've gone to lengths worthy of the CIA to protect your data, and still something goes wrong with your hard drive. What are you gonna do? If your hard drive goes ker-flooey, you can still start up your Mac with a System disk in the floppy drive. Ideally, that System disk (sometimes known as a *bootable disk*, *startup disk*, or *System disk*— choose your synonym) will also have some utilities on it to help you fix whatever went wrong with your hard drive.

Fortunately for you, you already have one: the *Disk Tools* disk from your original set of System disks. It contains a stripped down version of the Mac's System software, the HD SC Utility we talked about earlier, and a spiffy little program called Disk First Aid. In the computer-geek business, we call this a *Rescue Disk* because it can save your butt, not to mention rescue your disk.

Later on, if, or when, you buy a set of disk utilities, such as Norton Utilities for Macintosh or Central Point's MacTools, you can create a similar rescue disk with their utilities.

Disk First Aid is a disk-fixing application. It checks all of the things a Mac needs from a disk to operate, and if it finds something wrong, tries to fix it. You can use it on any disk, hard drive, or floppy. In fact, you should keep a copy on your hard drive, too, for fixing flaky floppy disks.

If you're trying to fix a flaky hard disk, you'd pop the Disk Tools disk in your floppy drive just after turning on your Mac. Your Mac will run from the System software on the disk, instead of from your hard drive (because Disk Tools can't fix any problems in an active—that is, running—System Folder, or on a disk with open files). When you get to the desktop, open the **Disk Tools** disk's icon, and launch **Disk First Aid**. It will look something like the following figure.

Shows all mounted disks and/or partitions

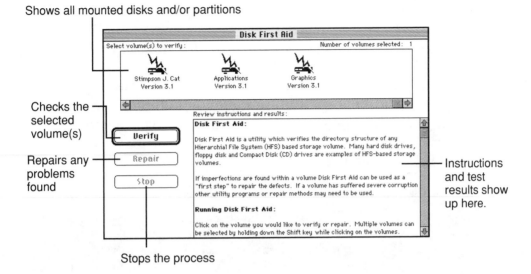

Checks the selected volume(s)

Repairs any problems found

Instructions and test results show up here.

Stops the process

Disk First Aid.

At the top of the screen, you can scroll through the display of *volumes* (hard drives, partitions, and disks are all volumes) and click on the volume you want to check out. If you want to check more than one, you can Shift-click to select more than one volume. When you've selected the volume(s) you want to check, clicking on the **Verify** button (or pressing **Enter**) will check them. If it finds a problem, it will tell you to click on the **Repair** button if you want to try and fix it. (You can also, if there are no active files on the selected disk, just click on the **Repair** button right at the start, to skip that intermediate step. Just a thought.)

To use Disk First Aid to fix a disk in your floppy drive, launch a copy of it from your hard drive. When it starts, pop in the disk you want to repair, click on its icon in the Select Volumes display at the top of the screen, and click on **Verify** or **Repair**. It works the same for disks as hard drives; hard drives just take longer to test. Disk First Aid can fix many of the common problems that plague disks and hard drives, but it can't fix everything.

Undelete Utilities

When your hard disk was finally repaired with the rescue disk, you discovered that your kid (or your co-worker) deleted a couple of important files that you didn't back up (shame on you). Now what? Well, if you don't already have a set of hard drive utilities, such as MacTools, The Norton Utilities, or one of the many others, you need to get some—especially if youngsters have access to your Mac. They love to throw things out and empty the Trash.

Most utility packages come with an *undelete utility* that tries to recover accidentally deleted files. It will scan your disks or hard drive, looking for intact files that have been marked as "deleted." When it finds one, you can tell it to remove the "deleted" marker, and the file will "exist" once more.

When you throw a file into the Trash and empty it, your Mac *marks* that file as deleted, saying that bit of hard drive real estate is back on the market (available for use). The file isn't actually *destroyed* until your Mac writes another file on top of it. Only then is the deleted file officially kaput. If you act quickly (before you save another file), your deleted file is still there and you can (usually) recover it with the proper utility.

The Least You Need to Know

In computing, as in life, bad things happen when you haven't provided for them. If you take precautionary steps, you may never have a problem. Even if you do have a problem, who cares? You're ready for it. In my opinion (and you may feel free to disagree), all of the information in this chapter was pretty important. I'd like to see you remember most of it because you can't be too safe. However, times being what they are, here are the really essential things for you to walk away with:

➤ If you don't want to *back up* your important files individually, you can use a *backup utility* to make a copy of your entire hard drive for storage. You should do one or the other. Doing both is best.

➤ Hard drives can be formatted like disks. They can also be *partitioned* into smaller sections to speed up your Mac and improve your file security. *Always back up your hard drive before formatting or partitioning it.*

➤ Save your files frequently as you work, using the **Save** (⌘-S) or the **Save As** commands under the **File** menu.

➤ Play it safe when other people have access to your Mac: protect the files you cannot live without. Lock them with the Get Info (⌘-I) dialog box, or use security software to password-protect files, folders, or hard drive partitions.

➤ Expect the best, but plan for the worst from your Mac: keep a rescue disk handy, such as a copy of the Disk Tools Disk from your original System disks. Or create your own rescue disk with utilities from a commercial utility package.

Part III
Macintosh—Behind Closed Doors... er, Folders

At this point (if you've been reading from cover to cover, that is), you can set up a Mac, launch applications, even fiddle around with files and folders. That'd be fine if you never had to print anything, or never ever wanted to fiddle around with all the customizing options that have made the Mac synonymous with coolness, fun-ness, and... er... ease-of-useness. (Cut me some slack here—synonymous is hard to rhyme with in this context.)

In Part III, we'll look at the parts of the Mac OS that work behind the scenes (where real work generally happens), the power behind the throne. We'll look at extensions and control panels, desk accessories, AppleScript, and those two chatterboxes PowerTalk and PlainTalk. In the process, we'll also learn about fonts, making stuff pretty, and putting it on paper for the world to see.

It's time to let loose with all those voyeuristic tendencies; we're going to poke around in the soul of your Mac: the System Folder.

Chapter 11

A Peek Inside the System Folder

In This Chapter

➤ The System Folder demystified

➤ Extensions explained

➤ Control panels condensed

➤ Items you can toss (if you don't need them)

The System Folder, more than any other folder on your hard drive, is like a Stephen King hotel: every folder is a room. Some of the rooms are used just for storage, some are haunted by creatures that work invisibly, others are a hotbed of activity. Put on some sneaky shoes and glasses that are good for peeking; we're about to get nosy.

Do Not Disturb

Some of the things stored in the System Folder (shown in the following figure) are only for the convenience of the System software. You can't do anything much with them except throw them out (we'll talk about unwanted baggage you can throw out at the end of this chapter), or just stare at them and wait for a cosmic revelation.

Inside the System Folder—are you peeking?

They aren't dead weight, by any stretch of the imagination. They're things that the System itself (or other applications) use. If you double-click on them, you'll get a message saying something to the effect of: Leave me alone, I don't work for you. How rude. Right now, you probably have these things lying around:

➤ **AtEase**   If you have it (you may not), AtEase is the application that creates the simplified Finder we talked about in Chapter 10. You don't do anything with the AtEase file itself; you control it with the AtEase Setup application. You'll also have an AtEase Items folder.

➤ **Clipboard**   The file where all the items you copy and cut hang out until you paste them into a document, or cut/copy something else. You can see what's in a file by using the **Show Clipboard** command in the **Edit** menu.

➤ **Finder**   The application that puts up the desktop, menus, and so on for you. You make changes to the Finder through your control panels and extensions, not directly through the application.

➤ **Scrapbook File**   Like the Clipboard, it holds whatever you have stored in your Scrapbook. You can only alter its contents by using the Scrapbook DA (in the menu).

Cold Storage

Other folders in the System Folder just hold stuff, keeping it all together for safekeeping and easy access by you, the System, and any applications that may care to use them.

➤ **Apple Menu Items folder**   Holds all of the DAs (and whatever else you care to throw in) that appear in your ⬛ menu. We talked about adding aliases and other things back in Chapter 7.

➤ **Startup Items folder**   Contains anything you want to launch every time you start your Mac. The easiest way to use this is to throw an alias of an application, sound, or document in there (rather than the original or a copy). When you start your Mac, the application launches, the sound plays, or the document opens with the application that created it. It's great for programs and documents you use every day.

➤ **Shutdown Items folder**   Works the same as the Startup Items folder, but (*duh*) at shutdown. Frankly, I can't think of a single practical thing I'd put in here—goofy stuff, yes, practical, no. By the way, using the Shut Down DA under the ⬛ menu sidesteps the Shutdown Items folder.

➤ **Extensions (Disabled)**   This is where the extensions you have turned off, using the Extensions Manager Control Panel, land. It prevents the extensions from loading at startup.

➤ **Control Panels (Disabled)**   his is where the control panels you have turned off, using the Extensions Manager Control Panel, land. It prevents the control panels from loading at startup.

➤ **Archived Type 1 Fonts**   You'll only have this folder if you've installed QuickDraw GX. This is where your PostScript Type 1 fonts will land, after using the Type 1 Enabler application, discussed in Chapter 14.

If you ever delete, up-grade, or reinstall an application, make sure you trash its preferences file, too. Otherwise, you can wind up with tons of preference files taking up space, and no application to use them. If you're reinstalling a program because it has started getting flaky on you, you should *definitely* trash its preference file. It may be part of your problem. If you don't delete it, it can pass the problem along to the fresh copy of the application.

133

➤ **Preferences folder** Most programs allow you to customize them to some degree. Whenever you tell an application that you always want it to do something a certain way, the program writes itself a note (a *preferences file*) and chucks it in this folder. That way, it'll do things your way each and every time.

➤ **PrintMonitor Documents folder** If you have a laser printer and you use background printing, this is where the *spooled files* go until the print monitor prints them for you. Chapter 13 has the scoop on printing and PrintMonitor.

Neither Fish nor Fowl: The System File and the Fonts Folder

Two things in the System Folder don't fall nicely into either category: the *System file* and the *Fonts folder*. Depending on what kinds of things you do with your Mac, you often may be poking around inside them, or not at all. They deserve some special attention.

The System File

Once upon a time (before System 7), just about all the cool things you added to your Mac were dumped into the *System file*: fonts, sounds, and Desk Accessories. In theory, it was like my grandmother's attic: full of all kinds of fascinating junk that you only dragged out once or twice a year, and then put back for safekeeping. Nowadays, all you'll see in the System file is your assortment of installed sounds and any funky *keyboard layouts* you may have. Fonts are in the Fonts folder, and DAs are in the Apple Menu Items folder, or wherever you dropped them. Got that?

A *keyboard layout* tells your Mac what letter, or symbol, you mean when you press a key on the keyboard. If you only use a standard QWERTY-style keyboard (such as a typewriter's), you don't have to worry about it. If you work in a foreign language, such as Japanese, or with an alternate keyboard layout (such as Dvorak, or a special one-handed layout), you can drop the appropriate keyboard layout in your System file and select it with the *Keyboard Control Panel*. (More about what control panels are and do in a minute.)

The Font Folder

Those little suitcase icons you see in the following figure are... well, *suitcases*. Your Mac uses them to pack related fonts together in one place. You open a font suitcase by double-clicking on it. Inside you'll find a bunch of font files, all variations of the font in the suitcase name (such as Chicago or Courier).

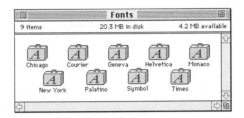

Inside the Font folder.

If you are the adventurous, creative type I think you are, you'll be in here a lot, tinkering and adding fonts all the time. All of Chapter 14 is dedicated to fun, fabulous, fantastic font facts.

Custom Mac Options

The two remaining folders inside your System Folder contain all the things that makes your Mac *your* Mac. They're the little snips and snails that let you customize the way you and your Mac work together. You can add extra capabilities by adding *extensions* and *control panels* to the appropriate folders.

Extensions

Extensions expand the capabilities of your Mac. In pre-System 7 days, Extensions were called *INITs*, which is a shortened form of *Initialization Program*. INITs or extensions load when you start up your Mac (they're those little icons popping up across the bottom of your screen) so their capabilities are available to you all the time.

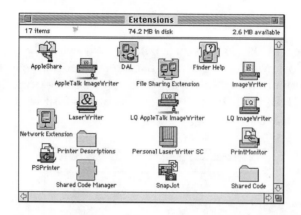

Inside the Extensions folder.

The AppleShare, File Sharing, and Network Extensions give your Mac the capability to interact with other Macs on a *network* (two or more Macs linked together by cables that allow them to communicate).

All of the X-Writer Extensions (StyleWriter, ImageWriter, LaserWriter, and so on, plus their GX variations) are Chooser Extensions that give your Mac the capability to send data to an Apple printer for printing. The PrintMonitor Extension lets your Mac print while you continue working on other things. (All of Chapter 13 is devoted to printing paraphernalia. Check it out.)

The EM Extension allows the Extensions Control Panel to deal with your extensions and control panels, keeping track of your sets, and moving individual items in and out of the appropriate *(Disabled)* folder as needed.

The Finder Help Extension gives you access to your help balloons all the time. All of the various *Guide* extensions (About Apple Guide, Apple Guide, and Macintosh Guide) are part of the Apple Guide system, and you'll be seeing more of them here as developers start to implement Apple Guide help in their programs.

The QuickTime Extension gives your Mac (if it can handle it) the capability to display what the technoids like to call "dynamic data," but which you and I call "movies." QuickTime is the coolest Extension that comes with your Mac; it allows you to show little movies in a window on your screen. However, unless you do multimedia presentation work or play multimedia games, it probably won't do more than amuse you for awhile. It is cool, though.

Depending on your Mac model, you'll probably have a few more extensions than those listed here. PowerTalk, PlainTalk, and any applications (especially Microsoft products) you install may add lots and lots of extensions to your system.

Many applications come with extensions: calendar programs that flash a message when you're scheduled to do something, backup programs that warn you it's time to back up your hard drive, among others. There are even extensions that come by themselves and make your Mac do entertaining things: make a vomiting sound when you empty the Trash, scream, and so on.

The best thing about extensions is that you don't have to do anything except drop them in the Extensions folder and forget about them. The worst thing about them is that they (and your control panels) take up RAM, and are the source of many of the problems you may experience with your Mac. Extensions sometimes squabble like spoiled children, resulting in a conflict that crashes your Mac. For just that reason, there's a whole section devoted to resolving extension conflicts in Chapter 21.

Control Panels

Control panels are more flexible than extensions. Most of them include a set of options you can set to your liking. You access your Control Panels folder (shown in the following figure) in one of two ways: either by selecting the **Control Panels** item in your ⌘ menu (or the individual control panel name from the submenu), or by double-clicking on the folder itself, which is inside your System Folder.

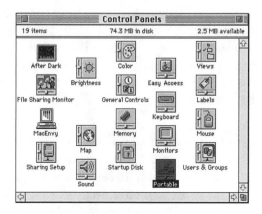

Inside the Control Panels folder.

For descriptions of the control panels features (alphabetically), read on:

➤ **Apple Menu Options**   Lets you turn the   menu's submenus on and off, and lets you specify how many recent documents or applications get added to either menu option. Submenus are a real time-saver.

➤ **Color**   Lets you pick the color of highlighted text. You can choose from several standard colors, or pick the **Other** selection. Selecting **Other** gives you a *color wheel* so you can pick the perfect color—something that matches your eyes, perhaps.

➤ **ColorSync System Profile**   Where you specify what kind of color monitor you have attached to your Mac so that your color output more closely matches the colors you see on your monitor, or vice versa. You'll have this only if QuickDraw GX is installed.

➤ **Date & Time**   You can set the current date and time here, as well as specify what formats your Mac uses for each. You can set dates in just about any standard date notation (Dec. 1, 1960, 1 December 60, 12/1/60), and display the time in 12- or 24-hour (military) format. This is also where you turn on and configure the menu bar clock (SuperClock!), and world travelers can specify what time zone they're in while on the road with their Mac.

➤ **Desktop Pattern**   Where you select the pattern that will appear in the background on your Mac's desktop. You can further customize it by copying and pasting a picture/pattern of your own from a drawing, painting, or other graphics program into the control panel.

➤ **Easy Access**   Easy Access, along with its companion control panel **CloseView**, gives your Mac special skills to make it easier for folks who can't handle a mouse or have limited vision or motor skills to use. These two aren't installed automatically. If you need them, use the installer's *Custom Install* option to pop them into your Control Panels folder.

➤ **Extensions Manager**   Very handy control panel that lets you turn off various extensions and control panels, and save different sets of them for different computing needs (for example, I have a set that turns off everything except the stuff I need to play RAM-happy CD-ROM games, freeing up lots of memory). You need to restart your Mac for any changes made here to take effect.

➤ **General Controls** Lets you specify whether you can see the desktop pattern while in an application and whether the Launcher starts up when your Mac does. You can also set the rate at which your insertion point blinks, and how many times a menu item blinks when selected.

The most *important* part of the General Controls is in the area called *Folder Protection*, which lets you keep anyone from deleting or renaming things in your System Folder, or (if you choose to use it) the Applications folder. Very important if children, strangers, or Mac-illiterates have access to your machine.

➤ **Keyboard** Lets you set the *Key Repeat Rate* (how fast the keyboard throws rrrrepeat letters up on your screen when you press a key). You can also set the *Delay Until Repeat* (how long you can hold down a key before it repeats itself). How you set these depends on how fast a typist you are.

➤ **Labels** Lets you set the color and word labels you can apply to any file with the **Label** menu in the **Finder** (as we discussed in Chapter 6). Double-click on the color to select a new one from the color wheel. Click-drag to select the word-label, and type in a new one. Choose colors and words that are significant to you, so you can tell at a glance what the file is for.

➤ **Macintosh Easy Open** Easy Open is part of the new suite of control panels and extensions (including PC Exchange) that make it easy to work with both DOS files and Mac files created with applications you don't happen to own. The control panel lets you turn Easy Open on and off and set your preferences. Once you set them to your liking, you probably won't need to bother with it again.

➤ **Map** Use this one to find different cities around the world by keying in a name. Cities are marked by flashing dots (handy for world travelers).

➤ **Memory** (No, don't sing that song from *Cats*, please, anything but that.) The *Memory Control Panel* does different things on different Macs.

All Macs can set a *Disk Cache* of various sizes, which speeds up your Mac by holding data in the cache (a block of RAM set aside to only store data) so your Mac doesn't have to go back to read from a disk so often.

139

How large a cache you set depends on the amount of RAM you have to start. If you have only 4 megabytes, a small cache (32–128K) can help without interfering too much with your ability to open other applications. With more RAM, you can set up a larger cache. Just be warned: memory you set aside for a cache can't be used for anything else. If you start getting **Application out of memory** messages, reduce the size of your cache and try again. It's all cache as cache can, anyhow.

Most current Macs have a *32-bit Addressing* option, which allows your Mac to use over 8 megabytes of installed RAM. If you have over 8 megs of RAM installed without 32-bit Addressing turned on, all the extra memory will be ignored. It's a case of use it or lose it.

Virtual memory uses part of your hard drive as a substitute for RAM. The information that normally gets stored in RAM gets written to an area on your hard disk. Virtual memory can fake applications into thinking you have more RAM than you really do.

Some other Macs have an option for *virtual memory*, which should only be used as a last ditch effort (in my opinion) because your Mac will slow down horribly. You'd be better off springing for more RAM and saving your hard drive for storage (Chapter 17 has information about adding more RAM to your Mac).

Some Mac models will also have an option for setting up a RAM disk. A RAM disk is something like a RAM cache (in that it's memory set aside to help speed up your Mac), except it acts like a kind of floppy disk, and it even appears on your desktop like a regular disk. You can copy frequently used applications (even your System software) to a RAM disk, and it will speed up the software because the data is already in memory—no time consuming disk reading is involved.

Power Macs have the Modern Memory Manager—check your manual for details.

➤ **Launcher** If you don't use the General Controls to have the Launcher start when you start your Mac, you can fire it up using the control panel. Read more about the Launcher in Chapter 7.

➤ **Monitors** The top half of this control panel lets you reset your monitor to display black and white, shades of gray, or color (if you

have a color monitor). How many
options you get depends on the capabilities of your monitor. The bottom
half is useful only if you have more
than one monitor attached to your
Mac. It lets you set which monitor will
show the menu bar and which monitor is secondary. You can tell which
monitor is which by clicking on the
Identify button.

Any changes you make in the Memory Control Panel won't take effect until you restart your Mac.

➤ **Mouse**   This control panel lets you set how quickly the cursor
moves in relation to how far or fast you move the mouse—that's
called *tracking*. You can also set the speed of your double-click so
your Mac knows what you mean by a double-click. (If you double-
click slowly, your Mac may read it as two single clicks unless you
set this to your own speed.)

➤ **Network**   You'll only use this if you're on a network. Check with
your Network Administrator if you have any questions about it.

➤ **Numbers**   Lets you set the decimal and thousands separators for
numbers (such as 2,001.367). You can also set the currency symbol ($) and whether it comes before or after the number.

➤ **PC Exchange** This control panel lets you specify which of your
applications you should use to open particular types of DOS files.
It helps if you know a little bit about DOS file suffixes (.BMP,
.PCX, .DOC, and so on) and what they mean before you try this.

➤ **Sharing Setup**   Like the Network Control Panel, you'll only use
Sharing Setup if you're on a network. Check with your Network
Administrator if you have any questions about it.

➤ **Startup Disk**   Specifies which hard drive (or hard drive *partition,*
as described in Chapter 10) you want your Mac to start up from.
This is convenient for users who keep different versions of the
Mac System software on different partitions or hard drives.

➤ **Sound**   Lets you set which installed sound in your System file
will be used (called the *Alert Sound*) when you do something your
Mac doesn't like. You can also set the volume of your Mac's
speaker (if it has one).

If your Mac came with a microphone (built-in or as an accessory), you can record your own sound by clicking on the **Add** button. You'll get a dialog box that looks and acts like the controls of a tape recorder. You can record any sound your Mac's microphone can pick up. If you like it, clicking on the **Save** button will bring up a dialog asking you to name the new sound. When you name it and click on **OK**, your Mac adds it to the sound files in your System.

➤ **Speech Setup**   You'll only have this if you have PlainTalk installed on your Mac. This is the control panel that lets you name your Mac, the voice it will use to speak to you, and how often you need to say your Mac's name to get it to pay attention to you.

➤ **Text**   With the Text Control Panel you tell your Mac what language conventions (alphabetical sorting, and so on) you use. Different languages handle them differently. Most English-speaking users won't have to mess with it.

➤ **Users & Groups**   For use on networks only. You can add new user and group names to the list of folks who have access to the information on your Mac. Check with your Network Administrator if you have any questions about it.

Whatever you do, *don't* select the Calculate folder sizes option because your Mac will slow down horribly. You'll sit there waiting while your Mac adds up the sizes of all the crap in all the folders in your window. You could go gray. Or bald. Don't do it. If you really need the size of your folders from time to time, simply turn the feature on and off. Just use it when you need it, and leave it off the rest of the time.

➤ **Views**   Gives you three sets of options for how your Mac presents information to you. You can select the font (and its point size) used for file and folder names. It's great for people like me, who have trouble reading teeny-tiny type all the doo-dah day.

You can also select how your icons land in your windows or on the desktop. You can have them line up in straight, neat lines (*straight grid*), or you can have columns of icons offset slightly (*staggered grid*) so there's less chance of name overlap (I hate that). If you click on the check box next to Always snap to grid, icons always fall into the nearest grid position.

Finally, you can specify the information presented in windows when you view by name. You can select the *size* of the icon

142

shown, as well as eight options for information displayed. Click on the check boxes in front of the information you want displayed, and turn off the rest.

➤ **WindowShade**   A very clever control panel that helps you manage multiple windows open on your desktop. With WindowShade turned on, clicking on the menu bar will roll the window up like, well, a window shade. Very handy, also very fun.

In addition to the control panels that are part of the Mac OS, there are millions of fun, helpful, funny, and just plain silly ones flying around. You can find them through your Mac User Group and just about any online service.

Junk You Can Throw Away

Now that you know where everything is and what it does, here's a big secret: You don't have to keep all of it! If you don't use it, why keep it? It's only taking up space on your hard drive and probably nibbling away at the precious little RAM you have. Ditch it.

When (or if) you discover you need these puppies, you can always reinstall them. There are step-by-step instructions for installing and reinstalling System software in Chapter 20.

Trashing Extensions

Right now your Extensions folder is choked with Chooser Extensions for every single printer that Apple makes. You own, what, one? Maybe two? Find all the ones that aren't for the printer(s) you own and throw them in the Trash.

Are you on a network? If not, you can safely trash the AppleTalk, File Sharing, and Network Extensions. Drag them

Don't throw away things that directly control your Mac. Without the Mouse Control Panel, you can't mouse around. Without the Monitors Control Panel, you can't control your monitor. Always think before you trash. Ask yourself, "Do I use this function or feature? Does my Mac need it to operate?" If you answer "No," you're probably safe throwing it away. If you trash something vital, your Mac may not work properly, and you'll have to reinstall either the item or the whole System software. When in doubt, leave it alone.

(kicking and screaming) into the Trash. When you've thrown away everything you want, select **Empty Trash** from under the **Special** menu and kiss those bad boys good-bye.

Surrendering Control (Panels)

Like the extensions, there are some control panels you can trash and not miss at all. If you aren't on a network, you can easily trash the File Sharing Monitor, Sharing Setup, and Users & Groups Control Panels. If you don't like (or don't use) the Map Control Panel, throw it out. If you don't deal with DOS disks or files from other people, you can trash PC Exchange and Easy Open as well.

Miscellaneous Trash

Here's more junk you can trash:

➤ If you don't like, need, or use AtEase, you can trash it, too. Its component parts are scattered throughout your System Folder.

➤ There are probably one or two Read Me files scattered throughout your hard drive. If you've read them, throw them out.

Instead of going on a search and destroy mission of your own, you can use your System 7.5 Installer to do your dirty work for you. The third installation option (after Easy and Custom installs) is Custom Remove. Using the Custom Remove feature, you can select everything you care to trash and let the installer do it all in one fell swoop.

➤ If you played around with any of the networking control panels, you've probably added a couple of *preference files* to your Preferences folder. When you've trashed the networking extensions and control panels, be sure to trash any preference or data files that may have been added to the Preferences folder. They'll be named so you can spot them.

The Least You Need to Know

Here are the few things you really need to remember about your System Folder. The rest of it may come in handy some time, but this is stuff you'll use frequently.

➤ Some of what's in your System Folder is only for use by the System software. It won't let you do anything to them (for example, the Clipboard and Scrapbook files) unless it's through the appropriate application or DA.

➤ Anything you put in the Startup Items folder will launch every time you start up your Mac. Ditto for the Shutdown Items folder, except these items quit when you shut down your Mac.

➤ Extensions (or INITs) add a wide range of capabilities to your Mac. To install them, drop them in your Extensions folder, and **Restart** your Mac.

➤ *Control Panels* customize the operation of your Mac to match your own computing style.

➤ Extraneous items may be in your extensions and control panels folder (*oy!* all those printer drivers). Keep only the ones you need to keep your Mac up and running, and you working comfortably. The rest can be thrown away.

Chapter 12

Your Mac's Goodies

In This Chapter

➤ What everything is

➤ What everything does

➤ What you can do with it

➤ Available replacements when you outgrow things

The future of your Macintosh is uncertain (not like the future glimpsed through one of those Magic Eight-Ball toys, "Future uncertain, ask again later") because what becomes of your Mac depends on what becomes of you. The junk that came with your System software (SimpleText, the Desk Accessories, and the rest) is just a place to begin. Some of it you'll outgrow quickly. Others may be useful for as long as you use a Mac. However, you can't outgrow them if you don't know what they are and how to use them, so let's get started.

Night of the Living DAs

You heard briefly about the Desk Accessories (DAs) when I talked about the ￼ menu in Chapter 6. DAs are available to you through the ￼ menu, no matter what application you're using. That makes them very handy indeed. Here they come, in alphabetical order.

AppleCD Audio Player

Everybody installing System 7.5 gets a copy of the AppleCD Audio Player. This handy little desk accessory (shown in the following figure) enables you to use your Apple CD-ROM drive as an audio CD player. However, it will only work with Apple-made CD-ROM drives, so if you have a drive by another manufacturer, you can throw it in the Trash. It won't help you.

Close Box

Click here to open/close the playlist portion.

Pretty standard audio CD controls

The AppleCD Audio Player DA.

If you own or have used an audio CD player, you know these controls already. If you've used a cassette player, you can probably figure them out. I won't belabor the obvious.

The Calculator

The Calculator DA gives you a basic add, subtract, multiply, and divide calculator right on your Mac's screen.

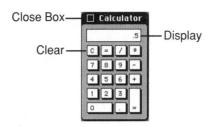

The Calculator DA.

I'm also sure you know how to use a calculator. You can use your mouse to click on the Calculator's buttons if you want, but using the number keys on your keyboard is easier. If you have a keyboard with a numeric keypad, it's even easier. The only difference between the Calculator DA and any calculator you may have used is that some of the math symbols are different, because there isn't a symbol for them on your keyboard.

The keyboard equivalents are:

+   Add

–   Subtract

*   Multiply

/   Divide

You can copy any number shown in the Calculator's display with the **Copy** command (⌘-C) and **Paste** it (⌘-V) into any document. If you need to do anything beyond these four basic functions, you'll either need to use a real calculator or replace this DA with one of the many shareware, freeware, or commercial calculator programs available. There are calculator replacements that do all sorts of zippy scientific calculations—all the ones I refused to learn in high school.

Find File

The Finder's **Find** command used to live only in the File menu. System 7.5's new and improved Find File is also a desk accessory, so you can use it in applications that don't have a similar function of their own.

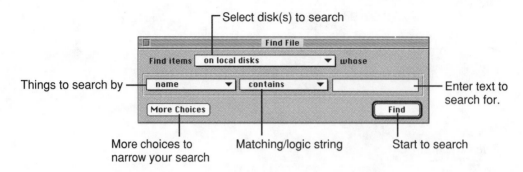

The Find File DA.

To begin a search, first tell the DA where you want to look: on one disk or every disk and hard drive currently available to your Mac. Next, tell it what you're searching for. In the figure, we're looking for a file name that contains a particular word (that word would be entered in the text box above the Find button). The pop-up menu in the center (showing the word "contains") is a logic string that tells your Mac how to look: look for something that has or doesn't have this word as part of its name. There are a number of ways to use this menu, depending on what you remember about the file you want to find.

By clicking on the **More Choices** button, you can narrow your search down by specifying as many as nine more things about the file, including file type, file label, and file size. Clicking on the **Find** button starts the search, and your Mac will get back to you as soon as it can with the search results: either a list of all the files that meet your search requirements, or a sad beep saying it couldn't find what you're looking for.

Jigsaw Puzzle

The Jigsaw Puzzle DA is great for wasting time. When you first launch the Puzzle, it's a puzzle version of the color world map that's included in your Scrapbook. You can, however, use any small PICT format graphic as a puzzle; just open it with the **Open** command (⌘-O) in the **File** menu. When the picture is open, select **Start New Puzzle** from the **Options** menu (⌘-N), and you'll be asked whether you want the puzzle pieces to be small, medium, or large. Choose whichever you like, just remember that smaller is tougher to solve.

150

A customized jigsaw puzzle.

After that, the puzzle works like any jigsaw puzzle you've ever done. Click and hold on a puzzle piece, drag it to the spot where it belongs, and let go. If the piece really belongs there, it will click into place, and you won't be able to pick it up again.

Can't solve the puzzle? You can see what the original picture looked like (as a reminder) by using the **Show Picture** command on the Options menu, or you can have the puzzle solve itself with the **Solve Puzzle** command just below it. When you solve it, you get a little musical salute.

Key Caps

The Key Caps DA finally solves the mystery of where all those special characters (_, , ¥) are hiding. The Key Caps keyboard will reproduce your keyboard, key for key. You select a font by pulling down the **Key Caps** menu. It works just like any other font menu. When you select a font, Key Caps shows that font's lowercase character set, like the one shown in the following figure.

151

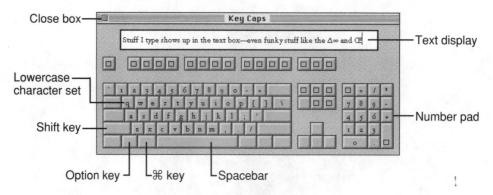

The Key Caps DA.

If you hold down the **Shift** key, the display changes to the upper-case character set. Release the **Shift** key, and press the **Option** key, and the display shows you what special characters are made with the

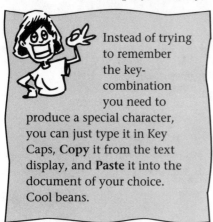

Instead of trying to remember the key-combination you need to produce a special character, you can just type it in Key Caps, **Copy** it from the text display, and **Paste** it into the document of your choice. Cool beans.

Option-character key combinations. Press the **Shift** key again, while still holding down the **Option** key, and the display shows you the characters made with the Option-Shift-Character key combination. Any key in the display that shows a box doesn't have a special character assigned to it. That's okay.

There are tons of other font utilities flying around that are variations on Key Caps, some are better, some are worse, and most of them are geared toward the special needs of designers and layout artists.

The Note Pad

The Note Pad is digital scratch paper (do people other than nuns say "scratch paper" any more?). When you launch it, the Note Pad looks like a blank pad of paper (there's that keen grasp of the obvious again). You can type short notes to yourself, lists of things to do, ideas for work, stuff to remember, and so on.

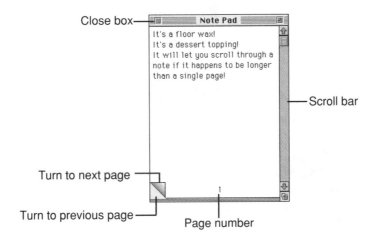

The Note Pad DA.

Everything you type in the Note Pad stays there until you delete it. Not only that, but you can also copy and paste from the Note Pad into any application. The System 7.5 Note Pad is greatly improved from earlier versions. It even *sounds* better. The Note Pad has only eight pages for notes, but (because the pages can be scrolled) you can write longer notes than fit on the visible page. The Note Pad is still limited in usefulness, but that's okay because Stickies pick up where the Note Pad leaves off—more about Stickies in a minute.

The Scrapbook

The Scrapbook DA is highly underrated and under-used in my opinion. Like a regular scrapbook or photo album, you can stick things in your Mac's Scrapbook for future use: pictures, logos, QuickTime movies, and just about anything else you can copy and paste (even System 7.5's new clipping files). As the following figure shows, I keep a scanned copy of my signature in the Scrapbook so I can slap it into documents I'm too lazy to sign.

A **scanner** is a piece of hardware that converts text, photographs, or line drawings into digital information that can be used on a computer. I'll talk about scanners and other hardware add-ons in Chapter 17.

153

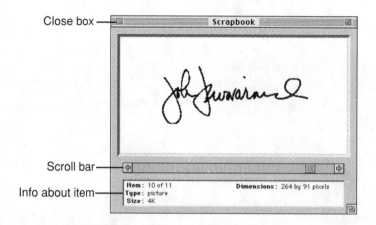

The Scrapbook DA.

When you open the Scrapbook DA, you can skim through its contents by sliding the scroll box or clicking on either scroll arrow. Apple thoughtfully added some things you may like, but you can't use all of them: there's a sound you can only listen to, and if you have QuickTime, there are two little movies. You can copy and paste the QuickTime movies into an application if it can cope with them. If you'd like to use something in the Scrapbook, here's how:

1. Scroll to it, and select **Copy** from the **Edit** menu.

2. **Close** or **Hide** the Scrapbook.

3. Open the document (or whatever) you want to paste into, and select **Paste** from the **Edit** menu. Voilà!

   To paste something into the Scrapbook, reverse the process:

1. Select the text or graphic you want to paste into the Scrapbook, and copy it to the Clipboard.

2. Open the **Scrapbook**, and scroll to the item after which you want your new one to land.

3. Select **Paste** from the **Edit** menu, and the Scrapbook adds a new page in front of the current page to hold your new scrap.

   The Scrapbook supports Macintosh drag and drop (discussed in Chapter 8) so you just drag and drop items from the Scrapbook into applications that also support drag and drop (and vice versa, of course). To permanently remove an item from the Scrapbook, scroll to it and select **Cut** (⌘-X) from the **Edit** menu.

There are some more advanced Scrapbook replacements available if you find yourself outgrowing the original Scrapbook: SmartScrap and ClickPaste are both more flexible and more powerful.

Stickies

If you, like myself, are memory-impaired (I have a mind like a steel trap. Unfortunately, it's rusted open), Stickies are a pleasure. Like those Post-It type notes you probably have stuck all over your desk area already, Stickies are notes you can stick all over your Mac's desktop to remind you of things you need to remember.

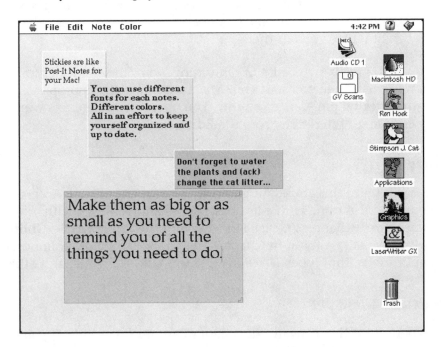

I am stuck on Stickies.

Stickies have all the functionality of a really small word processor: you create and edit Stickies pretty much the way you'd create and edit a file with SimpleText, but with these differences:

➤ Instead of a Font and/or Style menu, each note's font information is defined with the **Text Style** command (⌘-T) under the **Note** menu.

➤ You can't mix fonts or styles in a Stickie, it's only one per note.

➤ You specify what color each Stickie is by clicking on the Stickie (to make it active, just like you would a window) and selecting the color you want from the **Color** menu.

➤ While each Stickie behaves like a normal Mac window, there is no scroll bar. If your text runs off the Stickie, you can use your arrow keys to see the rest of it, or resize the note so the text fits.

➤ Closing a Stickie (by clicking on its Close Box) deletes the note *unless you tell your Mac to save it.*

➤ Quitting Stickies with notes on your desktop automatically saves the notes. The next time you open Stickies, your notes will be right where you left them.

If you really need a lot of reminding, you can set Stickies to launch every time you start your Mac by clicking the appropriate box in the Stickies' preference window. You open the preferences window by choosing **Preferences** from the **Edit** menu.

Other Stuff

In addition to this abundant and nifty assortment of Desk Accessories, your Mac also came with a few basic applications. Along with SimpleText (Chapter 7), Disk First Aid, and the Apple HD SC Utility (which we talked about in Chapter 10), you get some other important applications: the HyperCard Player, PowerTalk, PlainTalk, and others.

HyperCard Player

HyperCard is the software equivalent of an index card file. If you were using index cards for a research paper, you could write information about one topic on each card and refer to the information on other cards with little notes to yourself. HyperCard lets you do the same kind of thing, only with more flexibility. Its basic unit of information is a card. A collection of cards is called a *stack*. You can sort through these cards one at a time, or (if the stack is written that way) click on a word, phrase, or picture on one card, to automatically bring up a card of information related to that word, phrase, or picture. HyperCard is also a programming tool because its *scripting language* (way to write commands for it) lets you create stacks that are actual applications.

The HyperCard Player is basically just something to play stacks. You can tinker with them a little, but not much, nor can you create your own stacks (to do that, you need to buy the full version of HyperCard). You can launch the Player in one of three ways: double-click on the **HyperCard Player** icon, the **Home** icon, or the icon of the stack you want to play.

Your Mac churns a little as it reads the information. If you clicked on the **HyperCard Player**, or **Home** icons, you'll get the Player's Home Stack as shown in the following figure. If you clicked on a stack's icon, you'll see that stack, and it'll look like whatever it looks like (a Zen statement if I ever heard one).

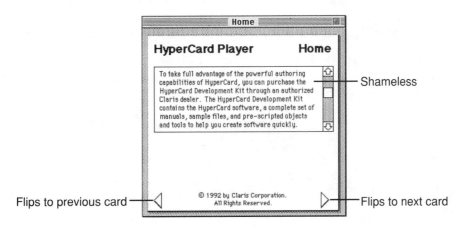

HyperCard Player Home.

You can use the right- and left-pointing arrows at the bottom of the card to flip through the rest of the Home stack. There isn't much to it. The last card of the stack is your *Preferences Card*. It lets you set the level of stuff you can do with the Player. Adjust the User Level by clicking on the level you want to set, or by sliding the white arrow to that level. From the Player's Home stack, you can launch another stack by selecting the **Open Stack** command from the **File** menu. It gives you a standard Open dialog box to navigate to the stack you want to open.

You don't really want to be reading about HyperCard; you want to be playing with it. That's okay. Learning by playing is much more fun than learning by reading. Launch the HyperCard Tour stack. Go play. I understand.

PC Exchange

Maybe you were suckered in by those commercials that said Macs will let you use DOS applications, documents, and disks. It wasn't a lie exactly, but it did stretch the truth a little. To run DOS and Windows applications on a Mac you need to buy additional software—something like Insignia Solutions' SoftPC or Soft Windows.

However, System 7.5 does come with everything you need to format and work with DOS disks like they were Mac disks. Two control panels give you that power: EasyOpen and PC Exchange (both were covered briefly back in Chapter 11). If you ever have the need to be able to read DOS files and disks, leave them installed in your Control Panels folder. They'll make dealing with DOS files practically effortless.

The capability to read and format (initialize) DOS disks is built in, and you don't even have to think about it. However, to open DOS files, you need to do a little work.

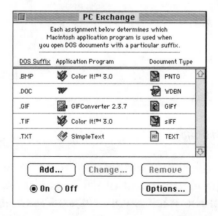

The PC Exchange Control Panel.

The PC Exchange Control Panel (shown above) was mentioned only in the most general terms in Chapter 11. In order to make opening DOS documents as effortless as possible, you need to tell the PC

158

Exchange what kind(s) of DOS files you'll be opening, and what Mac application you want to open them.

In the figure, you can see that I've associated .BMP (a DOS graphics format) with Color It!, and the PC Exchange will convert the .BMP (short for bit-mapped) into a Macintosh PNTG file (short for, you guessed it, painting).

To associate DOS formats with your Mac applications, click on the **Add** button. You'll get a dialog that asks you for the DOS file extension (like .BMP), the application you want to use to open it (which you can select from an Open-type dialog), and then click on the kind of Mac file you want the DOS file to become.

It isn't as difficult as it sounds—try it and see—but a knowledge of DOS files and their identifying extensions/suffixes (.BMP, .DOC, and so on) is very helpful. If you've worked with DOS before, you should already be familiar with them. If you're wading into uncharted waters, you may want to ask the person giving you the files what the suffixes mean, so you can assign an appropriate Mac application.

PowerTalk

PowerTalk is software that makes working with others on a network simpler. It gives you two more desktop icons: one is a mailbox that consolidates all your received e-mail in one location. The other is a catalog of information and resources that your work group shares.

PowerTalk will be of limited interest or use to folks who aren't part of a network. If you are part of a network, talk to your System Administrator to see if you can use PowerTalk. She'll be glad to walk you through installation and setup and show you how to use it.

PlainTalk

PlainTalk is the speech recognition software that works only with AV Macs. PlainTalk lets you tell your Mac what to do through speech commands, and it responds with a voice of its own—when it works, it's very cool, very *Star Trek*.

All in all, however (unless someone who uses your Mac is physically unable to maneuver a mouse, use the keyboard, or see the monitor), PlainTalk is a cranky memory hog that misinterprets what you say as often as it gets it right. In the following figure where my Mac (named Oscar) has interpreted my spoken commands as "Cut" and "Shut Down," I was actually just saying "Hello," to which the Mac is supposed to reply, "Hello. Welcome to Macintosh" in its scratchy electronic voice. Given practice, lots of RAM, and inhumanly clear pronunciation, PlainTalk can be put to good use. I suggest using the *Introduction to Speech* tutorial that comes with PlainTalk before you try it.

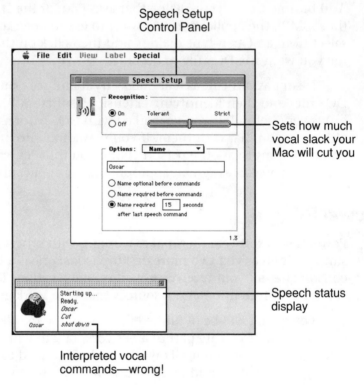

Speech Setup Control Panel

Sets how much vocal slack your Mac will cut you

Speech status display

Interpreted vocal commands—wrong!

Talking to your Mac.

If your Mac can't handle speech recognition, you can get Text-to-speech software (available from your favorite authorized Apple dealer, and Apple's areas on eWorld and America Online) that will let SimpleText read text files aloud. You just can't boss your Mac around with it.

Script Editor

AppleScript is (sort of) a programming language that lets you customize features and functions of your Mac, and some of your applications. To make use of it, you use the Script Editor (it will be in your Apple Extras folder after you've installed System 7.5) to write and edit your own scripts.

The squeamish (like myself) will probably be satisfied with the prewritten scripts available in the **Automated Tasks** folder in the **menu** and supplement those with more scripts from online services and user groups (like the one shown in the following figure). I don't feel like less of a man because I don't program or write scripts. Really. I don't. I *don't.*

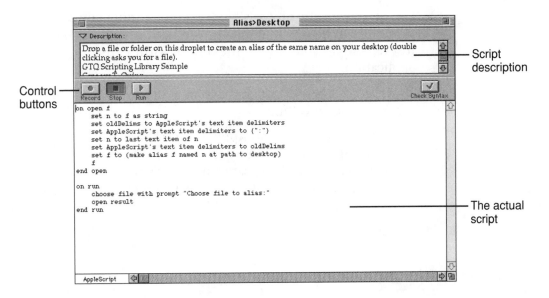

The AppleScript Script Editor.

The script shown in the figure was written by Gregory T. Quinn, part of the ZiffNet Script-A-File utility package, that makes dealing with AppleScript much easier. It, along with other Ziff-ware, is only available in the ZiffNet areas of America Online, CompuServe, and eWorld.

If you're a braver soul than I (and God bless you if you are) you should really pick up a good book on AppleScript before you begin: check your library or favorite computer bookstore, or ask a Script-head from your local user group for a recommendation.

The Least You Need to Know

Once you try all of the software accessories that came with your Mac, their use will quickly become second nature to you. Here are some things to keep in mind while you learn and explore:

➤ Your use of the DAs and applications that came with your System software will vary depending on how you work and grow as a Mac user.

➤ DAs all have really obvious names, so reminding you of what each does would insult your intelligence. Just remember you can use them from within any application.

➤ *HyperCard* is like a digital and dynamic index card file. Way cool and fun.

➤ PowerTalk, PlainTalk, and AppleScript will appeal to only certain Mac users or owners of certain Macs. You can live very full and satisfying lives without ever using any of them—but that doesn't mean you should be afraid to try them either.

➤ Fear nothing. This is Macintosh, after all.

Chapter 13

Printer Prattle

In This Chapter

➤ Types of printers

➤ Chauffeur-driven printers

➤ Choosing the Chooser

➤ QuickDraw GX

The only way to get that Great American Novel (or Great American Memo) you've been writing from your Mac's screen and into your hand is by printing it out. Printing can be, at once, the most rewarding and the most frustrating operation you perform. The two emotions are related: if it weren't so very satisfying to hold a crisp, clean printout (the result of your labors) in your hot little hand, it wouldn't be so very frustrating when things go wrong. I'll try and head some of that frustration off at the pass by arming you with a pile of printer preparedness.

Printer Types

The simplest path to pain-free printing is with an Apple printer. Because Apple designed the computer as well as the printer, you get everything you need to hook that bad boy up and just print away. Other manufacturers' printers will work with your Mac. However, unless it's a model specifically designed to work with a Mac (such as Hewlett-Packard's line of Mac-specific printers), you have to go through some Byzantine maneuvers to get a *third-party* printer to work with your Mac. We'll talk a little bit more about hooking up a non-Apple printer in a minute. First let's do a basic overview of your printer choices—in case you haven't bought one yet.

Dot-Matrix Printers

Dot-matrix printers are old and venerable machines. They've been around about as long as computers themselves. They work by means of an arrangement of 9 or 24 pins in a *print head* (the moving portion that holds the ribbon and the pin assembly). The print head moves along the paper. The pins poke out and strike the ribbon. The ribbon strikes the paper, and dots are left behind.

The **third party** is not the party you go to after the first two. Third party refers to a company that isn't you and isn't Apple. Most often, they're referred to as **third-party developers**.

The print head leaves an arrangement of dots in a small, defined area that form the letters, numbers, and lines of your document. That's the dot *matrix*, and the source of the name. The more pins you have in the print head, the more densely packed the dots in the matrix, and the better the print quality. Therefore a 24-pin printer can give you better printout than a 9-pin. The number of dots that fit in the matrix is called the printer's *resolution*, and it's one of the few times that being dense is actually a good thing.

Apple's ImageWriter line of printers are dot-matrix printers, but there are hundreds of other brands. Most of the other brands, however, are geared toward the DOS side of computing and require those Byzantine maneuvers I mentioned earlier. The attraction of dot-matrix printers, overall, is that they're cheaper (but not much cheaper) than inkjet printers, and loads cheaper than laser printers. But they're also noisy buggers, and most require form-feed paper (the kind with the holes down the side, so sprockets can pull it through the printer).

Usually when you look at an ad for a printer, you'll see *printer resolution* described as *300 dpi* or *360 × 360*. Clear as mud, eh? What that means is the first printer prints 300 *dots per inch*, which is a fairly standard print resolution; though you will see some laser printers that can print from 600 to even thousands of dots per inch. The second printer is a dot-matrix printer that is capable of printing a matrix 360 dots high by 360 dots wide. That's lots o' dots, and a fairly standard resolution for 24-pin dot-matrix printers and inkjets. The higher a printer's resolution, the better the printed page will look—and the higher the printer's price tag.

Inkjet Printers

In theory, inkjet printers work much the same as dot-matrix printers: there's a print head that moves back and forth across your paper leaving a matrix of dots to form lines and letters. In practice, however, there's one big exception.

Instead of pins striking a ribbon, the print head of an inkjet printer spits (eeeewww) those ink dots directly onto the paper to form your letters and lines. Because the spray of ink delivered by the print head is finer than the dots made by a dot-matrix printer, the resolution of an inkjet printer may sound the same (300 or 360 dpi) as a dot-matrix printer, but the quality usually looks better.

The attraction to inkjet printers is that they're quiet, the output is good, and they're a reasonable substitute if you need, but can't afford, a laser printer. However, there are a few drawbacks. They tend to be slow, and if you use the optional coated inkjet paper, the ink can smear if you handle the page too soon after printing. Plus, the coated paper (which keeps the ink from being absorbed into the paper, which in turn distorts the shape of letters) is expensive.

Apple's StyleWriter series are all inkjet printers. Hewlett-Packard, among others, makes a line of inkjets especially for the Mac (the DeskWriter line), many of which can print in glorious color.

Laser Printers

I know it's showing my age, but I remember when lasers were purely the stuff of science fiction. Now they're all over the place, thankfully without the destructive capability of their science fiction cousins.

Laser printers are the best, yet the most overrated, printers available today. They use laser beams to affix a black powder (*toner*) to the page in the shape of your letters and lines. Because the laser beam can be controlled so accurately and the toner can be so finely ground, even laser printers with a 300 dpi resolution produce a page that looks better than one printed on an inkjet or dot-matrix printer with a higher resolution.

Because laser printers can fool the eye into seeing more detail than other, higher resolution printer-types, the laser printer is the best output device available for personal and business use. The print just looks better, crisper, and more professional. There are a number of color laser printers, but they can be pretty expensive for average needs.

Specialty Printers

There are some printers that are geared toward specialized uses. The ones most readers may be interested in (since I don't think many will have the $20,000 to buy a 1000 DPI imagesetter on their own) are label and envelope printers.

On regular printers, labels and envelopes can be a pain: labels come loose and gum up the printer; envelopes print nicely (if they don't jam on the way through), but come out with the flap glued shut. There are special, small printers made to handle these annoying chores.

Label printers print labels—nothing but labels, and all kinds of labels. If you're a labelling fool, have a big video cassette, audio cassette, or diskette library, and handwritten labels just don't do it for you, you might want to check one out. Envelope printers print the mailing and return addresses on envelopes. Some will also accommodate postcards, and even a small variety of labels. Again, if you find yourself frequently cursing as you try and remove a massacred envelope from your printer's gizzards, you may want to think about an envelope printer. You can get either variety of printer (label or envelope) for between $150–$300.

Let Me Drive: All About Printer Drivers

Every bit as important as how (and how well) the printer gets your masterpiece on the page, is how (and how well) your Mac gets your page to the printer. The job of getting your Great American Novel (or memo) from your Mac to your printer is the job of the printer *driver*. The printer driver, like the driver of a car, issues instructions for the machine to follow. These drivers, also known as *Chooser extensions*, live in the Extensions folder inside your System Folder.

There are three kinds of printer drivers: those that use QuickDraw (built into your Mac's System software), those that use the new version of QuickDraw (QuickDraw GX), and those that rely on Adobe PostScript. QuickDraw and PostScript are known as *page description languages*, a hoity-toity way of saying they get your printer to print what you've created on the screen.

QuickDraw is built into your Mac's System software. It's the same thing that draws and redraws everything you see on your screen. If your printer driver relies on QuickDraw (and most of them do), then your Mac does most of the heavy math that figures out which dot goes where on the page. You can add QuickDraw GX to your Mac if you're using System 7.5, and your Mac has 8 MB of RAM (16 MB for a Power Mac). The GX version of QuickDraw includes better font handling and color printing and allows you to "print" documents to disk (PDDs, for Portable Digital Documents). There's more about QuickDraw GX coming up.

PostScript, on the other hand, is used mainly in laser printers, you'll see and hear them referred to as PostScript printers. PostScript isn't part of your Mac, rather it lives inside the printer on a chip. When you print, the page is sent to the printer, and PostScript figures out where the dots go.

Every printer made specifically for Macintosh comes with an appropriate driver. Apple provides you with *all* the drivers for all of its printers with its System software. As I said earlier, you *can* use a non-Apple, non-Macintosh printer with your Mac, but it takes some work.

Don't get confused. In addition to the PostScript page description language, we'll also be talking about PostScript *fonts* and *Adobe Type Manager (ATM)*, which lets you use PostScript fonts on a non-PostScript printer. These are three different but interrelated things.

Non-Apple, Non-Macintosh Printers

There are three problems that stand in the way of hooking up a printer aimed at IBM-compatible machines. First, they don't come with printer drivers for Macs. Second, they don't come with the round-ended serial cables to plug into the printer port on the back of your Mac (a DIN-8 cable, if you want to be really geeky). Third, many of these printers are *parallel* printers (as opposed to the *serial* printers Macs use).

Parallel and **serial** are distinctions based on how the printers receive information from the computer. Parallel printers receive bits of information in sets of 8 bits. Most IBM-compatible computers come with two parallel ports, so parallel printers are popular for PCs. Serial printers receive bits of information one at a time. The Mac's built-in printer port is a serial port, and the root of this particular problem.

Two terribly clever companies have sidestepped these problems for you. The first one, GDT Softworks, in the lovely state of Washington, puts out what it calls PowerPrint. It's a collection of drivers that print on over a thousand non-Mac printers. It also comes with a converter cable that converts your Mac's serial output into parallel output. The second one, Orange Micro, has taken a different tack entirely. Rather than provide another driver, Orange Micro will sell you a converter cable and software that fakes your Mac into thinking it's printing to an Apple ImageWriter printer.

The biggest advantage to buying a non-Mac printer is that they tend to be less expensive up front. However, they may not be less expensive once you add the converter gewgaws and consider the dollar value of your pain and suffering. If you already have an IBM-compatible printer or someone wants to give you an old one, then it can be a great savings to you. Whether the extra effort and any savings you may gain are actually worth it, only you can decide.

Choosy Users Choose the Chooser

Regardless of what printer you end up with, you need to tell the Mac what and where it is. To do that, you use the Chooser. Select **Chooser** from the menu, and a window similar to the one shown in the following figure will appear. You may have more, and different, printer drivers, and the Chooser will look slightly different if you're using QuickDraw GX.

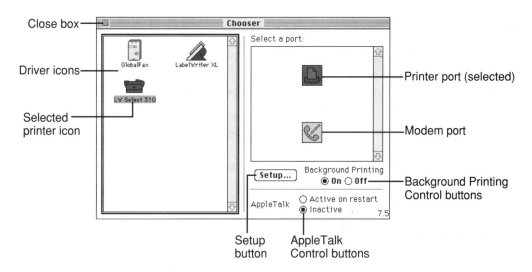

Close box

Driver icons

Selected printer icon

Printer port (selected)

Modem port

Background Printing Control buttons

Setup button

AppleTalk Control buttons

The Chooser.

Looking at the Chooser (clockwise, from the left), you'll see a window that displays the icons for all of the printers and other Chooser selectable devices, such as modems. If you have more printer drivers installed than fit in the window, you can scroll through the list to find the one you'd like to select. When you select a printer icon, the right half of the display changes to accommodate the needs of that particular printer.

Click on the icon for the port you want to connect your printer to. Depending on the type of printer you've selected, the bottom third of the right side of the window will be different.

If you have a **Setup** button, clicking on it brings up a window or dialog box where you can tell your Mac necessary information about the chosen printer. If a **Background Printing** option is available to you (and turned on), you will gain control of your Macintosh before the printer completes the print job. You don't have to wait for the entire thing to print before moving on to other work.

Background printing is accomplished by means of another little program called PrintMonitor, which your Mac launches automatically when you have the Background Printing option turned on. We'll talk more about PrintMonitor in a bit.

169

In its simplest terms, a **network** can be as small as one Mac hooked up with one laser printer via AppleTalk. At its most extreme, a network can be dozens of Macs hooked up to each other, as well as to several printers. If your network consists of one Mac and one printer linked by AppleTalk, the instructions here are enough to get you printing. If you're on a more complicated network, check with the network administrator (whoever manages the beast) to verify what you need to do to print.

Finally, the *AppleTalk* control buttons are at the bottom right of the window. AppleTalk is Apple's built-in networking feature. Many Apple laser printers rely on AppleTalk to pass information from your Mac to the printer.

If you connect your printer via AppleTalk (check your printer manual), be sure that AppleTalk is *active* before you try to print. If it isn't, click on the radio button in front of the word **Active**. You'll get a message warning you to restart your Mac before AppleTalk is activated.

Once you have the Chooser set up to accommodate your printer, you can close it by clicking on the **Close Box** in the upper left corner. If you've changed anything, you'll get a warning that you've changed printers with the Chooser, and you should adjust your Page Setup settings. The next section explains how to do that.

Setting Up to Print

The **Page Setup** command tells your Mac what kind of paper you'll be printing on. To use it, select the **Page Setup** option from the **File** menu. You'll see a dialog box similar to the one shown in the following figure. (The options available to you will vary slightly from printer to printer or from program to program.) You'll notice that the dialog box is specific to the printer selected in the Chooser.

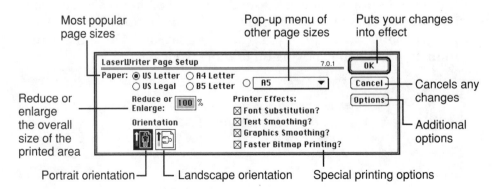

The Page Setup dialog box.

The most commonly used paper sizes are at the top of the dialog box: *US Letter* (8 1/2 × 11 inches), *US Legal* (8 1/2 × 14 inches), *A4 Letter* (8 1/2 × 11 2/3 inches, a size more common in Europe), and *B5 Letter* (another standard size in Europe, 7 × 10 inches). These are standard no matter what printer you use. To select one of these sizes, simply click on the radio button in front of the paper size of your choice. If those paper size options aren't enough for you, select the pop-up menu, and you have eight more choices.

Another dialog box option is the Reduce or Enlarge text box. You can type in the percentage you would like each page of your current document reduced or enlarged to. Below the Reduce or Enlarge option are the Orientation icons. The icon on the left, where the person is standing full length on the page, is called *portrait orientation*. A page in portrait orientation looks the way you normally think of an 8 1/2 × 11-inch piece of paper (taller than it is wide). The icon on the right, where the outline of a person is cut off at the waist (ouch) is *landscape orientation*. Landscape turns the page so that it is wider than it is tall: 11 × 8 1/2 inches. Portrait is the *default* (or preset) orientation, so only change it if you want to print in landscape. If you want to print several documents in landscape orientation, you must change the Page Setup for each one.

> "Reduce or Enlarge" is badly phrased. It seems to say you should enter the amount you want the page reduced or enlarged by. That's wrong! If you want each page *reduced* by 25%, you don't enter 25%. Instead, you enter 75%, because 100% minus 25% is 75% (100–25=75). (Who said this math crap wouldn't be useful after you left school?) If you want to *enlarge* each page by 25%, you'd enter 125%.

Next come the Printer Effects options. These vary from printer to printer, so check your printer's manual if you're not sure what your options do. Clicking on the **Options** button brings up an additional dialog box that lets you add some special effects to your printed page. You can select any combination of these options that you care to, or none at all. The options vary depending on your printer's capabilities. Check your documentation if you can't figure out what one of your options is, or just try them; you won't hurt anything. When you've chosen the special effects (if any) you want to inflict on your document, click on the **OK** button, or press the **Enter** key, and you'll return to the Page Setup dialog box.

Finally, click on the **OK** button (or press **Enter**) when you're through making changes to the page setup. The Mac closes the Page Setup dialog box and returns you to your document for printing. Clicking on the **Cancel** button abandons any changes you may have made and closes the Page Setup dialog box.

Printing (Finally!)

Now that you have informed your Mac of all your printing choices, you can finally print out a document. If you don't often change print-ers, paper size, or add special printing effects, you may not have to tinker with the Chooser or Page Setup settings again for a long time. So let's print while the printing is good.

Printing a Document within an Application

When your application is running and your document is open, click on the **File** menu. If everything is set to your liking and you have turned your printer on, select the **Print** command. You'll get a dialog box something like the one shown here.

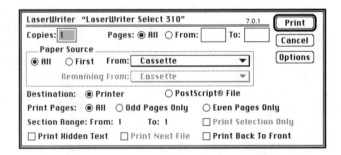

The Print dialog box.

Simply press ⌘-P to print.

As before, some of the features and functions of the dialog box will vary. Some programs, such as Aldus PageMaker, replace the regular Print dialog box with one of their own. Check with your application's documen-tation if you want to know the particulars.

When your dialog box options are set to your liking, click on **Print**, and in a few minutes or so (depending on your printer and the length of your document), you'll have a nice, crisp printout to ooh and ahh over.

Printing a Document from the Desktop

Yes, Virginia, there is a way to print a file you've already saved without having to open the application that created it. First, click on the document's icon to select it. Then, select **Print** from the **File** menu (or press ⌘-**P**). Your Mac automatically fires up the application that created the document, opens the document, and presents you with the Print dialog box. Click on the **Print** button or press **Enter**. Your file prints, and your Mac automatically shuts down the application, neat as can be.

From the desktop, you can also print the contents of the currently active window. This is way helpful for keeping track of what you have, particularly your extensions and control panels. To print the contents of the active window, do one of these two things:

➤ If the window's in Icon or Small Icon view, select **Print Window** from the **File** menu. Repeat the process for each folder in the original window (so you get a full printout of contents).

➤ If the window's in View by Name, click on the arrow in front of each folder icon to expand the view to include all items in nested folders. Select **Print Window** from the **File** menu.

This will save you *gobs* of time when/if you're on the phone with some company's technical support department and they say "What extensions and control panels do you have running?"

Monitoring PrintMonitor

If your printer gives you the option of *background printing*, you'll need to deal with *PrintMonitor*. It's a wee bit of a program that lives in the Extensions folder inside your System Folder. PrintMonitor accepts the printing chores you send it and handles them while you move on to other things.

When you print a file, all of the printing data is printed to disk in a folder called *PrintMonitor Documents* located in your System Folder. As soon as it's done printing to disk, control of your Mac is returned to you. This is called *spooling* a file (don't ask me why). Then, working quietly in the background, PrintMonitor then picks up the spooled file and sends it to your printer.

You don't need to be printing something to access PrintMonitor. You can open it like any other application. Locate the PrintMonitor icon inside the Extensions folder in your System Folder, and double-click on it. You'll see the PrintMonitor dialog box shown here.

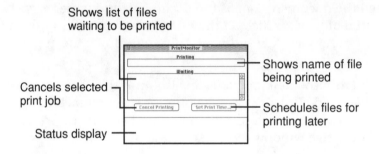

Here's the PrintMonitor.

When you're printing something, all those blank spaces you see in the figure get filled in, as follows:

The first box, labeled *Printing*, shows you the name of the file currently being printed, as well as the name of the printer it is printing on. Below it, the *Waiting* box shows you what files are queued up to print after the current file.

The **Cancel Printing** button stops the current file from printing or removes a selected file from the *Waiting* queue. To cancel a file, simply click on its name to select it, and click on the **Cancel Printing** button. It may take a second or two for PrintMonitor to register the **Cancel Printing** command. Don't panic.

When you cancel a print job with the **Cancel Printing** button, the spooled file is deleted from the PrintMonitor Documents folder. If you change your mind and want to print it again, you have to print it from scratch.

174

If you want to *pause* the printing process (while you change paper, run to the bathroom, or something), select **Stop Printing** from PrintMonitor's **File** menu. That stops the print job without deleting the spooled file. When you get back, select **Resume Printing** from the **File** menu (it's where Stop Printing was before), and the print job continues.

When the current file finishes printing, it's like the Mad Hatter's tea party: everything in the queue moves up one space, and the process starts all over again. If there's nothing else waiting to be printed, the display goes blank. If PrintMonitor is working in the background (it's not the active application), it shuts itself down automatically and goes away. If it is the active application, it sits there until you click on something else (the desktop or another application), and then it scurries away, back into its hole until you call it up again.

QuickDraw GX Printing

The process of printing doesn't change much when using QuickDraw GX. All of the previous information applies, but with the following differences.

The Chooser

Using the Chooser remains pretty much the same with GX printing (shown in the next figure). You still select the appropriate GX driver for your printer (though GX drivers are different from regular Chooser extensions). You also tell the Chooser whether you connected your printer to the printer or modem ports. However, you must also tell the printer whether you attached your printer to a serial port, via AppleTalk, or to a print server as part of a larger network (with the pop-up menu, as shown in the following figure). Most users will choose one of the first two—most home users won't be dealing with a large network. If you use a network at work, check with the network administrator for the proper Chooser settings.

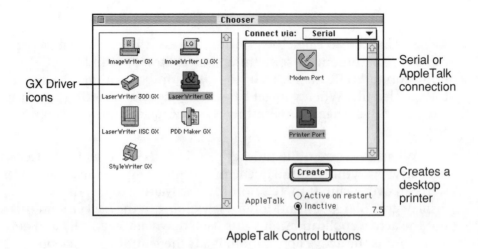

GX Driver icons

Serial or AppleTalk connection

Creates a desktop printer

AppleTalk Control buttons

The Chooser with QuickDraw GX.

Instead of using a **Setup** command with QuickDraw GX, you use the **Create** button to create a *desktop printer*. You can create two types of desktop printers: either for a physical, "here's a piece of paper" printer, or for a PPD (Portable Digital Document) printer.

Desktop Printer Icons

Desktop printers are icons, like those shown in the following figure, that sit on your desktop and give you access to drag-and-drop printing. Instead of selecting a document icon and selecting the Print command from the File menu (as discussed earlier), you can drag the document's icon and drop it on the appropriate printer icon. Printing will commence.

Desktop Printers and a Portable Digital Document.

The first icon, labeled LaserWriter GX, is a paper printer. You'll get a piece of paper with your words or pictures, or whatever, on it when you use that icon to print. The second, labeled PDD Maker GX, prints your document to your desktop as a file. A PDD file, when opened on a Mac, will look *exactly* the way it would if printed on paper, regardless of whether the person looking at it has the same application (perhaps a word processor) or the same fonts installed.

The third icon shown is a PDD file. They're very handy if you want to send someone a file and it's important that it looks the way you created it—it may be a newsletter that you busted your hump trying to make pretty, but you aren't sure the recipient has the same wild and crazy font assortment that you have, or the same application. The advantage to PDD files is that they do, indeed, look the way you intended them to look. The disadvantage (which is minor, really) is that PDD files are much larger than the original files because they contain all that font and layout information. A 6K SimpleText file with a few fonts will turn into a 92K PDD, more than fifteen times the original size.

Printing with QuickDraw GX

When you print from inside an application, such as a word processor, the file you're printing goes to the default printer—the one with the thick black border around it (in the last figure, that would be the PDD Maker). You set the default printer like this:

1. Click on the desktop printer's icon to select it. When you do, a **Printing** menu will appear in the menu bar, after the Special menu.

2. Click on the **Printing** menu and select the **Set Default Printer** option. The selected printer is now your default printer.

Pros and Cons of GX

Like most things in life, there are good and bad things about using QuickDraw GX. The good things include: simplified page setup and printing options, drag-and-drop printing, faster printing, better font handling, and better color output. PDDs are also good for folks who want to distribute disk-based documents to many Mac users with different system configurations.

The bad things (aside from the lack of GX-compatible drivers at the moment) include: you need 8 MB/16 MB of RAM to use it (you may want to look at the section on adding RAM in Chapter 17, or RAM utilities in Chapter 16); it eats up hard drive space; and you only get better font handling with GX fonts (which aren't widely available yet). It also increases desktop clutter with those printer icons, but that's minor. Do you need it? Probably not. Will you like it? Probably, if your system can handle it, and if you've been irritated by the limitation of plain ol' QuickDraw printing. If your Mac can handle it, try it and decide for yourself.

The Least You Need to Know

Here's a quick recap of what you need to remember about printing:

➤ You need a printer to print. The kind of printer you use is completely up to you.

➤ You have to have a driver (appropriate for your printer) installed in the Extensions folder inside your System Folder in order to print.

➤ The Chooser (on the ⌘ menu) tells your Mac what printer (and printer driver) you are using, and where it is connected to your Mac.

➤ Use the **Page Setup** command (on the **File** menu) to tell your Mac what size paper you'll be printing on, and what orientation it will be in.

➤ You can print an open document from within an application with the **Print** command on the **File** menu, or by pressing ⌘-**P**.

➤ You can print a document from the desktop by selecting its icon and issuing either of the print commands.

➤ QuickDraw GX has some nice features, but I don't think the world will come to an end if you don't use it.

Font Facts

Fonts are slightly schizophrenic. On one hand, they're mundane, everyday things: the alphabet, numbers, symbols, and punctuation. On the other hand, each font has its own personality, style (or lack there of), and color.

A single chapter isn't going to give you the skills you need to raise font use to an art form—it would take a big, fat, hairy book the size of the *Oxford English Dictionary*, and even then, there's no guarantee you'll become a font artiste. I'll introduce you to just the font basics. It won't make you an artiste, but it will help you use fonts more effectively and may put you in touch with the artiste within.

In the Beginning, There Was Bit Map

When Macs were first released, the concept of a graphical, icon-based interface was radical and new. In order to get the desktop on the desktop, all the different fonts had to be built into the System software. At the time, the simplest way of doing that was to create each letter, number, and symbol of each font in a way that would be easy for your Mac to draw on the screen or print on a printer. The easiest way of doing that was to draw the letters the same way your Mac or printer would: one dot at a time.

There are many words used in computing to distinguish one kind of dot from another. In a printout, dots are simply called **dots** (as in **dots per inch**) when they make up letters and lines. On your monitor, each dot is called a **pixel**, borrowed from the terminology of television design. It's a contracted form of *picture element.* In drawing, and in fonts, a dot that is part of a letter or line is called a *bit* because it takes one bit (the smallest unit of memory) to create and place that dot somewhere.

Since each dot in a letter is called a bit, and each letter is formed by drawing a map to tell your Mac where to place the dots, the earliest fonts were called bit-mapped. Because these bit-mapped fonts were first designed for use on your Mac's screen, they're also referred to as *screen fonts*. The terms were used interchangeably.

The trouble with bit-mapped fonts is that, because they're a collection of square-ish dots trying to form round-ish characters, the letter shapes would often look lumpy and jagged (if that's hard for you to visualize, try and build a smooth curve out of Legos). Lumpy letters are hard to read, especially at smaller sizes (for fonts, that's *point size*). At larger point sizes, the lumps get even more pronounced. You can see what I mean in this figure.

Lumpy bit-mapped letters.

The words in the figure were done with 24-point Times (a standard Mac font) and then enlarged to show the detail. The lumpiness (often called *jaggies*) is most noticeable in the curved portions of the S,

180

the 2, and even the diagonal part of the 4, which looks like a staircase instead of a smooth diagonal line.

Point size is a term borrowed from typesetters. One **point** is approximately 1/72 of an inch. Point is abbreviated **pt.** (as in 12-pt.).

The most you need to remember about point size (unless you get heavily into fonts) is that a *12-pt.* font is roughly equal to the size of type you'd get from a typewriter, and the size you'll probably use most often. Anything much larger or smaller would be reserved for special uses, like big headlines (like the chapter names throughout this book) or tiny captions (such as those under the figures). For each common point size (like 9-, 10-, 12-, and 14-points), there was a plain bit-mapped font file, one per size. If you needed special styles (like **bold**, *italic*, and ***bold italic***), your Mac manufactured them by thickening or slanting the plain bit maps. That added another level of lumpiness to the fonts, making them even harder to read.

Generally though, the jaggies were bearable if you had all the sizes you needed to do your work. However, bit-mapped fonts only came in fixed point sizes. If you needed to use, say, *12-point Venice* but only had the *14-point* version installed, the jaggies would get completely out of hand. Because the Venice bit map is only available in 14-point, your Mac gets creative when you specify Venice in 12-point and tries to compress the bit map it has to imitate the bit map you want. As you can see from the sample below, the Mac isn't very good at imitations. The lovely calligraphic lines and flourishes of Venice at 14 points get pretty well trashed at 12 points. The invention of *outline* fonts changed all that.

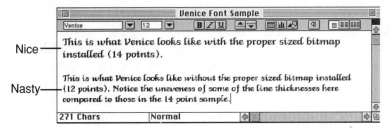

Venice font sample.

Shapely Fonts

Instead of telling your Mac where each dot goes to shape a letter, an outline font gives a mathematical description of the letter's shape (an outline) that your Mac can then fill in. Outline fonts are like digital coloring books; all your Mac has to do is stay within the lines. The following figure shows the kind of outline that outline-style fonts provide, and how they get filled in.

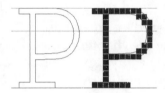

Font outlines.

The **P** on the right of the figure isn't really an accurate representation of how the outline gets filled in. You can see how some of the dots fall outside the outline (in the curve), and parts of the outline aren't filled in. Outline fonts do a little more fiddling to better fill in the outline. That's the blessing and curse of outline fonts.

Because font outlines are mathematical, it's easy for your Mac to fudge a number here and there to come up with the point size you need. Outline fonts are sometimes called *scalable fonts* (mostly in the world of DOS) because their size can be scaled up or down to meet your needs. The math to scale a font takes time, even for a computer. So, to keep your Mac from spending all of its time calculating the curves of S's, outline fonts work in tandem with their bit-mapped cousins. In fact, each outline font comes with a set of bit-mapped fonts at specific sizes. They also come with specific outlines for **bold**, *italic*, extended, and compressed formats. It improves the look of the type on the page, but all those additional font outlines can clog up your Font folder (more about that in a little while).

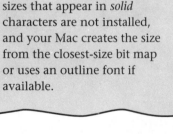

You can easily tell what sizes of a font you have installed. When you look at the **Font** or **Size** menu in any application, you'll usually see the sizes you can choose from. The font sizes that appear in *outline* characters are installed and look beautiful. The font sizes that appear in *solid* characters are not installed, and your Mac creates the size from the closest-size bit map or uses an outline font if available.

If you select a font at a size available in bit-mapped format, your Mac uses that one first. If you goose the size up (or down) to one that isn't installed, then your Mac resorts to the outline font. There are two competing outline formats. One is *TrueType* from Apple. The other is *PostScript* from Adobe Systems. Both will also be available in GX variations. Each font type has specific benefits and drawbacks in terms of their use. Don't get the idea that fonts are an either/or proposition. TrueType and PostScript fonts get along fine on your Mac. You can use both if you want.

PS: It's PostScript

PostScript fonts, from Adobe and other manufacturers, have been around as long as there have been laser printers. They were originally made to live inside your printer's ROM (read-only memory) or be downloaded to its RAM (random-access memory) to make your laser-printed output as crisp and clear as the technology allows. As I mentioned before, PostScript fonts have two parts: the bit-mapped font that turns up on your screen, and the part that lives in your printer (or in your Mac waiting to be downloaded to the printer).

In the past, the part that went to the printer (called a *printer font*) was the actual *font outline* and had no effect on what you saw on your screen. You still had the jaggies imposed by the limits of bit-mapped screen fonts. Then Adobe introduced *Adobe Type Manager* (*ATM*), which does two great things for Mac users. First, it lets your Mac use the *printer* fonts to create *screen* fonts in sizes you don't have a bit map for. The immediate benefit is less jagged type on your screen.

Additionally, ATM lets you use PostScript fonts on non-PostScript printers (such as dot-matrix, and some lasers) so you get the clarity and crispness of PostScript without shelling out big bucks for a PostScript laser. That's two big benefits. The only drawback to ATM is that it can slow your Mac down noticeably, and it can eat up its memory (RAM). System 7.5's QuickDraw GX comes with a special GX version of Adobe Type Manager. If you aren't running QuickDraw GX, you can get Adobe Type Manager direct from Adobe for about $30 by calling Adobe Systems at 1-800-521-1976.

Adobe's fonts currently come in three variations: *Type 1*, *Type 3*, and *Multiple Masters*. Type 1 fonts are the most common and easiest to find. You won't often see Type 3. Multiple Master fonts are for design pros: they're fonts that you can tinker with to create hundreds, even thousands of variations. Only real font freaks need apply.

There are also two other versions of ATM flying around: *ATM* and *Super ATM*. Super ATM has more functions (and therefore costs more). Super ATM comes with Multiple Master fonts and will create substitute fonts if you try to open a document that uses fonts you don't own. You can get Super ATM for about $95 by mail order.

True (Blue) Type

TrueType fonts, from Apple, were introduced with System 7.0. If you're running System 7.0 or later, you have TrueType and don't need anything extra. (System 6 users need to get the *TrueType INIT* from their local authorized Apple Dealer). TrueType looks good, both on the page and on your screen, and there are hundreds of TrueType fonts around—not quite as many as Type 1 fonts, but still lots of them. The big advantage to TrueType is that you don't need anything extra to use them, just fonts—and fonts are easy to find.

GX Fonts

With the introduction of System 7.5 and QuickDraw GX, there's a new font variation muddying up the waters: GX fonts. When you use QuickDraw GX (with an application that can make use of its special features and GX fonts that contain additional typographic information), you can get typographic effects that previously required extra fonts and extra work. Now you can get such esoteric typography as real fractions (one character instead of 3—*number/number*), ligatures (where two letters are set as one joined character), and alternate *swash* characters (where, say, the tail of a J drops down into an elaborate swirl).

GX fonts are a font variation, not a whole new kind of font. There will be GX fonts in both TrueType and Type 1 format, and the only difference between GX and non-GX fonts is the additional typographic information. The fonts you already have will work with QuickDraw GX—your TrueType fonts work automatically with it, your Type 1 fonts need to be *enabled* before you can use them. More about enabling fonts in a minute.

₳ Field Guide to Font Icons

Once you go poking around in your Font folder (System 7.1 and later) or System file (System 7.0 and earlier), you'll probably want to know which type of font is which. It's easy to tell them apart, simply by looking. Let the following figure be your guide.

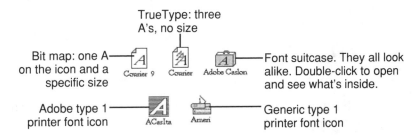

Here are some font icons.

Bit-mapped fonts only have one **A** on their icons and a point size after their names (as with *Courier 9* in the figure). All bit-mapped font icons look pretty much the same, whether from Adobe, Apple, or somebody else. TrueType fonts have three A's on the icon and no point size in the name (such as *Courier* in the figure). However, they specify **Bold**, *Italic*, or ***Bold Italic*** in the name.

Adobe PostScript printer fonts have a stylized **A** (for Adobe) as their icons, and many have seriously abridged names (*ACasIta* in the figure translates into *Adobe Caslon Italic*). PostScript printer fonts from other sources may have specialized icons. Many come with a generic icon, a LaserWriter with a **1** (like *Ameri* (for *American*) in the figure).

The suitcase icon is the font equivalent of a folder: a convenient container to group related fonts together (a font family) in one location. The one in the figure contains all of the Adobe Caslon variations I own.

Ins and Outs of Fonts

Since the history of fonts is speckled with innovation and change, there are different ways to install and remove fonts in different versions of the Mac OS. System 7.5 is the latest and greatest, so let's start there and backtrack.

System 7.1 through 7.5

A piece of cake: drag the font icons you want installed from their disks into your Font folder. When you're done, restart your Mac. To remove fonts, reverse the process: drag the font icons out of your Font folder and onto a disk, holding folder, or into the Trash. Restart your Mac. You won't even break a sweat.

System 7.0

Installing fonts in 7.0 is still pretty easy, just not as easy as in 7.5.

1. After making sure that you're only running the Finder (quit any open applications), find your System Folder.

2. Locate the fonts you want to install (open the disk or folder window where they're located), select them, and drag-and-drop them on your closed System Folder.

   You'll get a message to the effect of **Fonts should be stored in the System file, so I'm gonna put them there, Okay?** (The message varies according to the kind of font you're installing. Bit-mapped and TrueType fonts go in the System file, the PostScript *outline* (or printer) fonts go in the Extensions folder—don't worry; your Mac knows where they all go.)

3. Click on the **OK** button, and your Mac takes care of the rest. When it's done copying the fonts into your System, simply restart your Mac.

   To remove fonts:

1. Open your System file, and drag the fonts you want to remove out of it. They can go onto a disk, into another folder, or into the Trash.

2. If you're removing PostScript fonts, drag the matching outline/printer fonts out of your Extensions folder, too.

3. Restart your Mac.

Pre-System 7

For Mac OS versions before System 7.0, things are a little more complicated. You need to use an application called The Font/DA Mover that came on your original System disks. You also use it to install Desk Accessories in your System, too. Its icon is a little moving truck (so cute). You launch the Font/DA Mover like any application. When the application opens, you'll see a screen like the one shown here.

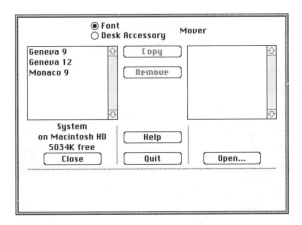

The Font/DA Mover.

The scroll box on the left displays the fonts already installed in your System file. Click on the **Open** button under the right scroll box. You'll get a standard Open dialog box. Use it to navigate to the fonts you want to install. Click, or Shift-click, on the font name(s) in the right scroll box that you want to install. When you have the names of all the fonts you want to install selected, click on the **Copy** button. Font/DA mover installs them. When it's done, **Quit** the Font/DA Mover, and restart your Mac.

To remove fonts, click, or Shift-Click, on the font name(s) in the left scroll box (the ones already in your System). Click on the **Remove** button. When you've removed all the fonts you want out of there, **Quit** the Font/DA Mover, and restart your Mac.

187

Enabling Type 1 Fonts for QuickDraw GX

While installing fonts with System 7.5 is still easier than with older versions, there is an extra step you need to perform if you're using QuickDraw GX and Type 1 fonts. You need to *enable* them, meaning you have to adapt them so QuickDraw GX can use them. To do that, you use the Type 1 Enabler application that comes in the QuickDraw GX folder with your System 7.5 disks or CD-ROM.

Launch the Enabler just like you would any other application. When it starts up, you'll see an Open dialog, asking you to locate the Type 1 font(s) you want to enable. The font can already be installed in your Fonts folder, or you can enable it right from a floppy disk or font CD (which will save you time). Then do the following:

1. Navigate to the Type 1 font you want to enable, and click on it to select it (you can enable a single font, a single suitcase containing several fonts, or an entire folder of fonts).

2. Press **Enter**. The Enabler will ask where you want the enabled fonts stored.

3. If the fonts you're enabling are already in your Fonts folder, just press **Enter**. If they're stored anywhere else, navigate to your Fonts folder (inside your System folder,) and then press **Enter**. The Enabler will do its thing.

4. Repeat the process for any other Type 1 fonts you care to enable, or **Quit** the Enabler.

5. You need to restart your Mac to make use of your newly enabled fonts. Use the **Restart** command under the **Special** menu.

   You're all set!

Font Management

Here's the trouble with fonts: the more you load into your System, the more memory and hard drive space they take up. If you turn into a font freak (like me), that can spell trouble unless you have a huge hard drive and mountains of RAM. Here are a couple of ways to keep your fonts under control.

Keep Track of What You Have

The first step to managing your fonts is keeping track of the ones you own—especially if you don't keep them all installed all of the time. One way to see what a mystery font looks like is to double-click on its icon. System 7 opens a window displaying a sample of the type. TrueType fonts shows you a variety of sizes. Bit-mapped fonts only show you the size of the font you clicked on.

This works well enough, but it isn't always convenient to go digging around double-clicking on fonts to see what they look like. I've found it easier to keep a binder full of printed pages of samples of all the fonts I own. The samples show the font name, the point size used, and every letter of the alphabet (upper- and lowercase) as well as all the numbers, punctuation, and symbols.

There are two ways to do this. One is to use a word processor to create and save a document of all the usual characters. When I install a new font, I open the sample document, select the text, and change the old font to the new one. Then I print it out and slap it into my binder. The other way is with a font utility. You can find *freeware* utilities that give you more information about a font than you'll ever need. These utilities are available on most online services and from Mac user groups. Whether you do it yourself, manually, or use one of the many font utilities, a binder of samples is a great way to remember what fonts you have and what they look like.

Saving Memory

I've mentioned it before, but it bears repeating: fonts take up memory. You may not see it directly, but you may notice that your System software RAM usage (when you check it with **About This Macintosh** in the menu) is getting piggy. One way to trim it back is to remove fonts you only use once in a blue moon from your System and re-install them when you need them. It's work, but it's pretty easy with any of the versions of System 7. Another way is to buy and install a font manager, such as Suitcase, from Symantec.

Suitcase used a Font folder before Apple ever thought of it. Suitcase is a desk accessory that manages your fonts, sounds, and Desk Accessories (three of my favorite things—right up there with raindrops

189

on roses and whiskers on kittens). You can store them anywhere on your hard drive that you like, outside the System Folder.

The great thing about Suitcase is that it lets you specify a set of fonts, sounds, and DAs to use whenever you start your Mac. Then Suitcase lets you open temporary sets for a special project, for a particular application, or just on a whim. You can see the Suitcase dialog box and some of the sets of fonts and stuff I have set up in the next figure.

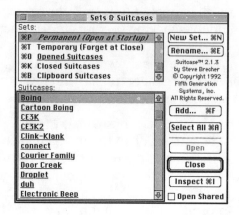

The Suitcase dialog box.

The immediate benefit is that the size of your System software's RAM usage only increases when you open fonts (or whatever), and can actually shrink (gasp!) when you knock stuff out. Suitcase does take some setting up, but it isn't difficult, and boy, does it cut down on font craziness. I think my Mac would explode without it.

Adobe Type Reunion

Another way to squeeze some extra space out of your Mac when you have piles of PostScript fonts installed is by using Adobe Type Reunion. The problem with PostScript fonts, as I mentioned before, is that not only does each font have at least two pieces (the screen and printer fonts), there are also separate fonts for bold, italic, and bold italic. All these different styles make up a font *family* and can include such exotic variations as: *semibold* (lightly bold), *heavy* (extra bold), *light* (thinner than the regular), *oblique* (mildly italic), and then combinations, such as *light oblique semibold*. Yikes! Each of these font variations takes up space in your font menu. To make matters worse, some of the names don't hang together alphabetically.

That's a problem. It's awkward to have to go sifting through a jam-packed font menu trying to find all of the family members of a font. It also wastes time. Adobe Type Reunion changes that. Type Reunion reorganizes your font menu so that font families are represented by only *one* entry in the main menu, with a submenu to display all of the variations. Oh, it makes the heart sing!

As long as we're on the subject of font families, you should be aware that some companies, when advertising fonts, put in letters six-feet high that the package includes OVER 100 POSTSCRIPT FONTS! It isn't necessarily a lie, so much as bending the truth a little. What they're doing is counting individual fonts, rather than font families. So, in truth, you are getting 100 fonts, but six or ten of them are, say, Helvetica variations. Saying OVER 100 POSTSCRIPT FONTS! sounds better than saying OVER 15 FONT FAMILIES!

Speed Up Your Laser Printer's Print Time

Now that you've filled up your Mac to its blow-hole with fonts, you're going to be tempted to use them, right? Well, you should know that using many fonts in a document can increase your printing time, or foul it up entirely. Here's why: Most laser printers come with fonts built into their read-only memory (ROM). Using the fonts already stored in the printer makes documents print faster. If you use a font that isn't in your printer, your laser and Mac start some heavy negotiating:

Laser: Hey! This says use Bodoni. I ain't got Bodoni. You got it?
Mac: Wait a minute, let me look.
Laser: Okay, but hurry it up.
Mac: Got it! You want it?
Laser: Yeah, send it down.
Mac: Sending it.
Laser: Getting it.
Mac: Got it?

Laser: Yeah, got it.
Mac: Good.
Laser: Hey! This says use Bodoni Bold. I ain't got Bodoni Bold.

It happens faster than that, but still, you may be old and gray before they're done shmoozing about fonts (thank goodness they don't gossip, too). If you load a document with too many fonts (and don't ask me how many too many is; it depends on your printer's memory), the printer's RAM can get so full of font outlines that it can't process the actual document. It just sits there chattering with your Mac about how cool all those fonts look.

There are two ways to avoid this back-and-forth chattering. The first (for maniacal font freaks only) is to attach a hard drive to your printer (if it has a SCSI port, like the one on your Mac). You can *download* all of your fonts that fit on the drive, and your printer never has to ask for them again.

Most of us, however, aren't so heavily into fonts (or rich enough) to just throw another hard drive at our printers. A cheaper way to do it is to download the fonts you regularly use (or ones you know you'll use today) to your laser printer's RAM. This isn't a permanent fix. It has to be done every time you turn your printer on because things in RAM go away when you turn off the power. You download fonts to your printer with one of two utilities: either the Apple Font Utility (it came with your System software), or Adobe's Font Downloader, which comes with every Adobe font you buy.

In general, both do similar things: download fonts and PostScript files (documents you've *printed to disk*, you'll recall from the last chapter) to your printer. Both give you a catalog/directory of the fonts already in your printer's memory and allow you to restart your printer without having to turn the power off and back on. Apple's Font Utility also lets you stop your LaserWriter from printing out that wasteful startup page every time you turn the power on. Simply select **Start Page Options**, and tell it to *stop that right now*.

Some Fonting Tips

When selecting fonts for various projects, I like to hold the KISS rule in mind at all times: Keep It Simple, Stupid. I like to keep the number of fonts in any document to a manageable number: two, maybe three. I figure if I can't get enough variety out of different point sizes and combinations of bold and italic, well, I'm not going to win any design prizes anyhow.

If I go for two fonts, say one for text and another for headings and subheadings, then I try to contrast them as much as possible while keeping them harmonious. I am prone to novelty fonts for headings, so I like to keep my text font tasteful, like Palatino. I like to use words set in a large, interesting typeface, rather than using a picture. I think it attracts more attention than a picture, anyhow. If I do use some sort of graphic, I still keep it simple: never underestimate the power of a well-placed line.

That's what I like to do. Other people like to do different things. You can go to your library or bookstore and find some books on design to learn all of the finer points (I've been tempted to write one of my own), but your own taste is the final deciding factor. It's like what that jazz great, Les Paul, used to say (and I'm paraphrasing here): If you make a mistake, but it works, then it's not a mistake—it's jazz.

The Least You Need to Know

Fonts are tough. They're deceptive. They only take a couple of minutes to master in terms of the technoid stuff (where they go and how to tame them). However, you can spend a lifetime combining them, arranging them, making them pretty, and still not learn everything there is to know about them. They're an adventure. Here's the least you need to know to get you started on your adventure:

➤ Bit-mapped fonts come in specific sizes and are sometimes called screen fonts.

➤ You can use outline fonts (such as TrueType and PostScript) at any size, but still use bit-mapped fonts for basic sizes.

➤ Fonts go in your Font folder in System 7.1–7.5. For System 7.0, they go in your System File (and PostScript printer fonts go in the Extension folder).

➤ You must enable your Type 1 fonts (with the Type 1 Enabler) before you can use them with QuickDraw GX.

➤ Managing your fonts can spare you hassles and time.

➤ When using fonts in your documents, work with the KISS rule, but live for jazz.

Part IV
Growing a Macintosh

Your Mac, out of the box, is full of potential, but you have to work with your Mac to realize that potential. You'll both grow as your skills increase and your needs get more specific and demanding; you'll do more complicated work as you learn about the more complex tools you can add to your Mac.

In Part III, we looked at all the stuff that comes with your Mac. That's the place where Mac potential starts to be realized. Now we'll look at some of the software and hardware you can buy to turn that potential Mac into the actual Mac you need and want. We'll also talk about modems, online services, PowerBooks, Newton MessagePads, getting emotional support, technical support, and self-sufficiency when things start to go a little flaky around the edges.

*Part IV: It's about growth, it's about needs, and most importantly, it's about **shopping**.*

MOMENTS IN COMPUTER HELL #607:

MISSING THE SAVE

Chapter 15

When the Going Gets Tough, the Tough Go Shopping

In This Chapter

➤ Lots o' lists of things to do (fair warning)

➤ Before you think about shopping

➤ Preparing to shop

➤ Shopping 'til you drop

➤ What I have

➤ What I'd buy (if someone else was footing the bill)

Computer users are easily tantalized: all you have to do is promise to eliminate some annoying problem, or add a nifto-swifto capability that wasn't there before. Like the old saying goes: *Build a better Mac mouse, and the world will beat a path to your door.*

Unfortunately, there are many add-ons and applications that promise Mac users the world but only deliver the marshy parts of New Jersey. That's because manufacturers and salespeople want you to buy what they have to sell. If they have to exaggerate the positives a little and overlook the negatives a lot, well, that's Marketing (with a capital M).

This chapter hopes to make you a little cynical when it comes to shopping. I hope to poke a hole in the lovely gauze of hype and advertising that surrounds most products (not just computer accessories). I'll talk about what you should do before you buy, what to do when you're ready to buy, and I'll even engage in a little healthy fantasy by telling what equipment I have now and what I'd buy if someone else was paying for it.

Before You Buy

Because somehow, someone found out you own a Mac, you've wound up on a bazillion mailing lists. Today, you received a catalog the size of the Manhattan Yellow Pages from the Mega MacMonger mail-order company (just call 1-800-PAY-MEEE), and already the pages are dripping with drool. You're lusting after a million dollars worth of stuff. What do you do?

Put the catalog away.

Companies design catalogs to make you want stuff. Never mind what you want; you know you want everything. Shush that inner child that's stamping its feet and screaming "Gimmee, gimmee." Now is the time to think about what you need.

To shush that greedy youngster inside me, I make a little list. I keep it near my Mac. When, in the course of human events, it becomes apparent that I need something (that will make my life easier, or help me and/or my Mac work better), I add it to the list. When there's a couple of things on my list, I'll look them over to see if they are things that I really need. If not, I cross them off the list. (I've crossed a big fat, full-page, full-color flatbed scanner off my list every month for the past seven months. I really want one, but I don't need it yet.) If, after I eliminate wants that are masquerading as needs, there's anything left on the list, I prepare to shop.

First, I'll take a quick inventory of my finances to see how much I can afford to spend and whether I have the cash or the space left on a credit card. I set my price limit first. Only then will I pull out the Mega MacMonger catalog and see how much what I need costs. If I can't afford it, I put the list and catalog aside and start saving up for it, either by setting aside the cash or paying off a credit card. There's nothing more frustrating than obsessing over a new computer gadget that I can't afford.

On the rare occasions that I can afford it (or must—sometimes you really have no choice), I start to do my preshopping drill. It's a couple of simple steps that make me an informed shopper. Mostly, I do it to save time and money, but it also ticks off manipulative sales clerks (and that's a good thing, too). I go through this process with everything I buy, from software to complete computers. The more expensive the purchase, the more thoroughly I do my homework. I'm cheap that way.

Ask the (Insert Gender-Specific Noun Here) Who Owns One

I know a few Mac users: my brother for one, people I've worked with, and electronic friends on America Online and eWorld. When I start lusting after a product, a hard drive, or other big-ticket item, I'll call them up or drop them a note online. Here's what I ask them:

➤ What's the make and model of yours?

➤ Where did you get it?

➤ What did you pay for it?

➤ Were you happy with it, and if not, why?

➤ Were you happy with the company you bought it from, and if not, why?

➤ If you had it to do all over again, would you buy the same thing? If not, why? (This usually provokes an emotional response: shopping as therapy.)

I always go to the people I know (whose opinions I trust) first. That gives me a place to start, either with products and companies to look at or to avoid like the plague.

The Reviews Are In

My next step is to go to the magazines: *MacUser*, *Macworld*, and the like. I'll pull out back issues and see if they've reviewed the particular product I'm interested in, or if they've done a round-up review ("10 PostScript Laser Printers Compared" or something similar). I'll read everything I can find on the product or class of product.

I don't read the magazines to buy the products they recommend. I find that most magazines have different priorities from mine. I've found myself buying stuff that reviewers hated, because what seemed a horrible problem to the reviewer didn't bother me at all. I read reviews and roundups for the factual information: components, speed, price, and problems. The opinion stuff is just opinion after all and totally subjective. I give the reviewer's opinion a fairly low weight in my buying decision.

Settling for the Best

After I weigh all the reviews from my friends and magazines, then I sit down and decide what I'm going to purchase. Sometimes, circumstances dictate that you settle for a product that meets fewer of your needs than some other. Price is usually the deciding factor.

In general, I try to get the most from my money that I can. I'd rather spend a little more money for something that will grow with me and meet my future needs (either real or imagined), than spend less money on something I'm going to have to replace in six months. I'd rather just wait out the six months and get exactly what I need, rather than throw good money after bad in an effort to make do. This is especially true of hardware: why buy a hard drive with only enough storage space to hold you for the next six months? As soon as you add new software and store some data files, you'll run out of space again. I waited until I could afford to buy a bigger hard drive, one that would hold me for a year or two.

So, the advice here is: Get as much as you can while staying close to your budget. If you can't afford to buy something you can grow with, it may be better to wait until you can.

When You're Ready to Buy

So you've weighed your options (and your wallet or purse), listened to your friends, and read the reviews. You're ready to put your money where your Mac is. Where do you go?

With Apple trying to penetrate the so-called "Consumer Market" by putting Performas and Newtons into more traditional stores (as opposed to "Computer Stores"), your shopping opportunities have increased dramatically. Each kind of store has its own advantages and disadvantages. Let's look at each kind, talk about the differences, and then you can choose the shopping experience that best suits your needs.

The Educational Market

Apple pretty much pioneered the educational market with the Apple IIe and the first Macs. To this day, they still have a very strong educational distribution channel, and they discount heavily. If you work in education or your child goes to a Macintosh college (that is, a school that requires all students to have a Macintosh), then you may be eligible for special educational pricing on Macs, software, and peripherals. Good for you!

Before you do anything else, find out what kind of deals are available for faculty, staff, or students (depending on which one you are) for hardware and accessories. Sometimes, all you have to do is flash your student or staff I.D. in the college store, and you get deep discounts on everything Macintosh. On other campuses, you may have to contact an Apple representative directly, or place orders through a specific staff member. Check with your school for details, but check there first. You have nothing to save but money.

Malls, Stores, Superstores

The way shopping has evolved in this country, you're most likely to find a store that sells Macintosh computers, accessories, and software in or near a mall. You can find Performas and all the to-go-withs (software and accessories) in Sears, office supply chains (Staples, OfficeMax, and so on), and in shopping "clubs" (Sam's Club and the like). You can find the rest of the Macintosh line, plus Mac stuff from other companies, in local computer stores, and in national chain "superstores," such as Micro Center and Computer Warehouse.

The main advantage of shopping locally is that the store is nearby. If you're lucky to be in an area with many stores, you can comparison shop and even buy pieces at different stores based on price. If your local store claims, "We'll beat any advertised price," you should definitely take advantage of the offer. When shopping locally, you also have the advantage of being able to test drive software and hardware, question a salesperson, and (should something go wrong) make a return without having to ship the defective merchandise across the country for repair or replacement.

The disadvantage of local stores is simple: overhead. Part of every dollar you spend in a retail store goes to pay the rent, the utilities, the sales staff, mall security... you get the idea. Prices may be appreciably higher. Superstores try to offset the cost of overhead by going for volume; they sell more stuff at lower prices and hope that quantity makes up the difference.

You may also (in noncomputer stores, such as Sears) not have access to a knowledgeable salesperson. That can definitely cause trouble. If the clerk doesn't know what you're talking about, how can he offer you merchandise that meets your needs? Or that even works with your computer? Of course, the closeness of the store to your home makes it easier to return or exchange things, but how much running back and forth are you prepared to do? There are ways to protect yourself:

➤ Select a reputable store: one that's been around a while and is likely to still be around a while. A great return policy is meaningless if the store goes out of business.

➤ Before you buy anything, check the store's return policy. Get it in writing, if you can.

➤ If a clerk says he'll make an exception to the return policy for you (because you're so nice), definitely get it in writing, and be sure to get the clerk's name.

➤ If you can, pay with a credit card. You can always try to get the card company to withhold payment if a dispute develops.

➤ Try to make your purchase on a weekday, or when the store will be open for the next two or three days. There's nothing more frustrating than discovering a problem when the store is closed. (It's happened to me—over a three-day weekend, no less.) You'll have to sit and grind your teeth until they open again.

➤ Save all of your receipts, and don't fill out warranty/registration cards until everything is working satisfactorily. Some stores won't accept returns unless everything (even little slips of paper) is in its original condition.

Mail Order: An Overnight Affair

You've seen them (or you soon will) scattered throughout the Macintosh magazines: mail-order companies that sell everything you can possibly want for your Mac, including complete new Macs. Their prices are good, and many offer overnight delivery for almost immediate gratification.

The advantages of going the mail/phone-order route are numerous. You'll generally find lower prices, because they aren't maintaining glitzy stores. You can also save money on sales tax, if you're ordering across state lines (at least until the Feds or state governments figure out a way to plug the loophole). Philadelphia has a 7% sales tax. On a $200 hard drive, I'd pay an extra $14 if I bought it in town. A lot of mail-order places have a knowledgeable staff to take your order. They can help you make up your mind and answer any questions you may have. Additionally, many mail-order places have toll-free technical support lines where you can call and ask heavy-duty questions before (and after) you buy. I like that.

The disadvantages, however, are just as numerous:

➤ You can't try things before you buy them. You pretty much have to know what you want before you pick up the phone.

➤ Return policies are a little more strict. Many places charge a re-stocking fee (except on damaged or defective goods), and you must call for permission to return things.

➤ There's no way to judge a mail-order company's reliability from their ads. There just isn't. You can, however, get hints: read their policies closely. If it looks like they're nickel-and-diming you to death with service charges and restocking fees, run away. If they have a 900-number for ordering, run away. 900-numbers always seem vaguely slimy to me. I mean, really: making you pay $2 a minute for the privilege of spending more money—ack!

Mistakes happen. It's how mail-order companies correct these mistakes (yours or theirs) that is the measure of their greatness. I'm usually willing to pay a little more at a place (mail order or walk-in) where I get excellent service. A painful shopping experience is still painful, even if you save a buck. I've been lucky. I've dealt with a couple of the larger companies such as MacConnection, MacWarehouse, and Mac's Place (now called Rocky Mountain Computer Outfitters—Prince, Roseanne, now Mac's Place all changing names, who can keep up?) and have had nothing but good experiences. MacConnection and MacWarehouse both fixed problems that were a result of my own (blush) ignorance, with no hassle (and no extra charges). The dealer formerly known as Mac's Place replaced a defective hard drive overnight, painlessly. Needless to say, they've all gotten repeat business from me.

I don't recommend that novices buy whole computer systems by mail order. There are too many switches and rip-offs that can happen, especially if you're not wise to them. They can happen in a local store, too, but locally you can wring someone's neck, scream, or cause a scene if you need to. That's hard to do effectively by letter or phone. Sometimes, you don't have a choice. Again, there are ways to protect yourself:

➤ Ask your Mac friends who they've dealt with and who they've kept dealing with. Ask them why, too.

➤ Check the Macintosh magazines. Consumer columns and letters to the editor are often ways of hearing horror stories about shady companies.

➤ Consider what's normal. A mouse comes standard with every Mac. They're one of the things that makes a Mac a Mac. If a mail-order place tries to tell you that the mouse is optional, hang up the phone. They're ripping you off.

➤ Scour the fine print in ads. Don't pay extra for using a credit card, for overnight shipping, or for placing an order.

➤ If you can avoid it, don't pay by check. Even reputable places hold your check until it clears the bank: that's only prudent. Once they have your money, however, you have no recourse. Use a credit card so you can at least try to withhold payment should a dispute arise.

➤ When you're placing an order, take names. Write them down. Have the salesperson confirm your order. Be clear and be sure you've understood (and been understood) to avoid any confusion over what you ordered.

➤ Take notes, too. Good notes help you sort out a problem with the company, or document a claim with your credit card company should you need to withhold payment.

➤ This is extreme, but if you're the cautious type (paranoid), record your phone conversation when you place your order. You can get a microphone that sticks on the ear piece of your phone to record both halves of the ordering process. If you do, tell whoever you talk to that you are recording while you are recording and before you get down to business! Otherwise, it's horribly, horribly illegal. I'd hate to have to visit you in the slammer.

Single Platinum Mac Seeks Same

If your budget won't allow you to buy new, don't despair. Bargains can be had in the used computer market. You can find ads for used equipment in the want ads of your local newspaper or local computer newspaper or newsletter, if you have one. In the Pennsylvania, Delaware, and New Jersey area, we have *The Delaware Valley Computer User*. It's good, and it's free!

Other good sources: bulletin boards at your local supermarket, high school, or college, and if you use a modem (see Chapters 18 and 19), local electronic bulletin boards. You can also turn up leads on used stuff if you belong to a Macintosh user group. The real propeller-heads in these groups are always upgrading their equipment and selling off the old stuff.

The advantage of buying used is price. You can get some real bargains. The disadvantages are the same as for buying a used car from a classified ad: you don't know the person you're dealing with, and (if you don't know a good bit about computers) you may pay too much for a lemon. There isn't a lot you can do to protect yourself after the purchase, unless your local laws provide protection. Even so, resorting to the law is mighty tiresome. It's best to protect yourself before you hand over the cash:

➤ Try the machine or component out before you buy it, preferably at your home, and for a few hours if not for a day or two. Make sure the disk drive drives, the monitor monitors, the mouse mouses: check the obvious.

➤ Check for signs of damage or abuse. Heck, check for dust: anyone who tries to sell you something without cleaning it first has no idea of how to take care of things.

➤ If you can, look under the hood. Lots of dust, dirt, and other crud inside a computer (while not necessarily evil) is another sign of poor maintenance.

➤ If you don't know what to look for, bring someone along who does. Buy him or her a nice lunch as a bribe.

➤ Ask if you can have a 30-day warranty (in writing) in case the dingus blows up when you get it home. If not 30, try for 15, 10, or 7 days—even 48–72 hours. Anything to give you a little extra leeway.

➤ Make sure you get a transfer of ownership (just a signed note saying what you bought) if hardware is still under a manufacturer's warranty, or if you want to re-register the software in your name.

➤ If you're buying used software, make sure you get the original manuals and disks. If you get photocopies of the manual and duplicate disks, you have a software pirate (arrgh, maties) on your hands. That's horribly illegal, unethical, and just not nice. Don't encourage it.

Computer Brokers

No, these aren't people who break computers for a living. These are companies that buy up other companies' (and individuals') computers, refurbish them, and resell them. Or they're companies that lease computers, then sell old models when they upgrade their line of machines. They're like used car lots for computers.

The advantage of going through a broker to buy used equipment is that (since they refurbish the machines) they usually offer limited warranties (30–90 days). You can find them advertised in large metropolitan newspapers (you can pick up the *New York Times* just about anywhere these days), or in *USA Today*. Computer resellers are cropping up everywhere there are businesses that rent computers, so you may even be able to find them listed in your local *Yellow Pages*. Treat them like you would any mail-order company, taking the same precautions listed above.

Shopping for Software

As if all that isn't enough, when shopping for software, there's one extra concern: will the bloody thing run on your computer? The easiest way to be sure is to have a list of your basic system information handy when you go to the store or pick up the phone. In the store, you can match the list of what you have up against the "System Requirements" section of the software package.

A typical set of requirements (right off the box of Insignia Solutions' SoftWindows for Macintosh, a program that lets you run Windows on a Mac) may go something like this:

➤ Any Macintosh computer with a 68040 CPU including Quadra, Centris, LC475, Performa 475/476, and PowerBook (500 series)

➤ System 6.0.5 or greater

➤ Memory minimum: 8MB, 16MB recommended (12MB minimum with System 7.5)

➤ 23MB free hard disk space

➤ 1.44MB floppy drive

➤ 32-bit color QuickDraw required for VGA and EGA graphics

➤ For PC 80287 emulation, Macintosh math coprocessor required such as the built-in 68040 (not 68LC040) or 68881/68882

Software that's written to run on any Macintosh (including Power Macs) is written in what's called *fat binary* so that it can take full advantage of whatever Mac you own. For example, before System 7.5, Macs, Performas, and Power Macs each had their own versions of the Mac OS. Now they can all run System 7.5 because it's written *fat*. Unfortunately, that means the application itself is fat, meaning it takes up a lot of space on your hard drive.

The first five items are absolutes in this list: you *absolutely cannot* run this software if your Mac doesn't meet or exceed these requirements. The last two are requirements if you want to use those particular features of the program—if you can't live without them, make sure your Mac has the right stuff. This set of requirements is a little more stringent than most, but it demonstrates the kind of information you need to have.

You can find out what CPU and coprocessor chips (and the type of floppy drive) your Mac has by looking in the "Advanced Features" or "Technical Specifications" section of your Mac manual. You can find out which version of the Mac OS you're running, and how much RAM is installed, by using the **About This Macintosh** option under the menu. You can find out how much free space you have on your hard drive by turning on the **Show Disk Info in Header** item in the Views Control Panel, and then double-clicking on your hard drive's icon. If you're running System 7.0 or later, you have 32-bit color QuickDraw installed—it's built in. With earlier versions, look in the System Folder for the 32-bit Color QuickDraw INIT. Write all this information down, and carry it with you when you go shopping. When shopping by phone, ask the sales representative what the software's system requirements are before you place your order.

Power Mac users get a double whammy. Since they can run both regular Mac software (in emulation mode) and software specifically designed for Power Macs, they have to look closely at software packages. Mac software run in emulation mode will (generally) run on your Power Mac, but it will run slower than software written for a Power Mac (it runs in "native mode"). Look to see if there's a Power Mac version of the software you're lusting after. Versions of classic Mac applications will have a label saying "Accelerated for Power Macintosh" or the system requirements panel will specify if the software will run in native or emulation modes, plus the usual assortment of hardware requirements.

What I Have Now

A lot has changed in this area since the first edition of this book. If you've read that version, you'll see that I've been putting my shopping tips through some extensive field research.

Hardware

➤ Mac Quadra 660AV with 12MB of RAM and a 250MB internal hard drive.

➤ 14-inch Apple color monitor.

➤ Datadesk 101e extended keyboard.

➤ Kensington TurboMouse trackball.

➤ DataPlace 120MB external hard drive partitioned into three drives.

➤ Apple's PlainTalk microphone.

➤ AppleDesign external powered speakers (because there's nothing like a Mac going "Boing" in stereo).

➤ NEC MultiSpin 3XP external CD-ROM drive.

➤ Apple LaserWriter Select 310 PostScript laser printer with 5.5MB of printer RAM. It's slow, but it gives me an excuse to run out for coffee.

➤ CoStar LabelWriter XL Plus, because I'm anal retentive and label everything.

➤ Global Village's TelePort Gold high-speed fax/modem. I still adore Global Village's line of modems.

➤ A hand-held grayscale scanner, Caere's OmniScan. It's a pain in the hindquarters, but it works.

➤ I picked up a bargain on an old Outbound Mac-compatible portable. The company was pretty much driven out of business when Apple introduced the PowerBook. It's big, it's heavy, but I don't travel much.

➤ A Newton MessagePad 110, because I write everything down—it lightened my backpack by about 10 pounds, letting me throw out calendars, planners, address books, notebooks, and more.

Principal Software

My hard drives are choked with software. Some of it I only use once in a while. I won't bore you with that. This is stuff I use every day:

➤ System 7.5 (I still have 7.1 hiding on my drive, too, just in case) including QuickDraw GX and PlainTalk.

➤ DataViz's MacLink Plus, to complement Apple's PC Exchange, for dealing with DOS files and disks.

➤ Fifth Generation Systems' Suitcase 2.1.4, because I am a font and sound freak. I have entirely too many fonts and sounds installed for my own good, and Suitcase lets me easily rotate sets of each in and out of use as I need or want them.

➤ MicroFrontier's Color It! 3.0 for tinkering with graphic images.

➤ Kevin Mitchell's excellent shareware program GIFConverter 2.3.7, for other graphic-image tinkering.

➤ Microsoft Word 5.1a, for big writing projects.

➤ Symantec's GreatWorks 2.0 integrated package, for less complicated things.

➤ America Online 2.5.1. I go into withdrawal if I don't check my mail at least twice a week.

➤ CompuServe Information Manager 2.3. I play on America Online, but I work on CompuServe.

➤ Apple's eWorld 1.0, because you can never get too much e-mail.

➤ Aldus PageMaker 5.0, for desktop publishing chores.

➤ Microsoft FoxPro 2.5b, because I do some volunteer database management for a local nonprofit AIDS service organization.

➤ Berkeley Systems After Dark screen savers—all of them. Yes, I am a toy-brain.

What I'd Buy with Someone Else's Money

This is my wish list right now, but I'm fickle. It's subject to change at any moment. If someone wants to try and bribe me with some of this, well, you're welcome to try, but don't get your hopes up.

First, I'm noodling around with the idea of a Power Mac upgrade—not lusting yet, just thinking about it. Then I'd like another Mac: a PowerBook 500, fully loaded. I'd settle for a used PowerBook 100, kind of loaded, but this isn't my money I'm spending.

I'd immediately upgrade both Macs' memory to their full capacity: The Quadra 660AV can take up to 68 megabytes of RAM. I don't think I could ever use all that memory, but I'd sure give it a try. I'd go for a larger monitor, too, 16-inch or 21-inch. I get tired of paging through long manuscripts. Since I'm spending someone else's money, maybe I'll get two: a 16-inch color monitor, and then a monochrome full- or two-page display. Or how about one monitor that does both; something funky like the Radius Pivot (the monitor swivels so it can be either long or wide).

I'd want to add another external hard drive: either a big, fat one with over a gigabyte of storage or one with ejectable media—a SyQuest or Bernoulli. That way, when I fill up one cartridge, I could just pop in another. With all that storage memory, I'd have to get into Kodak's PhotoCD (you know, where you drop off a roll of film and get back a CD-ROM disk of pictures). Picture files are real memory hogs, both in storage memory and RAM.

I'd also need a color scanner, preferably full page, with Ofoto, OCR software, and Adobe PhotoShop for some serious photo tinkering. I'd create my own *National Inquirer of the Weekly World/Not Necessarily The News*-type photos of Satan's face in a storm cloud and space aliens with senators, without the inconvenience of having to leave my home.

Because I'm such a toy-brain, I'd have to buy a camcorder to create my own QuickTime video clips and presentations. I can't think of why I'd need them, but they look like fun. I'd also load up on CDs, both music and ROM. I think it would be great to have the 1812 Overture blasting out of my Mac. Since I'm such a font freak (I've already gotten Adobe's Type On Call CD), I'd snap up any other complete font libraries I could get my hands on. While I'm at it, I'd lay in a supply of educational and entertaining CDs in case my godboys stopped by and wanted to play.

There isn't much other software I'd add right away. I don't wish more than a few months in advance. Like Dorothy said when she landed in Oz, "My, things come and go so quickly here." Technology changes so rapidly; it doesn't pay to plan too far ahead.

That's my wish list. What's yours?

The Least You Need to Know

Remember these little tidbits whilst doing your shopping:

➤ Don't buy on impulse: do your homework.

➤ Protect yourself however you can when you make a purchase.

➤ Don't forget the potential savings if you qualify for educational-market purchases at your school.

➤ Buy to anticipate your future needs, as well as your present.

Software Cavalcade

As you learned in the last chapter, your Mac came loaded with enough tools to get you working and playing. As good as the DAs, SimpleText, and basic utilities are, they aren't really suitable for major projects. They're supporting cast, not leading players. You'll need to get other software suited for the task at hand—whatever that may be. To that end, this chapter is a roundup of the major software categories. If specific kinds of software also need, or are enhanced by, certain hardware, I'll mention it. After you rip through this chapter, you may want to run back to Chapter 15 for some shopping advice.

Freeware, Shareware, and Commercial— or—No Money, Money, and Mo' Money

Commercial software is what you see every time you walk into a computer store or open a Mac mail-order catalog. When you buy commercial products, you're not only paying for the software, but also the glossy manual, the research and development department's next five projects, all those ads you see everywhere, and extraneous, but pretty, packaging. Plus, you're throwing a nice chunk of change at the company's CEO.

Freeware is software written by programmers and distributed free of charge. There are literally thousands of freeware extensions, control panels, and DAs that do practical, useful, and even foolish things. You'll never see a freeware store. Mainly you'll find this software on *electronic bulletin boards (BBSs)* and other *online services*. You can also buy disks of freeware from user groups, bookstores (in book-disk sets), and from some mail-order companies. Generally, you'll find the most recent copies of freeware programs through online services.

Online services and **electronic bulletin boards** are companies and just plain folks who (when you have a modem) let you access a wide variety of files and information on their computer(s).

Online services generally refer to corporate entities, and everything you do with the services costs you some money. CompuServe, America Online, and Prodigy are online services. Electronic bulletin boards (BBSs) are usually smaller, home-grown services, and charge little or nothing for you to join them. We'll talk more about the services and communications in Chapter 18.

Shareware is software that is distributed in the same open manner as freeware, but if you like and use the software regularly, you should send the author a *fee*. The money requested is generally much less (from $5 to $50) than what you'd pay for commercial packages, and it goes *right to the programmer*. It doesn't get filtered through some huge corporation, and you don't have to pay until you know you like the software.

Well, maybe this isn't exactly a technical thing, but it is an ethical/politeness thing. I don't think there's such a thing as an Ethics Nerd. Anyway, one of the tackiest, *tackiest* things you can do is use shareware and *not* pay the fee. Don't be tacky.

In terms of finding freeware and shareware, one of the best things you can do for yourself is join a *Macintosh User Group*, or *MUG*. A MUG (pronounced like a coffee mug) is a collection at people at all levels of Macintosh skills. The idea of a MUG is best expressed by the mission statement of the BMUG (pronounced "BEE-mug"), the largest (and bestest, if you ask me) Mac User Group on the planet: **We're in the business of giving away information.**

Apple encourages MUGs because they save Apple loads of time and money. You can find the name of a local MUG by calling Apple at 1-800-538-9696. You can get more information about BMUG by calling 510-549-2684, or writing to: BMUG, 1442A Walnut St., #62, Berkeley, CA 94709-1496. For more reasons to join a MUG, peruse the pages of Chapter 22.

Integrated Packages

Integrated software packages have had a rough year: there used to be five or six different packages contending for the title of King/Queen of the Works. They beat the stuffing out of each other, and now there seems to be only two actively vying for the crown.

Each package includes an array of software you would normally have to buy separately: word processor, database, spreadsheet, painting, drawing, and communications. Some even have calendars, outlining, and charting capabilities. What makes them integrated is that the features of each module are available in all (or most) of the other modules. If you need a drawing while writing a memo, you can draw one. If you need a spreadsheet in a report, you can add one.

What You Can Do with Them

You can do almost anything with an integrated package that you can do with its stand-alone counterparts. The difference is that since integrated programs have to fit all those applications into one tidy package, many high-powered, gee-whiz features get dropped. Almost none of the individual modules are as powerful as their stand-alone siblings, but that isn't necessarily a bad thing.

Depending on what you do, you may not need all of the features, for example, of Microsoft Word or Claris' FileMaker Pro. The limited range of integrated functions may be enough for you. Also, if money is tight and you can't afford to buy all the stand-alones you need, a less expensive integrated package will let you work while you save to buy the higher-priced packages.

The Popular Packages

Microsoft Works, shown in the following figure, was the first integrated package for the Mac. All the other integrated packages tried (and many succeeded) in knocking it off of its throne. I own it but don't use it much. The latest release is version 4.0, and it's been accelerated for the Power Mac. Suggested retail is sketchy, but you can find it mail order for under $100—for now. (These prices and version numbers are accurate at the time of writing, but, *hey*, who knows what they'll be tomorrow?)

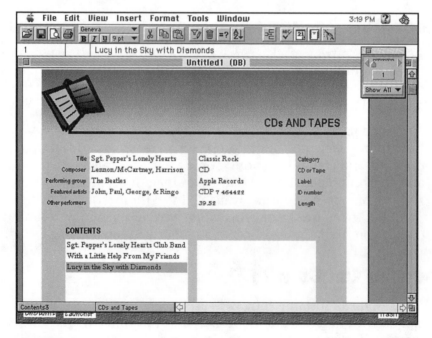

A database template in Microsoft Works 4.0.

The *Version number* refers to the (re)incarnation of the software. Version 1.0 is its debut. Version 1.1 fixes everything that should have been fixed before 1.0 was released. Version 2.0 is the next incarnation. Version 2.1 fixes the new incarnation, and so on. When the first number changes (1.0 to 2.0), it's called a *version upgrade*, a major overhaul. 2.0 to 2.1 (call it an incremental upgrade, maybe) means it's still essentially the same program, but now it works. Incremental upgrades (particularly ones that add a letter to the version number, like 5.1a) are sometimes called *bug fixes*. One more reason for sending in your software registration cards: when the company releases an upgrade to software you own, they'll let you know. If you can avoid it (sometimes you can't), never buy version X.0 of anything. Wait until there's a number or letter after the period.

ClarisWorks, from Claris, has the best overall integration of its modules. You can work with any module in any document, and the combination makes it a pretty fair replacement for a low-end page layout program. The integration is excellent. The latest version, 2.1, has been accelerated for Power Macs. ClarisWorks lists for $299, but you can get it mail order for about $199, or even under $100 if you own an earlier version of ClarisWorks, or any version of another Works program. That's called a *competitive upgrade*. It can save you big bucks if you're dissatisfied with the application you're currently using.

Extra Stuff

To make the best use of an integrated package, you don't need much in the way of additional hardware. To be completely practical, however, you'll probably want a Mac-compatible printer. Printers and printing are discussed in Chapter 13. A nice selection of fonts, in addition to the ones that came with your Mac, will also help you express yourself in new and attractive ways. Fonts are covered in Chapter 14.

Word Processing and Page Layout

There was a time when these would have been separate categories, but the dividing line has gotten decidedly blurry. Where word processors were once the domain of letters, reports, memos, and manuscripts, they've added enough graphic and layout features that you can use a word processor for simple to moderately complex page layout.

Meanwhile, page layout programs have improved in the text handling department. Once upon a time, it was faster to write your text with a word processor and *import* it into your page layout program. Now that page layout programs handle text entering and editing much better, you don't have to if you don't want to.

What You Can Do with Them

Word processors and page layout programs are all about words, words, words. Their sole duty in life is to get your thoughts down on paper in as attractive a manner possible. With a word processor or page layout program, you can express yourself. The final product (sort of) determines which kind of program you'll use.

An application's capability to use a document created with another application is called **importing**. When an application can save (with the **Save As** command) a file in a format easily imported by another application, it's called **exporting**. Many applications come with a set of **translators** that allow them to easily import and export files in other application formats. The PC Exchange control panel in System 7.5 (see Chapter 11) also allows simplified importing and exporting of DOS-based files.

In general terms, word processors are better for documents where the words are the main focus; however, many word processors let you add pictures and graphic elements (such as lines and boxes). Generally, word processors come with a *spell checker* and *thesaurus* built-in (sometime a grammar checker as well) so you don't have to use a separate application to check yourself. They also allow you to set margins (the space around the words on all four sides of the page), tabs, line spacing—all the things you used to have to fiddle with knobs on a typewriter to adjust.

Also in general, *page layout* programs deal with words, but their strength lies in arranging the words on the page with style, using columns, boxes, headlines, graphic elements, and pictures. Newsletters, newspapers, brochures, and flyers are the kinds of things you can create with a page layout program. Page layout programs give you some of the same features as a word processor, but their focus is on presentation: how those words look on the page. They give you complete control over columns and graphics (pictures, as well as lines and embellishments). They make it easier to create documents, such as booklets and brochures, where you aren't dealing with a standard 8 1/2 × 11-inch page, or you're folding it into new configurations.

The Popular Packages

Microsoft Word is the industry standard for word processing. Word boasts an impressive array of features: graphics capability, QuickTime compatibility (you can include a movie in your disk-based documents), voice annotation (you can actually attach spoken comments to your document, on disk only), an equation editor (for you scientific types), graphing, tables, and automatic indexing. It's very powerful stuff. If you have the space to store it and the memory to run it, and you can only afford one program, Word may be it. (They say a minimum of 2 megabytes of RAM with System 7, but that's wishful thinking. 4 MB is more like it.) Microsoft Word lists for about $500. You can get it by mail order for about $300. The latest version, 6.0, is accelerated for Power Macs.

MacWrite Pro, from Claris, is another full-featured word processor that almost crosses the line into the realm of page layout. Feature for feature, MacWrite Pro compares favorably to Word: it does a lot of that good stuff that Word does and is also a big, fat program that can hog up disk space and RAM—about half the size of Word, but still big. MacWrite Pro version 1.5, Power Mac accelerated (shown in the following figure) lists for about $250, and you'd normally pay about $170 for it by mail order. Lately, however, Claris has gotten aggressive with pricing, and you can pick it up mail order for under $100, while their largesse lasts.

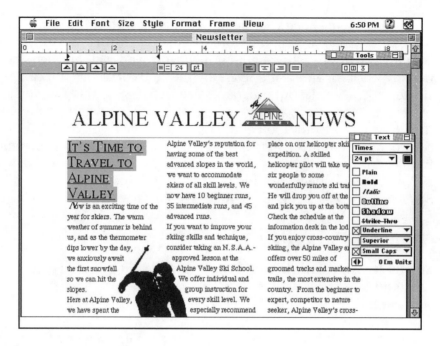

A sample newsletter in MacWrite Pro version 1.5.

WordPerfect 3.0 for the Mac and Power Mac, from WordPerfect Corporation, comes with a similar array of features and functions as Word and MacWrite Pro. Its features compare well and lists for about $500, with a mail order price of under $350. Competitive upgrades are dirt cheap (comparatively speaking) at about $50. Ask your local dealer to let you test drive it on one of their computers (you should always try before you buy, if you can).

WriteNow 4.0, from SoftKey, is an excellent contender for word processing for two reasons: it boasts a full complement of features (not as many as the higher-priced packages, but still a lot), and it's *cheap*. The advantages of WriteNow are that it takes up less disk space than the other full-featured word processors and runs with less RAM. That makes it ideal for PowerBook users. The price doesn't hurt either. WriteNow lists for $70, and you can pick it up mail order for about $45. The latest version (4.0) runs on Power Macs in native mode.

PageMaker, from Aldus, is the page layout program all others are trying to beat. PageMaker was introduced about the same time Apple introduced the first LaserWriter printer. The combination of the two resulted in the birth of *desktop publishing*.

PageMaker is exhaustive in its thoroughness. You can create a simple one-page flyer or an entire book-length manuscript. Its features include powerful editing tools (including spell checking), professional color handling, and total control of almost every aspect of typesetting. PageMaker lists for a daunting $900, but you can buy it by mail order for under $600. The current version is 5.0, and a Power Mac-accelerated version should be available any second now.

Desktop publishing is literally "publishing from the top of your desk," as opposed to having to pack up all your text and woes to send them to a typesetter and printer.

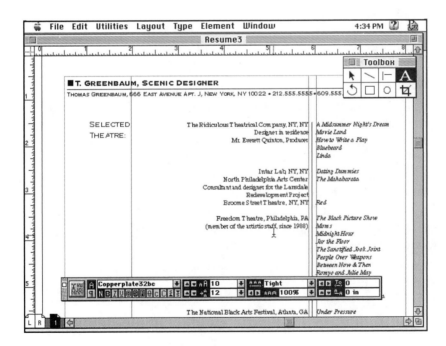

Aldus PageMaker 5.0 and a friend's résumé—the name has been changed to protect the goofy.

QuarkXPress, from Quark (the company, not the barkeep on "Deep Space Nine"), is PageMaker's biggest rival. For a while, they were neck and neck. Then Quark kind of squeezed ahead with a few more features and more flexibility. Now they're pretty much neck and neck again. On average, QuarkXPress and PageMaker are pretty evenly matched. I know people who are fiercely devoted to each. Quark also lists for about $900, with a mail-order price of about $600. The latest version, 3.3, is accelerated for Power Macs.

HomePublisher, also from Aldus, is a low-end version of PageMaker. It comes with an assortment of *templates* (predesigned pages), so all you have to worry about is selecting the graphics and writing the text. It isn't anywhere near as powerful as PageMaker, but it's okay for folks who want to dabble in page layout without investing half a grand to do it. HomePublisher lists for $80, and you can get it mail order for about $50.

None of the Above

In addition to straightforward word processors and page layout programs, there are applications that are geared toward specific processing needs.

For example, Final Draft, from MacToolkit, is a word processor aimed at television and film script writers. It automatically formats your script to industry-standard format and automates repetitive tasks like typing INT. and EXT. a billion times and adding MORE and CONT. where dialogue and scenes carry over to the next page. Doing all that funky film formatting can be tedious in a traditional word processor (trust me). It's worth the $350 ($250 mail order) price tag if you're a professional, aspiring, or just perspiring script writer. Version 3.0 wasn't available for preview at this writing but will be available by the time you read this.

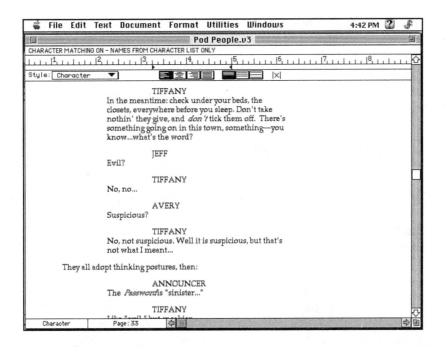

MacToolkit's Final Draft 3.0 and a scene from the deathless "Pod People" by yours truly. Any producers reading this?

You can also get programs that expedite entering mathematical and chemical equations and formulae into your Mac. I avoid math and chemistry, so check with your colleagues or professional journals and catalogs for information.

Extra Stuff

To make the best use of a word processor, as with the integrated packages above, a printer and an assortment of fonts will give you pretty pages of text. For page layout software, the same applies. Depending on the quality of output (your printed page) you need, a laser printer may be in order, especially if your pages will be duplicated and/or need to look professional.

You may also want to consider clip art (small drawings) and photographs to liven up your pages. You can either buy collections of pictures and clip art, or you can create your own. Painting and drawing programs (coming up shortly) will let you make your own clip art. A camera and a scanner (discussed in Chapter 17) will get photographs into your Mac.

Spreadsheets and Databases

Spreadsheets and databases are about manipulating information. Like word processors and page layout programs, these two do similar things with different kinds of data. Spreadsheets deal with numerical data (adding, subtracting, multiplying, and dividing columns of numbers). Databases deal with more word-based information (names, addresses, favorite colors, you name it).

Generally, both do little bits of what the other type of applications do best—you can enter text in a spreadsheet and add figures in a database. Spreadsheets and databases are information managers. They let you group bits of related information together, so you can look at various aspects without having to re-enter or manually reorganize the existing information.

What You Can Do with Them

Spreadsheets are all about numbers: working math on long columns of them; generating charts and graphs from numerical data; organizing a year's worth of financial information into smaller, month-sized segments.

Databases let you list, sort, and otherwise tinker with huge amounts of information: names, addresses, and other categories. You can create spreadsheets and databases as flexible and elaborate as you can imagine and design.

How much you expect the application to do for you will determine how much work you have to put in the spreadsheet or database. If you expect a database of all the members of your family to keep track of important events, you'd need to enter individual categories for birthdays, anniversaries, and so on, rather than a big, mixed bag of important dates.

Creating elaborate, yet elegant, spreadsheets and databases is an art form, one that I haven't mastered—though I have gotten better at it. I always want mine to do something I didn't anticipate when I designed them. For folks like me (with simple needs and little patience), the spreadsheet and database modules of an integrated package are probably enough. Others need the power of dedicated packages.

The Popular Packages

Excel from Microsoft (shown here) is the Word of spreadsheets. Part full-featured spreadsheet, it's also part page layout program, allowing you not only to do complicated and involved spreadsheets, but also make them pretty as all get-out. Excel lists for $495, with a street price of around $295. The so-new-I-don't-have-it-yet version 5.0 is accelerated for Power Mac and will look slightly different from the one shown below.

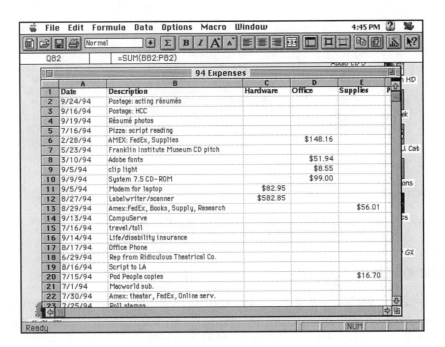

Microsoft Excel 4.0 with an expenses spreadsheet for (ack!) tax time.

225

FileMaker Pro, from Claris, is the industry standard database aimed at business users because it allows information sharing across a network, even to IBM-compatible computers running Microsoft Windows. (Don't get the idea you can't use it at home, though. You can.)

FileMaker Pro also has extensive report-generating capabilities, allowing you to print out exactly the information you need. FileMaker Pro 2.1 lists for about $400, and you can get it mail order for about $270. A Power Mac version will be available by the time you read this.

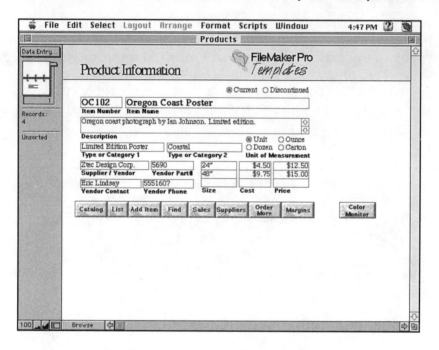

Using a product database template in FileMaker Pro 2.1.

None of the Above II

There are variations of database and spreadsheets that are customized or customizable for specific needs. You can use relational databases (such as ACIUS' 4th Dimension $900/$600) to build stand-alone applications that manage specific information. You need a certain amount of database and programming skill to create the application, but end users don't need to know anything too technical to use that application.

Instead of developing spreadsheets to track your business expenses and income, there are a number of accounting packages that save you that time and energy—packages that are appropriate for home use, some for business, and some that fall in between. You really need to shop to meet your needs.

There are also very specific database-like programs for tracking personal information (addresses, birthdays, appointments, and so on). Oddly enough, they're called PIMs (for Personal Information Managers). Claris' Organizer ($100/$50) is one such that can help you get your personal life, well, organized.

Extra Stuff

If you'll be making extensive use of a database or spreadsheet programs, you don't really need a lot of extras. However, if you'll be printing and sharing data (especially spreadsheets), a printer that can handle longer, legal-sized paper, may spare you some frustration.

Graphics Programs

Painting and drawing programs have been around as long as the Mac itself. They're graphic programs that let you draw and paint on your Mac's screen and save the graphics for use in your other documents. The pictures you produce (depending on the program) can be as simple as the stick-figures you drew in third grade, or as complex as a recreation of "La Giaconda" (that's the "Mona Lisa" to you and me). There are graphics programs for all levels of artistic skill. Graphics programs tend to fall naturally into several general categories:

➤ **Drawing programs** Create objects (a box, a circle, a line) that you can select and move around to create a picture, or in the case of computer-aided design (CAD) programs, a blueprint.

➤ **Painting programs** Let you create bit-mapped images. Bit-mapped images are collections of dots. They allow finer detailing than drawing programs. Programs for editing and enhancing photographic images fall (loosely) into the paint category.

➤ **PostScript-based programs** Generally referred to as illustration programs. You can scale PostScript illustrations to any size and they will still look good.

➤ **3-D Rendering programs**   Let you take basic two-dimensional images (showing height and width) and add simulated depth. (That's the third dimension—not to be confused with *The Fifth Dimension*; or that dimension of sight and sound and mind, known as "The Twilight Zone.")

Naturally, the more a program tries to do, the more complicated it can be to use, and may require a more high-powered Mac to be effective.

What You Can Do with Them

With the right application, and the right equipment, you can really do anything you like. You can create your own assortment of clip art for your reports and newsletters. You can create a logo for your business. You can do magazine-quality illustrations with a PostScript illustration program or draft the plans for a house or a machine with a CAD (computer-aided design) program.

Popular Packages

This particular software category is already huge, and new programs are introduced all the time. Any kind of exhaustive list of what's available, and what it does, could fill a volume on its own (and would go rapidly out of date). Because there are so many products, this is a listing of a few names from each category. Use the list (plus the comparison shopping advice from Chapter 15) to select the program that meets your needs and artistic skills.

Clip art is a collection of graphic images meant to be copied and pasted into other documents. The term comes from the days when you could buy a book of illustrations, clip them out with scissors, and literally glue them on your pages. Now clip art collections come on disks, but you still copy and paste them into your digital pages.

ClarisDraw from Claris. Drawing, color, advanced text handling (see the following figure). Extensive libraries of predesigned graphics. List: $400, street: $200.

ClarisDraw 1.0 from Claris—go figure.

IntelliDraw from Aldus. Intermediate/Advanced drawing. Funky tools. Color. List: $299, street: $200.

SuperPaint from Aldus. Does paint and draw functions. Color. List: $80, street: $50.

BrushStrokes from Claris. Huge selection of tools, capability to use add-ins from other major applications. List: $139, street: $100.

Painter from Fractal Design. Advanced paint tools. Comes in a cool paint can. Recreates actual oil paints and pastel textures on-screen. List: $400, street: $270.

PhotoShop from Adobe. Editing/enhancement software for scanned photographic images. High-powered, professional tool. List: $895, street: $550.

Freehand from Aldus. Professional-quality PostScript image creation, full-featured and flexible. List: $600, street: $390.

Illustrator from Adobe. A professional-quality flexible package from the people who created PostScript. List: $595, street: $390.

addDepth from Ray Dream. Converts 2-D PostScript fonts and illustrations into simulated 3-D. List: $179, street: $125.

Ray Dream Designer from Ray Dream. Similar to addDepth but lets you create images from scratch as well. List: $130, street: $90.

Three-D, from Macromedia. Lets you create and render 3-D images and add animation for video production. Amazing. List: $700, street: $500.

Extra Stuff

Many graphics programs benefit from adding a *drawing tablet* to your Mac. A drawing tablet is like a cross between your mouse and a piece of paper. Instead of rolling a mouse around, you draw on the tablet with a stylus (a pen without ink), and your pen-strokes appear on your Mac's screen.

Additionally, if you want the color picture from your screen to remain a color picture on the page, you may want to consider getting a color printer. There's a wide variety available, from low-cost inkjets, to very expensive laser printers.

Speaking of pictures, you may want to consider adding a scanner or digital camera to your hardware wish list. Scanners let you turn a paper photograph into a digital one you can include in your documents. A digital camera (Apple's QuickTake 100, for one) skips the paper stage and sends digital photographs right to your Mac. Either will give you something to play around with in Photoshop, or other image editing programs.

Applications with 3-D rendering capabilities take a very spunky Mac to work. You may need/want to add an accelerator and/or math co-processor to get your Mac (you should pardon the expression) up to speed. Likewise, you probably should invest in more RAM (the next chapter has tips on hardware, such as accelerators and RAM).

Utilities

Utility is a catch-all phrase that covers a lot of territory. Generally, it means an application that does something useful but not necessarily productive (meaning that you won't hold a finished product in your hand when you're done). Utilities come in all shapes and sizes. The kind(s) you need really depends on what type of things you do with your Mac. There are a few that will be of use to just about all Mac users.

Disk Utilities

I've already mentioned some disk utilities that you'd probably find handy: Central Point Software's MacTools and Symantec's Norton Utilities for Macintosh. Both provide tools for painlessly backing up the valuable data on your hard drive. Both also try to repair damaged disks (including hard drives) and try to retrieve deleted files.

Most disk utilities also have applications devoted to *optimizing* or *defragmenting* your hard drive. A disk optimizer reorganizes all that data so that files and applications are stored together, so it takes less time for your Mac to find the information. You should make a *complete backup* of your hard drive before you use an optimizer on it because if the optimizer goofs rewriting an important bit of System information, your hard drive is toast.

Fragmenting occurs when you save data to your hard drive and your Mac has to stash it as quickly as possible. It writes it in whatever space it can find, which is not necessarily all together. You can wind up with files being **fragmented**: a bit-bit here, a bit-bit there. That's okay in terms of writing the file, but when you want to use that file later, your Mac has to search all over your disk to find all those bits, and it can slow your Mac down.

Finder Enhancements

As much as I love the Finder, there are always things I wish it would do better: format disks faster, find files faster, have more flexible menus, and even better desktop patterns. Never ones to slouch, the software companies leap into the breach trying to add more features to the Finder. There are dozens of commercial and shareware solutions to some of the Finder's quirks. As of this writing, most are being retooled to deal with the new features and quirks of System 7.5.

Virus Protection

A computer *virus* is a small bit of programming that (when you use the file it's hidden in) does something funny (puts a silly message up on your screen) or something dangerous (overwrite all of your data files with gibberish). Either way, viruses are bad news. Because you don't see viruses before they strike, there's no way to tell if one will be benign or not. The better course is to avoid them, or destroy them before they can attack your system.

Many utility packages include *virus detection* software that scans your hard drive for those digital cooties and wipes them out before they strike. You can also get stand-alone virus protection with packages such as Virex (from DataWatch) and SAM (Symantec AntiVirus for Macintosh). However, the best virus detection program is absolutely *free*. Disinfectant, by John Norstad of Northwestern University, can detect and eliminate any viruses that may already exist on any of your drives (disk or hard), and prevent any from insinuating themselves into your system later.

The chances of a virus infecting your Mac increase every time you use software or data from other sources. If you do any of the following, you need virus protection:

➤ Trade disks with friends, colleagues, or strangers.

➤ Access a network's file library or download files from an online service.

➤ Let someone else use your Mac with his or her own disks (you don't know where they've been).

Hardware Diagnostics

As the name implies, hardware diagnostics test and try to diagnose any problems that may be plaguing your hardware. Most test the logic (or mother) board, hard and disk drives, video, and other hardware circuitry. Many also check your System Folder and desktop files for damage and will attempt to repair. These aren't a substitute for disk utilities—general disk utilities have more features and functions—but may help you identify and fix intermittent problems that are hardware related.

Compression Utilities

Another hotbed of growth in the utilities market has been *compression utilities*. Before compression utilities, you had only two options when you started running out of space on your hard drive: deleting old stuff to make room for new, or buying a bigger hard drive.

Compression utilities free up space by removing repetitive data and replacing it with smaller placeholders so the files take up less space. When you decompress (expand) the file, the application replaces the placeholders with the original information, and you have your file back. The cool thing about compression utilities is that they do it invisibly so you hardly notice (hardly because it does slow things down a little). Instead of spending a couple of hundred dollars on a bigger hard drive, you can compress your old one for under a hundred.

RAM Expansion Utilities

As a class, RAM utilities fake your Mac into thinking it has more RAM than it actually does. They're a less expensive alternative to buying more RAM. OptiMem, from the Jump Development Group (about $80 mail order) reduces the huge chunks of memory applications take for themselves when you open them, doling out more as needed, and taking it away when not being used. Applications will occasionally crash if they don't get enough memory fast enough. OptiMem learns, though, and crashes less frequently as you go along.

RAM Doubler, from Connectix, somehow (but don't ask me) fakes your Mac into thinking it has twice the installed RAM. My brother uses it and claims that it has no problems at all.

Screen Savers

A *screen saver* is a utility that blanks your Mac's monitor after a set period of inactivity. Why? Because, if you leave your monitor displaying the same screen for an extended period of time, it will get burned into the chemical coating on the inside of your monitor. You will forever see a ghost (*booooo*) image of that particular screen.

By far, the most popular screen saver is After Dark from Berkeley Systems. There's a whole line of them: After Dark, More After Dark, Star Trek: The Screen Saver, and The Disney Collection (and more coming). I'm ashamed to admit I have them all.

233

Popular Utility Packages

Central Point MacTools, from Central Point Software. List: $150, street: $85.

Norton Utilities for Macintosh, Symantec. List: $150, street: $90.

Apple Personal Diagnostics (shown below), Apple Computer. Checks out your hardware and System software for trouble. List: $129, street: $100.

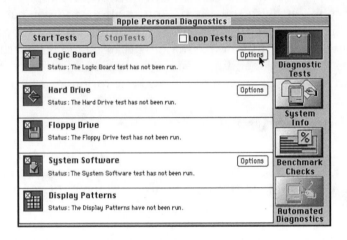

Apple Personal Diagnostics, version 1.1 and its diagnostic tests.

Now Utilities, Now Software. Has hierarchical Finder menus, better file and folder access during saves, file compression, and so on. List: $129, street: $70.

Kaboom!, Nova Development Corporation. A replacement for your Mac's Sound Control Panel that lets you assign sounds (mostly goofy) to dozens of Finder functions, instead of just a beep or eep. List: $50, street: $30.

Symantec AntiVirus for Macintosh (SAM), Symantec. List: $100, street: $65.

Disinfectant, John Norstad, Northwestern University. Free! You can get Disinfectant from most online services and MUGs, or send a self-addressed stamped envelope and an 800K floppy disk to: John Norstad, Academic Computing and Network Services, Northwestern University, 2129 Campus Drive North, Evanston, Illinois, 60208.

Stuffit Deluxe, from Aladdin Systems, is a manual compression utility for files or folders (as opposed to your whole hard drive). List: $120, street: $70.

Disk Doubler, from Symantec. Stuffit Deluxe's chief competition, with a similar range of functions. List: $110, street: $75.

RAM Doubler, from Connectix. Fakes your Mac into thinking you have twice the RAM you really do. List: $100, street: $60.

Stuffit SpaceSaver, from Aladdin Systems, is a transparent hard drive compression routine. List: $60, street: $35.

After Dark, from Berkeley Systems. The coolest. The basic module (After Dark) lists for $50, but you can get it for about $30 by mail order. More After Dark gives you updated and totally new modules but requires After Dark. List: $40, mail order: $25.

Star Trek: The Screen Saver, from Berkeley Systems, is a stand-alone spin off of After Dark. Features funky characters, scenes, and sounds from the original "Star Trek." List: $50, street: $30. At the same price are Simpsons, Marvel Comics, and Disney versions.

Giggles and Yucks: Games and Stuff

Macs used to be pathetic machines if you wanted to play games. There wasn't much around except for some bad freeware and shareware games. The computer that was thought of as a "toy" when it was first released suddenly became too serious to play games. Thankfully, that situation has changed. The introduction of the Mac LC, with the optional Apple IIe emulator card installed (allowing the LC to behave like a IIe), brought a huge increase in sales of Macs to schools. Now, there's an enormous assortment of educational titles available, too.

The Popular Packages

There's way, way too many to even try and pick a few measly samples. Games aren't like one-size-fits-all. They need to suit your personality. I like logic puzzles. You may like shoot-em-up war games. Do yourself a favor and browse the game and education aisles in your local software store. Buy yourself a treat; you earned it.

If you're not into games, but like to be entertained and educated (and have a CD-ROM drive), you may want to think about From Alice to Ocean from Claris. I've traveled almost entirely across Australia this summer—not in person, unfortunately, but partly through film and partly through CD-ROM. The first leg of the journey was from Melbourne to Alice Springs, the trek undertaken by the hearty drag trio in the movie *Priscilla, Queen of the Desert*. The second leg of the trek was From Alice to Ocean, a CD-ROM/book combination that documents Robyn Davidson's incredible seven-month journey across the outback, from Alice Springs to the Indian Ocean.

From Alice to Ocean, Ayers Rock.

From Alice to Ocean is a synthesis of Robyn Davidson's own record of the trip (selections from her book *Tracks*) interwoven with amazing images captured by photographer Rick Smolan (of the *A Day in the Life of...* photo book series). It's part of the Claris Clear Choice software collection. It lists for about $70, but you can find it mail order for about $50. I'd lend you mine, but it's not leaving my house. No way.

This is what CD-ROM is all about: a multimedia adventure that just draws you in and holds you tight through about an hour of images, music, and narration. It's a documentary film on your Mac, PBS on your PC. As an educational tool, it's marvelous. You can lure computer-addicts away from your Mac with the promise of even more information and lush photographs in the companion book. You can lure the computer-wary to your Mac by waving (but don't hurt yourself) this big, fat, gorgeous book under their noses, and introduce them to the world of CD-ROM.

The Least You Need to Know

There are more kinds of software available for the Mac than you can, well, shake a Mac at. Here are the important things you need to come away with from this particular chapter:

➤ Freeware and shareware are great, cheap alternatives to the pricier commercial packages.

➤ Macintosh User Groups (MUGs) are an excellent source of freeware and shareware (as well as other information and help for you and your Mac). You should join one.

➤ If there's something you want to do with your Mac, there's probably a software package around to help you accomplish it.

➤ Learn how to shop for the software that meets your needs. Chapter 15 will help.

Chapter 17

Hardware in a Nutshell

In This Chapter

➤ Macintosh brain surgery: CPU upgrades

➤ What was that? Oh, yeah: adding memory

➤ Pedal to the metal: accelerators and math chips

➤ SCSI peripherals

➤ I hate meeces to pieces

If you thought the small sampling of software was a smorgasbord for your Mac, just wait 'til you get a peek at all the hardware goodies you can add on.

Hiking the Upgrade Path

For starters, if you've had your Mac for awhile (and the way Apple keeps cranking 'em out, anything over three- or four-months old is suspect), there may be a newer version of your Mac on the market. Your Mac may have suddenly become a discontinued model. You may have bought a Quadra the week before Power Macs became available. You may be grinding your teeth to dust over the unfairness of it all. Stop it; your dentist will be mad.

The **motherboard** is the main component inside your Mac's housing. Sometimes called a **logic board**, it's the sheet of plastic that contains and connects the CPU chip, the system and video RAM, and your expansion slots, among others. Some Mac models also have a secondary logic board, called a **daughterboard**. Can aunt- and cousinboards be far behind?

Usually, when Apple releases a new, spiffier version of an existing CPU (like turning the Quadra 840AV to the Power Mac 8100/80AV), they generally offer an *upgrade*. That is, you bring your Mac into an authorized Apple dealer, and they'll rip the guts out of your old Mac and install the guts of the new one. The price is usually a lot less than the price of a completely new machine—it still isn't cheap, but it's less. In the case of some of the '040-based Macs, you can upgrade to a Power Mac with the addition of an expansion card, rather than a whole new *motherboard*.

However, that's *only* if the innards of the new machine fit in the box of the old. Sometimes, the architecture is too different, won't fit, and your only option is to buy the new CPU or remain satisfied with your current model.

Just because Apple replaced your current model with a newer one doesn't mean you have to upgrade. The only compelling reasons to upgrade your Mac are:

➤ If keeping current in Mac technology is your bread-and-butter (you're a consultant, a Mac writer, or something).

➤ If your old model can't keep up with new software and peripherals (say you can't run System 7.5), you should probably upgrade to a newer model.

➤ If you succumb to upgrade fever. That's when no matter what it is, if it's the latest and greatest, you have to have it.

"Because I can" or "because it's there" are not really good enough reasons to upgrade. If you keep upgrading simply because Apple and software companies keep releasing upgrades, you'll wind up in the poorhouse, babbling and drooling while you wait for your afternoon dose of Thorazine.

SIMMply the Best: Adding RAM

Short of upgrading your Mac to a zippier model, the kindest thing you can do for your tired, overworked Mac is to increase its supply of random-access memory (RAM). You add RAM by means of SIMMs (single in-line memory modules). SIMMs are tiny cards (about four inches long) with eight or nine memory chips on them. Most Macs have a couple of slots built-in to accept SIMMs (some Macs have more than others).

Adding RAM is like sending your Mac to college: it will be able to work with larger applications, do more stuff with those applications, and create bigger and better documents—all without the hazards of Friday night fraternity parties and high tuition bills.

SIMMs are simple to install in all but the compact Macs (the Classics) and PowerBooks, so you can do it yourself. Most mail-order companies are kind enough to send you an easy-to-follow installation guide, sometimes even a video tape, to make the process even easier. But technically, installing RAM yourself voids your Mac's warranty. If you're at all squeamish about that, have the RAM installed by your Local Authorized Apple Dealer.

Each Mac's memory capacity is different. Different Mac models also take different kinds of SIMMs (most use Mac SIMMs, others use the same kind as DOS computers). SIMMs come in different sizes: 1, 2, and 4 megabytes (even 8, 16, and 32 MB SIMMs). They also come in different speeds: 150 ns (for nanoseconds or billionths of a second; it's for how long it takes your Mac to access the memory), also 120, 100, 80, 70, and 60 ns. The lower the number, the faster the SIMM (and more expensive). The easiest way to find out which SIMMs your Mac needs is to ask.

If you're a do-it-yourself kind of person, mail-order companies are very good about specifying packages of SIMMs by Mac model and memory size. They'll also let you know if you need any special tools to install (such as the special wrench you need to crack open a PowerBook). Best of all, their advice is free, and their prices are usually better than your Local Authorized Apple Dealer. Of course, you have to do the work yourself.

If you'd rather have root canal (can you tell I have a dentist appointment later this week?) than poke around inside your Mac, call your Local Authorized Apple Dealer and let them do the work—if they don't know what kind and how many SIMMs your Mac can handle, well, we're all in big, BIG trouble.

Ahead Warp-Factor Seven: Accelerators and Such

Does your Mac seem pokey and slow compared to some other Macs you've seen? Can you type faster than your word processor can process? Do you have to take a coffee break while your spreadsheets recalculate? Your Mac doesn't need vitamins or iron supplements: it needs a silicon supplement.

Math Coprocessors

If you do a lot of math-intensive work with your Mac (not only spreadsheets, but 3-D rendering, PostScript illustrations, and so on), your Mac may benefit from the addition of a *math coprocessor,* or *FPU* (for Floating Point Unit) *chip*. A math coprocessor takes away the burden of math (and it is a burden) from your Mac's central processor. With the central processor freed up to do other things, your Mac can zip along, but only with applications designed to make use of a coprocessor (check your application manuals before you spring for one).

Some Macs come with math coprocessors as a standard feature. Others come with an empty socket where you can plug one in. Still others won't accept a coprocessor at all. If your Mac won't accept a coprocessor, don't despair: you have other options.

Accelerator Cards

If your Mac is generally sluggish, you can add an *accelerator card* to give it a boost. An accelerator card supplements your Mac's central processor by giving it another processor, or even bypassing your Mac's processor with a bigger, faster one.

The accelerator card goes into one of your Mac's expansion slots, which are empty sockets that accept cards that add speed or functions (such as an internal modem for communications) to your Mac. If your

Mac doesn't have a socket for one, some accelerator cards come with a math coprocessor on the card, so the socket isn't an issue.

Here's the trouble with accelerators: they're expensive. In some cases, almost as much as a whole new Mac CPU. It's a case of think before you buy. If your Mac is so pokey and slow that you think you want to accelerate, shop for the accelerator, but before you buy it, compare its price with the price of a more powerful Macintosh CPU. It may be less expensive (and more reliable) to cough up the bucks for a faster Mac.

Accelerators come made for specific Mac models, because some Macs have *NuBus* slots, others *PDS*, and still others have both. NuBus and PDS cards are not generally interchangeable, but the line is blurry: some manufacturers make accelerators that fit either type of slot, but you must purchase a separate adapter. Shop carefully.

NuBus is a high-speed slot that accepts cards that work along with your Mac's central processor to supplement its functions. The information is fed along a data path called a **bus**, like your Mac's ADB (Apple Desktop Bus) that feeds your Mac information from your mouse and keyboard. **PDS (Processor Direct Slot)** is a slot that feeds information directly into the central processor of your Mac rather than through a bus.

Because of the variety of Macs, slots, and accelerator cards, your path of least resistance is to figure out what you want your Mac to do faster. Then call your Local Authorized Apple Dealer, Macintosh Users Group, or favorite mail-order company, and pick their brains for suggestions. Shopping well is half the battle (see Chapter 15 for shopping tips).

Talk Scuzzy to Me: All About SCSI Devices

If you aren't considering buying any peripherals right away but want to know what your options are, skip this section and read about the hardware. SCSI is often confusing and troublesome to the biggest propeller-head. Don't hurt yourself unnecessarily. Wait until you need to read it, okay?

Many of the peripherals you'll read about in this section are *SCSI* (pronounced "SCUZ-zy") devices that require some special handling. Hard drives are SCSI devices, as are scanners. No matter what a SCSI device does, they all connect the same way (that's what makes them SCSI), so here's a little SCSI primer.

SCSI stands for Small Computer Systems Interface. It's another way of connecting peripherals to computers.

You can hook up a total of six SCSI devices to your Mac. (You can really install eight, but your Mac and its internal hard drive already count as two SCSI devices, leaving you only six available for add-ons.) Because your Mac only has one SCSI port, you connect SCSI devices to each other (they come with two SCSI ports), and only connect one of them to your Mac. That's called a *SCSI chain* or sometimes, a *daisy-chain*.

Having all those devices connected can confuse the heck out of your Mac (and you); that's why each device needs to be assigned a *SCSI ID Number*. The SCSI ID Numbers are 0 through 7. Typically, your Mac's ID Number is 7, and its internal hard drive is 0. That leaves you with the numbers 1 through 6 to assign other SCSI devices.

The ID Number tells your Mac what order to check-in the devices at startup. Usually your Mac looks for ID number 0 first, and backtracks through numbers 6 to 1. The ID Number has nothing to do with the physical order that the drives are hooked together—put that thought right out of your mind. That would be too easy.

You set the SCSI device's ID number with some sort of button, wheel, or set of *dip switches*. Check your doodads manual for its particular method of setting ID numbers. Let me tell you right now: dip switches are a pain in the butt. Do yourself a favor: buy SCSI stuff that has an external *wheel-* or *dial-set SCSI number*, or a *push-button*. It'll say so in the ad, or if you're shopping in person, you can look for it. (Did I say this was easy? I don't think so.)

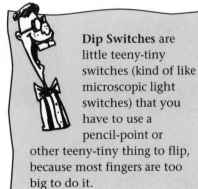

Dip Switches are little teeny-tiny switches (kind of like microscopic light switches) that you have to use a pencil-point or other teeny-tiny thing to flip, because most fingers are too big to do it.

When you're connecting a chain of SCSI devices, you have to terminate the first and last devices. A terminator stops the signal that runs through your SCSI cables from bouncing back and forth eternally through the chain, giving your Mac a nervous breakdown. When the signal hits the terminator, it stops, and your Mac can get on with its life. The first item in the chain is your Mac's internal drive. Its termination is built-in, and you never ever have to worry about it. You should also terminate the last item in the chain, the one that's physically farthest away from your Mac. Don't terminate anything in between.

Termination of a SCSI device is either *internal* (inside the device, and a pain in the butt—so avoid it), or *external* (on the outside of the case, often a cap plugged into one of the device's two SCSI ports, and very easy to change). To remove internal termination, you have to open the device and pull a little plug-kind-of-thing or cut off a resistor-kind-of-thing. Don't try it yourself. Take it into your Local Authorized Apple Dealer. Better still, don't buy anything with internal termination, if you can avoid it.

One last thing: the total length of the SCSI cables in any chain shouldn't be any longer than about 20 to 24 feet. (That's why most SCSI devices only come with two- or three-foot long cables). Otherwise, the signal gets too weak before it reaches the end of the chain. You can add a *signal amplifier* somewhere in the middle of a longer chain. It boosts the signal so it can travel farther, but they, naturally, cost money. If you can avoid that, you can save some shekels.

> The easiest termination to deal with is an on/off switch. Flip, it's on. Flip, it's off, just like the Clapper. I wish more manufacturers would use it.

Okay, one more one last thing: SCSI devices can be cranky. You can follow the rules to the letter, and it still won't work. If that happens, chuck the rules and try anything. (If you're adding one SCSI device, it's pretty painless. Even two isn't too bad. It's only when you get up to three or more that things may get kind of wonky.)

Storage Space

If your Mac's hard drive is choked with data, despite your best efforts to keep up with housekeeping (see Chapter 10 for more on that), or the best efforts of your compression software (Chapter 16) to give you some elbow room, it may be time to buy a new hard drive or other mass storage devices.

Fixed Drives

The easiest way to add a new hard drive to your Mac is to plug in an *external* hard drive. An external hard drive is one that sits near your Mac. You connect it to your Mac through your Mac's SCSI port.

Installing an *internal* drive is a little more difficult because you have to open your Mac to do it. There are screws to screw, cables to cable, but if you have the nerve, I say go for it. The biggest benefit of replacing your Mac's internal drive with a new, larger one (in addition to the extra space) is that you can still add six more SCSI devices. (Do I need to remind you again about how installing things inside your Mac can void Apple's warranty?)

A hard drive is also called a **fixed drive**. Not fixed as in neutered, but fixed as in not removable. It means the magnetic media is fixed in place. It doesn't come out.

Hard drive capacity (internal or external) is measured in megabytes. By today's standards, 40 or even 80 MB is pretty small, especially when you consider that a full installation of Microsoft Word takes up to 8 megabytes of space! That's 20% of a 40 MB hard drive. When shopping for hard drives, buy as large a drive as you can afford. I wouldn't get anything smaller than 80 MB, and you can find hard drives that hold as much as a gigabyte (1,000 megabytes), and more. Trust me, sooner or later, you'll fill it.

Removable Media Drives

Removable media drives work exactly like a hard drive, with one big difference: you can pop out the magnetic media when it gets full and pop in a new blank one—like a regular floppy disk. Imagine that: infinite storage potential! Removable media drives are a good idea for people who work on huge files that have to travel to another location. You pop out the media from your drive and toss it in your briefcase or backpack. No more lugging thirty or forty floppy disks around.

Removable media drives come in several varieties and capacities, but they're all SCSI devices:

➤ **Bernoulli drives**, from Iomega Corporation, work with what looks like a big ol' floppy disk. They come in capacities of about 45, 90, and 150 MB disks. The drives cost (mail-order pricing) between

$300 and $500. The Bernoulli disks cost about $100 each. The *cost per megabyte ratio* (the price divided by the number of MB of storage) only gets competitive with fixed hard drives if you know you'll use more than one or two Bernoulli disks.

The *cost per megabyte ratio (or $/MB ratio)* is a good rule of thumb for deciding if a hard (or other mass storage) drive is really a bargain. All the other options have to be equal (warranty, ease of use, and so on). Sorry, but it involves math. A 170 MB hard drive, at $349 (349/170= $2.05 per megabyte) is not as good a bargain as a 270 MB hard drive (with otherwise identical features) at $429 (429/270= $1.59 per megabyte). Of course, it's all meaningless if you only have about $349 to spend.

➤ **SyQuest** drives work with cartridges as well but come in more capacities. 5.25-inch cartridges can hold 44, 88, and 200 MB. 3.5-inch SyQuest cartridges can hold 105 and 270 MB. The drives cost (mail order) between $200 and $600 (depending on capacity). The cartridges cost between $75 and $100. The cost per megabyte ratio is a little easier on the wallet, but you still need to use a few disks regularly to make it cost-effective.

➤ **DAT Drives** or **Digital Audio Tape** drives can hold enormous amounts of data (up to 2 gigabytes per tape). They're good for voluminous backup copies of large or networked hard drives. They're a little pricey for personal use, since they run between $1,000 to $1,500.

➤ **Optical Drives** work something like standard 3.5-inch disks with a big difference: they use *VHD* (*very high-density*) disks that, when combined with the precision of an optically driven write-head, can store up to 128 MB per disk. The 5.25-inch versions can hold up to 1.3 gigabytes of data. Optical drives cost between $900–$3,000. In addition to being pricey, the optical mechanisms have special cleaning requirements, and I hate to clean.

If your circumstances make an ejectable media drive both necessary and cost-effective, go for it. Otherwise, a regular run-of-the-mill hard drive should be more than sufficient.

CD-ROM

CD-ROM drives (compact disc read-only memory) are SCSI devices that hold huge amounts (over 700 MB) of read-only data. You can hold the entire contents of a multimedia (pictures, sounds, movies, as well as words) encyclopedia on one CD. The advantages of CD-ROM drives are these:

➤ Huge libraries of reference and educational materials (excellent for children and students) are available.

➤ Lots of interactive games (if you're into gaming).

➤ The ability to play music CDs and Kodak Photo CDs (where you get your pictures back on disc, instead of on paper).

There are also disadvantages of CD-ROM drives. There are suddenly hundreds of drives to choose from, all with different speeds (an important factor) and capabilities:

➤ CD-ROM drives access data at between 180 ms (milliseconds, or thousandths of a second) and 400 ms. 180 ms is fast, 400 is slow. Compare that to most hard drives that access data at an average of about 20 ms. CD-ROMs are slloooowww.

➤ Some drives also only come with one SCSI port (most SCSI devices have two for easy daisy-chaining) which is a pain.

➤ Some drives you buy are just the drives: you have to buy cables, connector kits, driver software, speakers, headphones, and anything else you may want separately. I hate that. When you're pricing them, make sure the price includes everything you need, or else the drive you think is a bargain could start running you big bucks.

➤ Most computer peripherals go in boom-or-bust cycles. Right now, CD-ROM drives are a boom item: everyone is making them, trying to cash in. That's good because prices are competitive, but that's bad because you have to do your homework so you can buy the drive that's best for your needs. Flip to Chapter 15 for shopping tips.

PLUG! PLUG! You may also want to pick up *The Complete Idiot's Guide to CD-ROM* (by yours truly) for in-depth information, coupled with all the foolishness you've come to expect from me.

Input Devils—er, Devices

Anything that gets information into your Mac is an *input device*: a mouse, a keyboard, a scanner... you get the idea. Some come already packaged with your Mac, but you may want to replace them. Others make nice additions because of the benefits they give you.

Mice and Trackballs

Mice are nice, but you can do so much more with them if they get a little more complicated: one button (for some) just isn't enough. Two- or three-button mice let you program specific commands to each button: say the first button is your basic click; the second button is a double-click (but you only have to click once); and the third button is something you use frequently. You can program it to send a command like ⌘-W to close a window, or a click-lock (like holding down the button) for dragging stuff around without wearing your button-finger down to a nub.

Trackballs, on the other hand, work like mice turned over on their backs. Instead of sliding the mouse around, you roll the ball of the trackball to move the cursor. Your hand remains pretty much stationary.

Buying a replacement mouse or trackball also gives you (usually) a new control panel to replace the original Mouse Control Panel. What they do varies from manufacturer to manufacturer, but generally they let you assign a *tracking speed* (how far the cursor moves in relation to how far you move the mouse or trackball), a click speed (how quickly you click), and (for a multibutton device) what number of clicks or other commands the additional buttons send when pressed.

There's a lot of confusion about which is better for your health: a mouse or a trackball. Does heavy mouse-use cause Carpal Tunnel Syndrome (a very painful condition that affects the tendons of your wrist and forearm)? Does a trackball alleviate the problem? Or is the whole thing one of those high-fiber-like hypes only to sell peripherals?

I don't know. I do know that a multiple-button mouse or trackball can make it easier for you to work. On the other hand, I'm not a doctor, and I've never played one on TV. In terms of how I work and whether or not it may cause Carpal Tunnel, I follow the medical advice of Groucho Marx's Dr. Hackenbush: "Does it hurt when you do that? Then don't do that." If you have concerns about arm, wrist, or even neck or back pain when using your Mac, don't ask a computer geek; ask your doctor. That's why she's there.

Drawing Tablets

If you've ever tried drawing a free-form shape with your mouse, you know that it's no substitute for a pen and paper. A drawing tablet gives you the same sort of control of your drawing as a pen and paper. (I talked about this briefly while talking about painting and drawing software in Chapter 16.) A drawing tablet is an ADB device (like your mouse) that plugs into one of your Mac's ADB ports. It behaves like a pad of paper: you draw on it with a stylus, and the lines you draw show up on your Mac's screen in your painting/drawing program.

Drawing tablets come with many different functions and capabilities. The important thing to remember is that all the tablet capabilities in the world won't help you if the software you use can't make use of them. If you buy your software first, look for a drawing tablet that gives you all the functions it can handle. If you buy a super-duper full-featured tablet first, shop for software that can make use of the features, otherwise you've wasted money on the tablet. Probably the easiest way to do it is to buy the painting/drawing program when you buy your tablet so you can be sure the two work together. Some mail-order places even offer you a deal on a set: the software with the best tablet for it. That can save you time, and maybe even some money.

Keyboards

The best thing I ever did was add an *extended keyboard* to my Mac. An extended keyboard is longer than your normal keyboard. It has a number-pad for speedier entry of numerical data, arranged like the keys of a calculator. With practice, you can really speed up your numerical data entry. They also come with Function Keys (you know, those F1 through F15 keys) across the top of the keyboard. With a macro utility, like QuicKeys, you can assign all sorts of funky functions to the F-keys.

Apple makes several extended keyboards for the Mac, including that fabulous one that splits and bends (I think it even turns into a spy plane and an origami swan) so you can adjust it to your own typing comfort. Apple's keyboards are expensive, though. Other manufacturers make keyboards for Macs too, and for less. Mine even came with a bundled copy of QuicKeys. Too cool.

Scanners

A computer scanner is a SCSI device that takes an image, either photographic, graphic (such as a line drawing), or type (text), and converts it to digital information you can display and play with on your Mac's screen as shown in the following figure.

An embarrassing shot of the godboys, scanned with Caere's OmniScan, a grayscale, hand-held scanner. They're never that cute in real life.

Physically, there are two kinds of scanners: hand-held or flatbed. A hand-held scanner is small enough to fit in your hand. You slowly and carefully drag it across the image you want to digitize. A SCSI cable links it to your Mac (or your SCSI chain). A flatbed scanner looks like a small photocopier: it sits on your desk and you lay whatever it is you're scanning on a glass plate. The scanner does its thing (also like a photocopier) and the image shows up on your Mac.

Hand-held scanners are less expensive than flatbed scanners. They're also more difficult to use—you need to have good eye-hand coordination, for one thing. Because they're small, you may have to make several passes at whatever you're scanning, and stitch the pieces together with an editing utility (one usually comes with a scanner).

If a person is in a dither, they're all confused. When a picture is **dithered**, the dots that make it up are all confused. The dots get jumbled and tinkered with so the eye is faked into seeing many more shades of gray than are really there. Dithering reduces the quality of an image by making it look blurry.

Flatbed scanners are easier to use, but more expensive. You're also limited to stuff that fits on the glass plate: loose pages, photos, and so on. It's hard to scan things from thick books. For larger images, you can still scan parts and stitch them together. Flatbed scanners can usually be fitted with attachments that feed in multiple sheets, or even scan from slides or film negatives. They also cost extra.

Other considerations when selecting a scanner, include:

➤ Is it color (expensive), grayscale (less expensive), or black-and-white (practically cheap)?

➤ If it's grayscale, is it real grayscale (256 shades of gray), or does it take a few shades of gray and *dither* them? If you want to work with photographs, avoid the ones that dither if you can. Look for ones that say "true 256 shades of gray" or "true grayscale."

OCR stands for **optical character recognition**. A scanner only makes a picture of the words. If you want to be able to edit them and use them in a word processing document as words, you have to run the picture through OCR software to turn it into words again (one character, or letter, at a time).

➤ What's its resolution? *Resolution* is the number of dots per inch the scanner can create in an image. More dots improve the quality but are bad for the wallet, and high-resolution scans also take up lots of hard drive space.

➤ Does it come with OCR software? If you want to be able to scan stuff like quotations from books or magazines for use in reports and such, you need OCR software.

Monitors

Monitors come in many sizes, like their TV cousins. If you do extensive page layout work, you may want to get a two-page display. They're wider, so you can look at two full-sized pages at the same time. If you're heavy into QuickTime, or do a lot of presentation work, a big ol' 21-inch color monitor can give you a better idea of what your presentations will look like on the big screen. If you're a Classic II or monochrome PowerBook user, you may have the option of adding a larger color monitor to supplement your small built-in screen. These are all options, and there are many more.

You should know, before you shop, you may need to add a video card to control the monitor, or beef up your Mac's built-in video by adding video RAM to get the most out of it. Some models of Mac may also need special adapters to add additional monitors at all. Check your manuals or ask at your local MUG, or Local Authorized Apple Dealer for advice.

Sound-In, Sound-Out

If you bought a new-ish Mac, you may not have received a microphone with it for recording your own sounds. That's too bad, but it can be fixed. For about $25, you can buy the microphone set that Apple used to include with their Macs.

The big advantage to buying Apple's microphone is that it comes with a *phono-plug adapter* that you can use to dub sounds from other sources (such as the radio, audio, or video cassettes). The PlainTalk Microphone, the kind that comes with AV Macs, doesn't come with the adapter, but is (overall) a better quality microphone. If you have an older Mac that doesn't have an audio-in jack, you can still add your own sounds, but you need to buy a microphone package.

As long as we're on sound, you can also buy special computer speakers to give your Mac blazing sound. Or if you're the shy type, a pair of headphones (such as the kind you use with a WalkMan) will let you impress only yourself with sound. You can plug either kind into the audio-out jack.

Video-In and Out

With the advent of QuickTime, it has become very cool to use video clips on your Mac. For the practical-minded, they make for spiffy presentations. For toy-brains (like *moi*), they're just fun.

If you aren't satisfied with the selections of QuickTime clips you can buy, or if you need custom clips for a presentation, you can buy video boards that let you record your own clips from your VCR or camcorder. They're cards that you pop into one of your Mac's expansion slots. They give you both video-in and video-out ports. There are specific models for specific Mac slots (PDS or NuBus). Be sure you get the right one for your Mac.

When you're set up, you can also transfer your QuickTime creations to video tape (with the video-out port) to share your masterpieces with the Macintosh-impaired. Naturally, you don't need such a board if you have an AV Mac, since video in and out are built-in—that's what makes them Audio Visual Macs.

Baudy-Bits: About Modems

A *modem*, as I mentioned way, way the heck back in Chapter 2 (and will again in Chapter 18), is a device that allows two computers to talk and share files and information over common telephone lines. If you have access to two modem-equipped Macs (say one at work and one at home, or a desktop Mac and a PowerBook), you can stop shlepping disks back and forth between them.

With software (such as Apple Remote Access), you can dial up your home-based Mac from work (or vice versa) and access any file on the hard drive. On the road, you can hook into your job's network and check your e-mail (electronic mail), or just work like you were still in the office. I didn't want to have to drag work and business into this. This is Macintosh. It's supposed to be the fun one. But hey, you forced me into it.

Miscellaneous Hardware

There are many other goodies you can fling at your Mac. This was only a sample. By the time you read this, there will have been whole new families of hardware introduced. You'll see lower-priced CD drives that you can write to, instead of read-only. There will be fleets of add-ins for the new Power Macs to augment and accessorize the new technology. The only thing you can count on in the fast-paced world of computers is growth and change.

There's also tons of goofy stuff you can add: mouse-pockets that stick on the side of your monitor to hold your mouse when you aren't using it; or dopey ears and tails you can stick on your monitor to make it look like a monster or a dinosaur. It isn't really hardware, but it can be fun. And it's more fun to find them for yourself. My telling you everything would take all the mystery out of life.

The Least You Need to Know

There are almost as many hardware add-ons available for your Mac as there is software. Until you're ready to actually buy one, here's the least you need to remember from this chapter:

➤ There are many hardware upgrades available to rejuvenate a sluggish Mac.

➤ You can never go wrong with more RAM.

➤ Many peripherals (hard drives and CD-ROM readers) are SCSI devices.

➤ You can add up to six SCSI devices to your Mac.

➤ A big, fat, roomy hard drive would be a fabulous addition to any storage deprived Mac.

HEY, WHAT'S UP?

Chapter 18

Let Your Fingers Do the Talking

In This Chapter

➤ What modems are and how they work

➤ What communications software can do for you

➤ What electronic services are out there and how to access them

In telecommunications, the two components, hardware and software, are so perfectly entwined that you can't talk about one without the other. So, you'll hear about both. In this chapter, you'll learn about getting your Mac in touch with the whole, big, wide, wonderful world of digital communications.

Let's begin, shall we?

You Gotta Getta Modem

Modems are almost mystical. One little piece of hardware, one little piece of software, and suddenly you have the ability to be in two places at the same time. You can be all cozy and warm in your own little corner of your own little room, and at the same time, you can be inside a computer at a remote location chatting with folks or doing a pile of other cool stuff. Simply by making a phone call, you and your Mac can hook into a computer on the other side of your hometown or even into an international network of computers. How is this possible? It's the mystical combination of hardware and software.

What Modems Do

The communications software takes and interprets the things you type (commands, text, even mouse clicks) and converts that digital information into discrete, little packages of data. The little packages of data travel to the modem that converts the data to sound pulses. The modem compresses them and then shoots them out through your phone lines to the computer at the receiving end.

The receiving modem reverses the process: unwraps the little packages of data, expands them if necessary, and then hands the information off to the software and hardware at that end. The receiving computer then deals with the information you sent, either executing either that command or click, or sharing what you typed with whoever may be waiting for it.

With a modem and the appropriate software (there are different kinds, which I'll spell out in a minute) you can:

➤ Access a local bulletin board to get (and share) information, as well as freeware and shareware files.

➤ Access a national (or international) online service.

➤ Access another modem-equipped computer at work, at school, or even at a friend's house.

Modem Varieties

Modem technology has blossomed in the last couple of years. Where once you could choose only from slow, pokey, or super-pokey-slow modems, now there's a huge range of speeds—and some spiffy extra functions you can get, too. Modems are classified in two ways: first, by how fast they transmit data; second, by where you install them.

Modem speed is measured in *bits per second* (*BPS*), or *baud rate*. Most commonly, you'll see modems advertised as being 1200, 2400, 9600, 14400, or even 28800 BPS or baud.

Technically speaking, a modem's baud rate isn't exactly the same as the number of bits per second it transmits. However, the distinction is fine and only applies in certain circumstances. You don't need to worry about it. You can use the two terms pretty much interchangeably. Some snooty propeller-head may correct you, but just slap him.

1200 BPS is considered snail-slow these days. 2400 BPS modems are considered low-end. 9600 and 14400 BPS modems are pretty much standard, and with error correction and data compression features, they let you transmit data wicked-fast. 28800 BPS modems are fairly new, but with everyone buzzing about accessing the Information Superhighway, they should catch on as fast as they transmit data. Note that not all BBSs and online services can deal with the high speed (9600 BPS and faster) modems. If you can, check it out before you log on for the first time. If you can't check it out, don't panic. Most modems will automatically step down to the appropriate speed before they connect to another computer.

The differences in where you install your modem are pretty obvious. *An internal* modem goes right *inside* your Mac; it has no outer cases, no frills, only a bunch of circuits and chips on what looks like a plastic card. You install an internal modem in one of your expansion slots. If you decide to get an internal modem, make sure you purchase one appropriate for your type of Mac—in other words, ask before you buy (Chapter 15 has other helpful shopping tips). An *external* modem sits on your desk, *outside* your Mac. The only physical attachment is the cable that plugs into your Mac's modem or printer port (you can skip back to Chapter 2 if you need a refresher on ports and what they're for).

You can also further distinguish modems by any additional features they have: what else they do besides communicate with other computers. The added functions, naturally, are also phone-related. You can get a modem, called a *fax modem*, that doubles as a *fax machine* allowing you to send files to another fax machine right from your Mac's screen. You can choose a fax modem that only sends faxes to a fax machine (a *send-fax modem*); or one that receives faxes as well (*send and receive fax modem*, or simply a *fax modem*.)

Fax modems have three drawbacks. They're great for sending a memo or letter you've written on your Mac, but there's no easy way to send a fax from a piece of paper: a fax modem only deals with digital information. If you need to fax a paper document, you need a regular fax machine.

The second drawback is that when you receive a fax, you receive it as a *picture* of the document, not a text file that you can work with. Some fax modems, (the Global Village line, for one) come with *OCR* (optical character recognition) software that translates the picture of text into actual, editable text. The third drawback is that with a fax-modem you either have to leave your Mac and modem turned on most of the time, or you have to baby-sit the machine whenever you think you're going to receive a fax.

Some modems also give you a digital answering machine with *voice mail* capabilities. You've dealt with voice mail, I'm sure: "Press 1 for customer service. Press 2 for a company directory. Press 3 to leave a message." Pretty annoying to talk to, but I guess it's convenient for the user (and cheaper than hiring a receptionist). I can't imagine many home-users needing voice mail, unless you run a home-business, or have teenagers in the house who refuse to miss a single message.

Enter and Sign On Please...

When you buy yourself a modem, the manufacturers know you want instant gratification. They always include a generic telecommunications program (often referred to as just *telecom* or just *comm* software), and usually software or coupons for free trial time on a major service, such as America Online or CompuServe. You may get two or more kinds of telecom software because some online services require their members to use special *proprietary* software to access their service.

Proprietary means the property of, or specific to, a particular computer or service. America Online and eWorld are proprietary because you need their software to access their services and because the software won't work with any other service.

You can access some services (such as CompuServe) two ways, either with generic communications software or with their proprietary software (for CompuServe, that would be CompuServe Navigator, or CompuServe Information Manager).

The generic communications software that comes with your modem may be a freeware or shareware package, or it may be a scaled-down version of a commercial package with an offer to upgrade to a full-featured version at a special price. Because you want instant gratification when you unpack a modem, you're vulnerable to anything that sounds like a good deal. Don't bite yet, wait. The coupons may be a good deal, but the product may be something you don't need. Once you get some experience online, you'll know what kind of features you need. You may not need anything more than that generic package. If you get into telecommunications, you may need something more high-powered. Don't buy one until you know.

Once you have the modem and software installed, and a phone line hooked up to the modem (installation varies, so be sure to read the modem's manual), you're ready to roll. Whether you're using generic software to access a local bulletin board, or proprietary software for a big service, you have to do a couple of things before you can dial into a board.

Setting Up

For generic communications software, "setting up" may mean telling it where you installed the modem, what baud rate you want to use, and what phone number(s) to dial for what service. The setup procedure varies somewhat from modem to modem, software to software. Check the software or modem manual for details on how to configure your particular brand.

Proprietary software also requires some initial setup. In addition to the same kinds of information a generic telecommunications program would need, you'll also have to let the service know how you're going to pay for it; that means credit card information, too. Although I can't give you setup and configuration specifications for every kind of telecommunications software out there, I can certainly show you the kinds of information you'll need to supply to most applications. The next figure shows the setup dialog box for America Online's software.

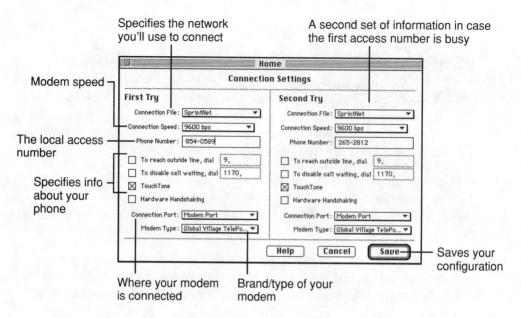

America Online's Setup dialog box.

As you can see from the figure, your communications software needs some basic information to function:

➤ The kind of telephone line you'll be using (Touch-Tone or rotary), so it knows what kind of noises to make to dial your phone.

➤ What port you plugged your modem into, so it can send the information to the right place.

➤ What phone number you want it to dial to reach the other computer or online service.

➤ What speed you want your modem to operate at (most are switchable from its highest speed down to about 300 baud).

The Connection File entry is only applicable to big services that let you call a local phone number for access. Even though America Online's computer is in Virginia, you dial a local number to reach it. My local number gives me access to SprintNet (a national phone network for computer users), which patches me into Virginia, while only making a local phone call—much less expensive than calling long distance.

The check boxes are for specifying particular dialing prefixes if you need to dial a special number (like 9) to get an outside line when calling from work, or if you have call waiting and want to disable it while you're online. You can edit these entries to suit the needs of your phone system.

You should always disable call waiting (if you have it) before using your modem. The clicking sound an incoming call makes can disrupt the flow of information to or from your computer and knock you offline. You'll have to start over with whatever you were doing. Very annoying.

You can add **1170,** to the beginning of any phone number your Mac is dialing (like: 1170,555-1212) to disable it. In some areas you may have to use ***70,** to disable.

The comma (,) makes your modem pause before dialing the rest of the number. The pause gives your phone a chance to accept the command before dialing the rest of the number. You can manually disable call waiting on a regular telephone by dialing either 1170 or *70 before you dial a number to talk to someone, too.

The Hardware Handshaking check box only applies to some high speed modems (over 9600 baud) with special cables. It adds an extra step where all the hardware involved chat for a second before the connection is made to establish what extra high speed features can come into play. Check your modem manual to see if you need it.

The Modem Type pop-up menu at the bottom lets you choose your exact make and model of modem for maximum efficiency. If your modem isn't listed, you can choose a generic entry. For most modems, a generic *Hayes compatible* setting will work fine.

Hayes compatible is a term that identifies a modem that conforms to the standard set of modem commands developed by the Hayes Corporation. Hayes compatibility is fairly standard among modems. I wouldn't mess with one that isn't—it can complicate your life unnecessarily.

Signing On

Once your hardware and software is set up, you're ready to dial out and *sign on* (also known as *logging on*) to a bulletin board for the very first time. What happens then varies from service to service, but generally a few standard things happen:

America Online, CompuServe, eWorld, and Prodigy are commercial companies that rely on credit cards to handle the high volume of payments they receive. Registering yourself with them is pretty much the same as using a credit card in a department store. You can be sure all they're interested in is getting paid for what you're buying from them—access to their service. You give them that information once, the first time you sign on, and that's it. Local bulletin boards usually don't accept credit cards. If someone online (on a local or national service) asks for your credit card number (in the course of normal conversation, or trying to sell you something), DON'T GIVE IT OUT. Credit card numbers are just as valuable as cash money—more so, in some cases. You wouldn't hand over your wallet to anyone who asked for it, would you?

➤ When you connect to the service, you'll be asked to identify yourself.

➤ Sometimes, you'll be asked to choose a *screen name*.

➤ If it's a pay service (like America Online or CompuServe), you'll have to register and set up a method of payment (usually a credit card number that will be billed monthly).

➤ When you register with a new service, you will also be asked to provide your real name (not your screen name), address, and telephone number for verification. Some local bulletin boards may get confirmation of the information by phone before you can use the service. It's a security precaution on their part.

➤ After you provide your name, you'll be asked to enter a *password*, which is your "open sesame" to the service. No one will be able to log on to your account (including you) without that password. Make sure it's one you can remember without writing it down somewhere, but not so obvious that anyone who knows you can figure it out.

➤ If you don't have to be verified (with a phone call from your local bulletin board's SysOp), you should be done—go on and explore. Learn. Have fun.

> A **screen name**, literally, is the name that appears on the screen whenever you "speak" to someone else on a service. Try to pick one that suits your personality, but keep it G-rated.

Around the World in 80 Ways

There are thousands upon thousands of bulletin boards in the world. Some are easier to find than others. You'll get information on the big commercial services when you unpack your modem. The little ones are harder to find.

Local Boards

Local boards come in all shapes and sizes. Some can only take one user at a time, others can take dozens. Many of them are geared to special-interests of their users: specific brands of computers, operating systems (like MS-DOS and System 7), computer games, sports, hobbies, sexuality, you name it.

> **SysOp** is short for System Operator. That's the propeller-head in charge of the bulletin board. It's pronounced "SIS-op."

There are three easy ways to find out if there's a bulletin board in your area:

➤ **Ask.** Ask members of your local MUG. Ask at your local computer store. Ask at your local college computer club. Just ask.

➤ **Read.** If you have a local computer newspaper or if your MUG publishes a newsletter, some local bulletin boards may advertise (though the ones that advertise probably want you to pay to join) or get mentioned in an article about modems or telecommunications.

➤ **Look.** If you join one of the major services, look in the area devoted to telecommunications or other special interest areas. There are usually many listings for bulletin boards across the country.

When you find one local bulletin board, log on to it. There's usually a listing of other bulletin boards in your area, or you can ask other subscribers for recommendations.

America Online

If you haven't noticed, America Online (*AOL* for short) is my favorite service. I use it a lot. (If you decide to sign up, drop me a note there— my screen name is Piv.) AOL is ideal for beginners: it has an excellent Mac interface, it's easy to find your way around, there's live help available most of the time, and the staff of Guides (those who do the helping) is well-trained, very helpful, and loads of fun.

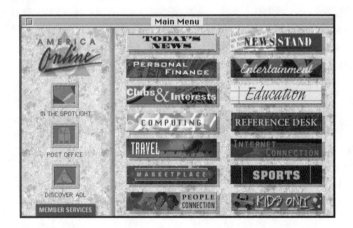

America Online 2.5.1.

The monthly membership fee of $9.95 includes five hours of use each month, and additional time is $3.50 per hour (there's a $2 per month surcharge if you pay by check). The rates are effective 24-hours a day, seven days a week. Special holidays (like Christmas and the Fourth of July) are free whether you've used your five hours or not.

You can pick up a free access kit by calling 1-800-227-6364 (tell them Piv sent you). Or you can buy a kit in book and software stores, which comes with a complete manual (very helpful) for $19.95, and includes 10 hours of free usage. Keep an eye out for *The Complete Idiot's Guide to America Online*—it's due soon.

CompuServe

CompuServe is the oldest and largest of the online services. It has millions of members world-wide. It is an excellent service, but it isn't quite as easy to navigate as America Online, nor are there as many opportunities for getting assistance if you run into trouble.

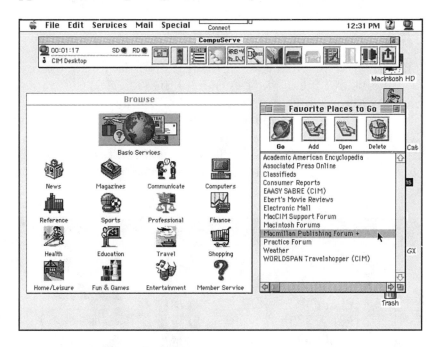

CompuServe Information Manager 2.4.

You can sign on to CompuServe without special software (the how-to information probably came with your modem), but I wouldn't recommend it for a beginner: there are no menus; everything is done with typed commands. Ack.

You can pick up a proprietary software package for CompuServe in most book and computer stores, or a friend with access to CompuServe already can download the latest version by using the command **GO: MACCIM**. In stores, the CompuServe Information Manager lists for about $50, but you can pick it up mail order for $25. The CompuServe Navigator lists for about $100, but you can buy it mail order for about

$50. Both come with a usage credit, so it actually winds up costing you less in the long run. It costs $10 to download the latest MacCIM version, but you get a $10 usage credit so it works out to be free-ish (just the cost of the phone call).

After the initial software investment, CompuServe charges a flat rate of $8.95 per month for basic services, with additional charges for extended packages. They always warn you before you try to enter a service that costs extra. (You can drop me a note here, too. My CompuServe address is 70713,3554—think you can remember it?)

PRODIGY

I don't care for PRODIGY. One of the reasons is demonstrated in the screenshot below: the old Mac version of the PRODIGY software won't run on my Mac. If it does run on your Mac, the software is completely un-Maclike. That annoys me, but don't let my prejudices sway you. (PRODIGY has recently—like yesterday—released a new Macintosh version of their software. I haven't seen it, so I can't comment on it. Maybe they've fixed it, and it's fabulous. Maybe it's more of the same. I don't know.)

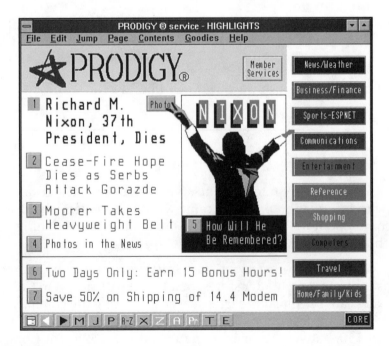

PRODIGY (Windows version... sorry).

To give PRODIGY its due, the service does corral an impressive array of celebrity guests, with related contests, to the service. The last time I signed on, Sue Grafton (author of the mysteries *A is for Alibi, B is for Burglar*, and so on), one of my personal favorites, was the *celeb du jour*. You can also shop 'til you drop, get gobs of news, weather, and sports, check out your horoscope, and read and post to lots of different special interest message boards.

If you're interested, you can get a PRODIGY startup kit in book and software stores. You may also have received software with your modem, or you can call 1-800-PRODIGY and get the kit just for the cost of shipping and handling (about $7). PRODIGY offers seven different pricing plans, but the basic "Value Plan" is $14.95 per month, which gets you unlimited access to core areas, 2 hours in the "Plus" (extra charge) areas, and 30 e-mail messages of about 100 words. Additional charges are $0.06/minute, and $0.25/e-mail page.

eWorld: the New Kid on the Block

1994 saw the launching of Apple Computer's own online service, called eWorld (for electronic world). It's built on a version of America Online's software, so it's easy to use and (as you can see here) very pretty.

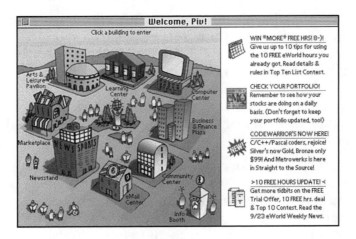

eWorld's welcoming screen. Oooh, pretty.

eWorld uses a city metaphor. Want to send mail? Click on the *eMail Center*. Meeting friends? Go to the *Community Center*. An impressive list of folks have signed on to offer services online, including user groups, such as BMUG and the Boston Computer Society, and news services from *USA Today* and Tribune Media Services. Naturally, you can get hot-off-the-ePress news direct from Apple about all their products and services, which is handy.

The service is fun, but population is a little thin right now. With service recently extended to Canada, that should start to change. Like all new things, eWorld needs to get a sense of itself and go through some growing pains. We'll see what happens. Drop me a note with your impressions. If you join, my screen name on eWorld is *Piv* too.

eWorld costs $8.95 per month, with two free hours of usage. Additional hours are $4.95 each. Access during prime time (6 a.m. to 6 p.m., Pacific Standard Time) will cost you $2/hour more. You can receive a free startup kit by calling 1-800-775-4556.

Internet and Others

The four services above are not the be-all and end-all of information services. A peek inside the coupon envelope that came packed with your modem tells you that much. There's lots more out there.

Don't think that because it wasn't mentioned here that a service isn't worth investigating. These four, plus any local boards you find, are a great place to start. Because this book works under the assumption that you're a beginner, I don't want to overwhelm you with choices. Once you get comfortable with the online world, you may be interested in exploring GEnie (the service run by GE), Delphi, the Internet (the international scientific and educational network), or one of hundreds of others.

Internet is a hot, hot ticket these days. If you think you want to dip your digital toe in those waters, most of the big online services offer some level of Internet access. America Online and Delphi are the most comprehensive. See the America Online section above for details about joining AOL. Information about Delphi is available by calling 1-800-544-4005. If you like what you see, you may want direct access to the Internet—be prepared to search for a service provider. Start with a good, Mac-based book about the Internet. Your local bookstore is swamped with Internet titles.

The Least You Need to Know

It would take a whole book to clue you in to the wonders that await you online. This was merely a taste. The least you should remember from this section:

➤ Modems connect you to a vast electronic world.

➤ Modems can be internal or external. If you're buying an internal one, ask to be sure it's appropriate for your Mac model.

➤ With a modem, you need some kind of communications software, either a generic one for general telecommuting, or a proprietary package to access a commercial online service.

➤ Your software needs to be configured for your modem, type of phone line, and the service you are using. Check your manual(s).

➤ You can find the phone numbers for local bulletin boards by asking at your local MUG or computer store, or by looking in computer publications.

➤ Have fun, and I'll see you around the planet.

Chapter 19

Computing on the Road (with Charles Kurault Nowhere in Sight)

In This Chapter

➤ Dealing with airports and airplanes

➤ Checking out hotels and motels

➤ File synchronization tips

➤ PB & J (PowerBooks and junk)

➤ NJ & U (Newton junk and you)

Portable users (whether that's a PowerBook, Newton MessagePad, or something else) have special concerns, the biggest of which is keeping their portables up and running as long as possible before the batteries croak. To make y'all happy, here's a special little chapter all your own, with tips and tricks for making your computing on the road just a little less harrowing.

In this chapter, you'll get tips for dealing with airport security, airlines, hotels, and motels. You'll also get some tips on keeping the files on your PowerBook and desktop Mac synchronized, so you always have the most recent version of a file handy.

Airport Security

The biggest pain in the butt, when traveling with techno-toys, is getting through the bloody airport metal detector and X-ray security check. (I always forget and wear a metal belt-buckle, so security has to poke me in embarrassing places with a hand-held metal detector. I don't enjoy it. Really.)

Airlines have gotten all kinds of weird when it comes to using electronics in the air. Some ban the use of radios, even with headphones. Others don't want you to use a laptop computer. Unfortunately, none of the airlines seem to agree on what you can and can't use. If you know you have to work in the air, check with the airline for their rules before you buy your ticket. Nothing's more irritating than needing to work and being told you can't.

If you're a savvy business traveler, you're carrying everything you need with you: a garment bag or overnight case, the obligatory briefcase, and perhaps another separate bag for your PowerBook/MessagePad and accessories. (How many arms do you have, anyhow?)

Your plan is to pass off the garment bag to a flight attendant, jam the overnight bag in the overhead compartment, and keep your precious computer case stowed under the seat until you can take it out and work—if you can convince airport security that none of your work tools is a bomb in disguise.

The easiest way to muscle your way through security is to drop everything but your computer case on the X-ray belt. Hand your electronics and accessories (disks, PCMCIA cards, and so on) over to the security guard and ask to have it hand-searched. That will spare everything from an X-ray bombardment. You will be asked to power up your PowerBook so security can see that it actually works and isn't a device of terrorism masquerading as a Mac.

You can turn it on and off for the guard; however, that's going to drain your battery needlessly (spinning up the hard drive, and then powering it down). If you plan to work while waiting for your flight to be called, you can (before you hit the security desk) power up your PowerBook and then put it to sleep with the **Sleep** command under the **Special** menu. When you get to security, all you have to do is open the lid and touch a key: your PowerBook will snap to attention. When you satisfy security, use the **Sleep** command again to conserve your battery until you're ready to work. With a Newton MessagePad, or other PDA, the "Prove that's not a bomb" display won't have a major effect on your battery, since there's no hard drive spinning.

Up in the Air

When you get onboard the plane, you can work until they tell you to prepare for takeoff. Then you must stow your PowerBook (in the overhead compartment, or under the seat in front of you), at least until you're in the air. Put that bad-boy to sleep (I almost said "put that puppy to sleep," an unfortunate choice of words), or turn it off if you plan to snooze and not work.

The Bates Motel

"Norman? Norman? You evil child, put that computer away and come help your mother..."

Hotels and motels that cater to business travelers have been getting more and more understanding of folks who tote around laptop computers. If your PowerBook or MessagePad has a fax modem, when you make reservations, be sure to ask for a room that has a phone jack you can plug into—not the typical hotel kind where you can't unplug the phone.

Before you leave on your trip, also be sure to get a couple of local access numbers for your destination from any online services you may use (America Online, CompuServe, NewtonMail).

Get in Sync

One of the most trying things about computing on the road is remembering which files are the most recent versions of documents you use on both your PowerBook and desktop Mac. System 7.5 has a built-in suite of PowerBook utilities, including file synchronization tools. The PowerBook File Assistant automatically synchronizes any two files, folders, or disks between PowerBook computers and other Macintosh systems.

However, since System 7.5 takes up gobs of hard disk space (over 21 MB for an Easy Install of the full System—without PowerTalk or QuickDraw GX), and RAM (4 MB minimum—8 MB on a Power Mac), many PowerBook users may blanch at the price of hardware add-ons to make 7.5 practical for their laptops. There are other steps you can take to make synchronization easier.

First, you can use the Views Control Panel's **List Views** options (shown in the following figure) and set your options to show date and comment information.

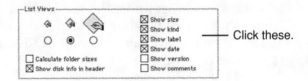

List Views from the Views Control Panel.

When you're ready to move the current version of a file between your computers, select **View by Name**, and then **View by Date** with the **Views** menu in the Finder. Your files will sort themselves out by the date/time that's automatically stamped on every file when you save it. Your most recent files will float to the top of the list (as shown here).

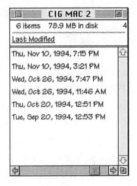

Files sorted by last modified date.

Second, you can attach comments to any file, which will appear if you select **Show Comments** in the Views Control Panel. To attach comments to a file:

1. Click on the file icon to select it.

2. Select **Get Info** from the **File** menu (⌘-I).

3. When the Get Info window appears (shown in the following figure), click in the Comments box to activate it, and type in a reminder.

4. Close the Get Info window. Your comments will appear whenever you change the view to **View by Name**.

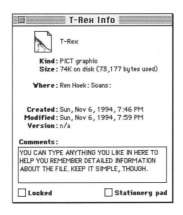

The Get Info window with comments.

You can also apply a set of naming strategies to help you recall which file is most recent. You can number your files like application versions: **Text 1.0** for a first version; **Text 1.2** for an intermediate phase; **Text 2.0** for a total revision. If that sounds like too much work, you can get applications that will synchronize your files for you automatically—it's still work, though. You should be aware of one more thing: If you ever rebuild your desktop (by holding down the ⌘-Option key combination at startup), be aware that rebuilding erases all of the comments you have attached to files. (You can get a shareware utility called CommentKeeper, available online and from MUGs and shareware libraries, that will save your comments.)

PowerBook Utilities and Other Doodads

The instant success of the PowerBook line left it wide open for third parties to try and fix the foibles of portable computing. There are scads of utilities, hardware add-ons, and effort-saving devices you can spring for. In addition to getting yourself a comfortable carrying case (that's padded to protect your PowerBook *and* your carrying shoulder) that will hold all of this, there are some other very handy items.

PowerBook Utilities

There are dozens of PowerBook utility packages available. The current crop all seem to address the same half-dozen or so concerns of the common PowerBook user: making batteries last longer, keeping tabs on battery charge, security, cursor control, speedy access to information about your system, and file synchronization.

To make batteries last longer, the utilities give you faster and better control of your PowerBook's automatic sleep settings (also much improved in System 7.5). Some will let you set different sets of conservation tools (such as controlling your monitor's display—a very power-hungry device) for different computing situations, even different applications. All of them provide an Instant Sleep command that bypasses the one in the Special menu, saving you time and battery power.

There's usually some sort of built-in monitor function to keep track of your battery's usage (so you know when it's time to buy a new one), its charge (so you know when you can plug that puppy in again), and its condition (totally draining the battery before recharge extends battery life), or to let you know that the battery isn't charging at all (very bad news).

Security functions generally provide password protection, either at startup, when you "wake" a sleeping PowerBook, or both. The goal is to keep casual observers from accessing your information when you aren't looking.

All the PowerBook utility packages give you help finding the PowerBook's cursor (which tends to vanish during periods of inactivity). Some let you set a larger cursor, so it's easier to find; others will find it for you whenever you touch the trackball. They also all enhance the PowerBook's battery display. Different packages add other displays: time and date clocks; computing time left to the battery; disk activity; and even whether AppleTalk is active.

Since the PowerBook utility packages vary greatly in their usefulness, it's silly for me to try to recommend one because I don't know how *you* use your PowerBook. As always, Mr. Phelps, shop for the package that gives you the tools you need at a price you can afford. If your PB can handle it, you may want to try System 7.5 before investing in a pile of accessory software.

Synchronization Utilities

Many, if not most, people working on PowerBooks use them as travel machines and rely on desktop Macs and Duo-docking stations at home or in the office. That presents the problem of knowing which hard drive has the latest-greatest version of any given file.

All of the stand-alone file-synchronization utilities provide you the means of specifying which files and folders on which of the Macs you access are to be kept current with your PowerBook's files, and which are not. All of them are more or less comparable in terms of basic functions, while some have extra whiz-bang features, such as automatic virus checking (a nice touch) and the capability to synchronize two Macs via floppies, since not everyone has access to a network.

If you need one, shop to meet your current needs. If you think you may need only one, and (again) if your PB can handle it, you may want to try System 7.5's new File Assistant before springing for additional software.

PowerBook Hardware

The kindest hardware additions you can give your PowerBook are similar to those mentioned in Chapter 17: more RAM, a bigger internal hard drive, a modem, and an external monitor, keyboard, and mouse for those times when your PowerBook isn't on your knees.

Additionally, there's some PowerBook-specific junk that may make your life easy: an extra battery or two (some of which will give you 5–9 hours of computing time); a free-standing battery conditioner (one that drains the battery completely before recharging it, to extend the battery's life), and a security kit (the laptop equivalent of a bicycle chain) that will let you anchor your PowerBook to some immobile piece of furniture to keep it from traveling without you.

Dressing Up Your Newton MessagePad

Like PowerBooks, everybody uses their Newton differently, so I hesitate to recommend software. However, you can't go wrong by getting a Newton Connection Kit so you can share data back and forth between your Mac and Newton (why enter all of those birthdays and phone numbers again?), plus you don't have to buy software or expensive cards—you can buy less expensive floppy versions and load them onto your Newton from your Mac. If you work with a Windows PC at work, you can also get a Windows version of the Connection Kit, so you can share that data with your Newton, too.

The Connection Kit will let you make entries in your Newton address and phone book, appointment calendar, and so on, right on your Mac, and then update the files on your Newton when you synchronize. That's especially handy if you have a lot of data to enter and find writing it all into your Newton a slow and tedious affair.

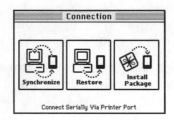

The Newton Connection Kit 2.0.

While you're at it, get yourself some extra batteries or a convenient on-the-road recharging option. You also can't go wrong with a nice case to protect and hold your Newton, plus any extra PCMCIA storage cards you may have. You can even do both. The BMI X-pack for Newton is a leather carrying case with space for three PCMCIA cards, space for credit and business cards, pockets, and a built-in (okay, Velcroed-in) rechargeable battery that will give you up to 15 hours of battery life.

Okay, I can't resist—my favorite bit of Newton software is GoFigure from Dubl-Click software. Aside from a great name, GoFigure gives you fifteen different kinds of calculators, my favorite of which are the Sales Tax and Restaurant Tip calculator (very handy), and Babies. The Babies calculator will easily figure out how much you owe the baby-sitter, but the really cool function is, if you enter your (or a friend's) date of birth, it will give you more information than you will ever need about when you were conceived. For those working in the other direction, it will give you an estimated delivery date for your pending bundle of joy. It's quite a giggle, in addition to being very handy.

The Least You Need to Know

Here are some easy-on-the-brain reminders to keep you happily computing on the road:

➤ Check with your airline (before you buy your ticket) to be sure you can use your PowerBook or MessagePad in flight.

➤ Make sure any hotel you make reservations with is computer friendly—especially toward your modem.

➤ You can synchronize files between your PowerBook and desktop Mac without buying additional software; it just takes some organizing strategy.

➤ The right utilities and accessories can make your life on the road much easier.

Chapter 20

Installing System (and Other) Software

In This Chapter

➤ How to install System software

➤ How to re-install System software

➤ Custom installations

➤ Installing practically anything

Did you get your hands on a Mac without installed System software, or is something all boogered up in the System that was installed on your hard drive? I've said it before and I'll say it again: *Don't panic*. Likewise, don't panic if you have a hot new software title you want to install. It's a piece of cake—with sprinkles and everything.

If you're upgrading to System 7.5 from an earlier version of the Mac OS, you may want to run the **Safe Install Utility** before you take the plunge. Safe Install will check your existing System folder to make sure there isn't anything potentially incompatible with it hiding in there. If you choose the Detailed check, it will also list all of the applications installed on your Mac, with the software company's phone number in case you need to call and see if the application(s) in question run under System 7.5. You'll find Safe Install on the Before You Install disk, if you're installing from floppies, or in the Before You Install folder inside the Installation folder on the CD-ROM version.

Extra Steps When Re-installing

If you're re-installing the same version of your System software to eliminate a suspected (or confirmed) corruption problem or upgrade to a new version, there are some extra steps you have to take. Naturally, if you're installing from scratch, you may skip blithely ahead to the next section, "Installation Included."

Before you re-install your System software, you want to get rid of the items you think, know, or think you know are causing you grief. Double-click on the **System Folder** to get at its contents. It will prevent the problem from being passed on to your fresh copy of the Mac OS. To be safe, click-drag the following out of your System Folder and into the Trash:

➤ The **System Suitcase**

➤ The **Finder** file

➤ Any suspicious extensions or control panels from the appropriate folder

➤ The **Preference** files (located in the **Preferences** folder) associated with the files you've already thrown out (for example, the Finder Prefs file)

Chuck them all, empty the Trash (using the **Empty Trash** command under the **Special menu**), and follow the steps in the next section.

Installation Included

With the introduction of System 7.5, Mac users have the option of getting their System software on one single CD-ROM disc, instead of a pile of floppies. However, floppies are still the media of choice for many Mac users. We'll look at both ways to install your System software.

From Floppy Disks

If you're installing from floppy disks, here's what you need to do first:

1. Dig out the set of System disks that came with your Mac (or if you were very good, the backup copies you made).

2. Start your Mac if it's off, or restart it (using the **Restart** command under the **Special** menu) if it's already running.

3. At the startup sound, pop in the first **Install** disk from your set of System disks. It has a scaled-down version of the System software installed so you can run your Mac from it.

4. When you reach the desktop, open the Install disk's window (if it doesn't open automatically) by double-clicking on its icon.

5. Scroll around in the window until you spot the **Installer** icon shown here. Double-click on it to fire up the Installer program.

The Installer icon.

You're ready to install; skip ahead to the "Easy or Custom?" section.

From a CD-ROM Disc

If your System software came on a CD-ROM disc, your procedure is a little different. First, when you start or restart your Mac (as in step 3 above), you'll need to be sure that the appropriate driver software for your CD-ROM drive is on the floppy disk you're using as the startup disk. If it isn't, your Mac won't know it has a CD-ROM drive attached, much less that there's a disc in it.

The CD version of System 7.5 comes with a Disk Tools disk, with minimal System software and drivers for an Apple CD-ROM drive already installed. If you have an Apple CD-ROM drive, you can use that disk. If you have a CD-ROM by any other manufacturer, make a copy of the Disk Tools disk (that's covered in Chapter 8). Then you can delete the Apple CD driver from the copy (by dragging it from the disks Extensions folder and into the Trash), and copy the appropriate driver software from your hard drive's Extensions folder to the Extensions folder inside the System Folder on the Disk Tools disk. Check your CD-ROM drive's manual for details about which driver(s) you'll need to copy.

Make sure you lock your copy of the Disk Tools when you're done tinkering with it. Copying files is discussed back in Chapter 8, locking and unlocking disks in Chapter 9.

With your altered, duplicate Disk Tools disk in hand, you're ready to begin. After your Mac starts and you're at the desktop, you should put the System software CD in your CD-ROM drive. Here it is step by step:

1. Start your Mac if it's off, or restart it (using the **Restart** command under the **Special** menu) if it's already running.

2. At the startup sound, pop in the **Disk Tools** disk with the appropriate CD-ROM driver(s) installed on it.

3. When you reach the desktop, insert the System 7.5 CD into your drive.

4. When the CD's icon appears on your desktop, double-click on it to open it (if it doesn't open automatically).

5. Scroll around in the window until you spot the **Installation** folder icon. Double-click on it to open it.

6. Scroll around in the **Installation** window until you spot the **System Install** folder icon. Double-click on it to open it.

7. Scroll around in that window until you spot the **Installer** icon. Double-click on it to launch the Installer.

Now you too can proceed with an Easy or Custom installation.

Easy or Custom?

Whether you're working with floppy disks or a CD, when the Installer application opens, you'll be presented with a Welcome screen. To proceed, click on the **OK** button. That puts you right into the Installer's **Easy Install** option.

Easy Does It

The Easy Install option assumes you don't want to be bothered (or you're too intimidated to be bothered) selecting the exact installation you want. If you're installing from scratch and have no idea what your custom options are, simply click on the **Install** button and skip the section on custom installations.

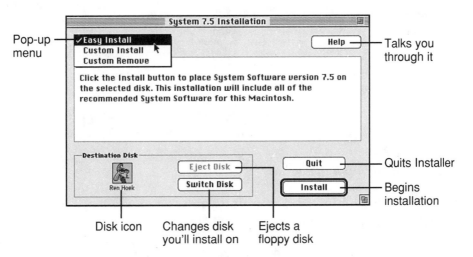

The Easy Install dialog box.

Easy Install simply throws everything that can possibly be relevant to your Macintosh model onto your hard drive—entirely too much stuff. When you're done installing, turn to the "Junk You Can Throw Away" section in Chapter 11, decide which junk you don't need or want, and throw it away.

The next time you need (or want) to re-install your System software, you'll feel more confident about choosing a custom installation. If this is a re-installation you're doing and you want to pick and choose what will be put on your hard drive, click where it says **Easy Install** and the pop-up menu will pop up (funny how that works). Select the Custom Install option.

Custom Installations

Selecting the **Custom Install** option changes the Installer dialog box to the one shown here. By scrolling through the list in the middle of the dialog, you can click on one basic installation, or you can click in the check boxes to select several installation options.

The Custom Install dialog box.

Clicking on the right-pointing arrows beside each option will show what System software is included with each option. In the figure, System software for just about any Mac is chosen. You can select or deselect any of the suboptions by clicking in the check box, and the check mark will go away; that item *will not* be installed.

If you find all these options confusing, you can (without regret or shame-based feelings) choose the **Easy Install** option from the pop-up menu and opt for the full installation without any thinking on your part. It's okay.

If you want to install System software on a hard drive other than the one named beneath the **Install** button, click on the **Switch Disk** button until the name and icon of the hard drive you want to install on appears in the Destination Disk area.

Don't be afraid. You'll notice that almost every screen shown throughout this section gives you the opportunity to Quit the Installer, or Cancel the installation once it has begun. You aren't working without a net.

When you've selected the disk to install on and the options you want installed, click on the **Install** button, and *a-waaaay you go*. If you're installing from a CD, you can go get yourself a beverage or a nice snack—just check back in ten minutes or so. If you're installing from floppies, put on your red shoes and get ready to dance the floppy shuffle.

Doin' the Floppy Shuffle

When you click on the **Install** button, your Mac will think and churn, think and churn, deciding what all it needs to install to make your Mac happy.

System 7.5 comes on a pile of high-density floppy disks. When you click on the **Install** button, the Installer decides which disks it will need, and lines them up in the status display. You're bound to have to shuffle floppies around, inserting and removing them from the disk drive.

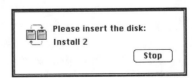

To save yourself some time, stack the disks in order by your floppy drive; that way you won't have to go searching for a disk each time your Mac asks for one. Keep the first disk separate from the rest; your Mac will ask for it again at the end of the process.

When your Mac needs the next disk in the series, it will spit out the current disk in the drive, and flash the message shown in the following figure (of course, the name of the disk will change). Simply remove the ejected disk and pop in the one requested. The installation will proceed along its merry way.

```
┌──────────────────────────────────────┐
│  ┌─┐   Please insert the disk:        │
│  │ │↕                                  │
│  └─┘   Install 2                       │
│                          ┌────────┐    │
│                          │  Stop  │    │
│                          └────────┘    │
└──────────────────────────────────────┘
```

The Installer disk request.

When the installation is nearly complete, your Mac will request that you insert the disk labeled **Install** again. It wraps up a few things, tidies up after itself, and you're done. To celebrate, your Mac will throw the message shown in the next figure up on your screen. Click on the **Restart** button, and you're good to go.

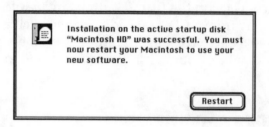

Installation successful!

Installing Other Software

These days, most other software comes on several disks with an installer program, just like the one for the Mac's System software. The steps for installing are similar to installing System software—down to the Easy and Custom installation options—*except:* you don't have to start your Mac from a floppy disk before you install.

You should, however, turn off any virus protection software you have installed before trying to install new software. It can really booger up the process. You can turn it off by using the Extensions Manager control panel (covered in Chapter 11) and restarting your Mac.

After you Restart, remember to turn back on your virus protection, extensions, and control panels that you had turned off. Then you'll need to **Restart** yet again.

To be completely free of interfering extensions, you can simply restart your Mac and hold down the **Shift** key as soon as the little Mac icon appears on your monitor. That'll turn off *everything*. (You can't use the Shift key trick if you're installing software from a CD-ROM disc; it will also turn off your CD-ROM drivers. Use the Extension Manager instead, and turn off everything but your CD-ROM drivers.)

Re-installing Other Software

If you're re-installing an application that has suddenly gotten cranky on you and you think parts of it have been damaged or corrupted, you should throw out *all* of the suspect application before you install the new copy. As with System software, this prevents the problem from being passed on to your new copy.

The kinder, gentler software publishers put a listing of what gets installed where in their manual (usually in the installation instructions, but check elsewhere if you don't see it). If you're lucky to have one, follow the map to remove all the software's tentacles from your hard drive.

In addition to the obvious application and accessory files (that are probably all lumped together in a folder on your hard drive), be sure to check in the System Folder for:

➤ Preference files

➤ Extensions and/or control panels

➤ Accessory applications (such as spell or grammar checkers) that are usually installed in the System Folder. Look for a folder with the application or software company's name as the folder name; get rid of it.

Throw everything in the Trash, empty it, and proceed with your installation.

The Least You Need to Know

Re-installing System software is something that you really shouldn't have to do on a regular basis, but you should remember a few things when the need arises.

➤ Turn on/Restart your Mac and immediately pop the Install disk into the drive (or a startup disk with CD-ROM drivers installed for CD software).

➤ When in doubt, choose **Easy Install**. You can always trash the excess later.

➤ When installing software other than System software, remember to turn off or disable any virus protection programs you may have running. To be completely confident, turn off all of your extensions and control panels (either with the Extensions Manager or by holding down the Shift key at startup).

➤ If you used the Extensions Manager to turn off extensions and controls panels before the installation, remember to turn them back on and restart your Mac again.

Chapter 21

Troubleshooting: I Think We're All Bozos on This Bus

In addition to the above information, I also hope you'll get a solid grounding in how Macs work, so you'll be able to search and destroy problems on your own.

Before You Panic

Macs are, in some respects, just like babies: sometimes they spit up for no good reason. It doesn't mean your Mac is sick if something weird happens; it could simply be an odd collision of circumstances that threw your Mac for a loop. Before you go packing it up to drag into your nearest Authorized Apple Service Center, there are some things you can try before you panic.

Check the Obvious

Your Mac won't start. Your communications software can't connect to your favorite bulletin board. You can't get a certain file to print. Your external hard drive doesn't want to mount. They all sound like serious problems. In some cases, they may be. In others, they aren't. Before you reach for the phone, check the obvious:

➤ Is everything plugged in and turned on?

➤ Are cables connected securely to your Mac and the peripheral?

➤ Are the correct cables plugged into the correct peripherals?

➤ If it's a monitor problem (say, no picture), check the contrast and brightness controls, as well as the above.

➤ Are you using the right software for the hardware (the correct printer driver in the Chooser, the right telecommunications software for the service, and so on)?

➤ What's the dumbest thing you could have forgotten to do? Check that, too.

Always, always, always check the obvious. The more obvious it seems, the more you should check it. Trust me on this. I once had to make three trips to a computer store trying to get my brand new LaserWriter Select 310 to print. I tried everything you'll read here, plus more. (I also hurled some colorful language at it that you probably will never see in print.) Even the technician at the store was flummoxed because it always worked there. To make a long story short, it turned out to be the printer cable. I had the wrong kind, but no one noticed because Mac cables all look kind of alike. Trust me here, if professional tweaks can be faked out by a cable, so can you. *Check the obvious!*

Upgrade Gremlins

If something weird starts happening just after you've, for example, upgraded to System 7.5 from an earlier version, don't necessarily blame your Mac. Sometimes, all your favorite software isn't quite comfortable with the new System software—this was a major headache when System 7.0 appeared, less so with 7.5.

The thing about software upgrades (both for the Mac OS and your favorite applications) is they're *supposed* to behave at least a little differently from what you're used to. New versions of stuff (especially, it seems, the Mac OS) often have little things wrong with them that may not be pretty, but are not really problems, or at least not problems that are really traumatic. They're called *bugs*.

For example: sometimes with System 7.5, when dragging an icon into the Trash from a window that's showing its contents by name, the window may not redraw itself properly. File names may look like they're double-printed. They *are* double-printed. It isn't a Mac-threatening problem; it's just ugly and impossible to read. Close the window in question and reopen it, and things will look fine (or, if you have WindowShade turned on, just roll the window up and back down). This falls into the category of ugly but not dangerous.

In the traumatic category, System 7.5 sometimes seems to have some memory problems. You may get **Out Of Memory** messages trying to open an application, when you bloody well have tons of memory available. The only way I've found to clear it up is to save open files and quit open applications (if any) and Restart. That isn't really traumatic, but it is a pain in the hindquarters.

A judicious Restart works in other situations, too.

Start Again

If strange things happen while you're working on something, stop. If you can, save everything (⌘-S), quit (⌘-Q) any and all open applications, and **Restart** your Mac.

Sometimes, a heavy-duty work session, with a lot of opening and closing (and reopening) of applications and documents, confuses your Mac. A restart is like a slap in the face to your Mac. It forces it to clear out its memory (which is why you save your work before restarting) and load your documents and applications again from scratch. If the problem recurs, then you have to start sniffing around for another solution.

Rebuild Your Desktop

Your Mac keeps track of everything on every disk by building these big, fat, invisible files that are collectively called *The Desktop File*. Sometimes, the information in the Desktop File gets screwed up, mismatched, or disconnected. Your Mac may tell you it can't find an

If you use the **Get Info** command to attach comments to any of your files, rebuilding the desktop will delete those comments. You'll have to redo them.

application that you know is right under its digital nose. Some of your file icons may become boring generic ones. When your Desktop File gets screwy, it's like Wednesday on the "Mickey Mouse Club"—anything can happen. You have to tell your Mac to rebuild its Desktop File.

Restart your Mac while holding down the ⌘ and **Option** keys. When you reach the desktop, you'll get a notice saying, **Are you sure you want to rebuild the Desktop?** Click on **OK**. The message repeats for every disk, hard drive, or hard drive partition on your Mac. To rebuild the Desktop File on a floppy disk, hold down the ⌘ and **Option** keys while you insert the disk in your floppy drive.

Zap Your PRAM

That's pronounced "pea-RAM," not "pram" like a baby carriage. PRAM is where your Mac stores parameter information: how you like the time and date displayed and other custom settings you use control panels to set. If your PRAM goes wonky, your Mac doesn't know how to behave. So you have to administer another open-handed slap across your Mac's face.

I could never remember the key combination to zap PRAM until I noticed the letters made a nice little mnemonic device. Simply remember COPpeR, (Control-Option-P-R) as in pennies, or "You'll never take me alive, COPpeR!"

This time, as you **Restart**, press **Control-Option-P-R** (you may have to get a friend to help), and hold them until your startup screen blinks. That clears the parameter setting and starts you with a clean slate: that means you need to open your control panels and reset them to your preferred settings.

Re-install Suspicious Applications

If your problems persist, try re-installing the suspect application. Delete all of the application files (they can be scattered all over your hard drive and in your System Folder). Be sure to delete the application's preference file(s) in your Preferences folder. Re-install the application, following the directions in your manual. If you suspect your System software, you can re-install that, too. See Chapter 20 for details on installing System and other software.

When All Else Fails

(Re)read the manual. Who knows, there may be some useful information in it.

Problems at Startup

Many of the problems discussed so far happen while you're already up and running with your Mac, and then something jumps out and goes, Boo!

More frightening, to me at least, are the problems that happen right after you power up your Mac, and you immediately know something is wrong. Your Mac's life flashes before your eyes. Don't Panic. Here are some specific (and generic) startup problems and what you can do to remedy them.

Plenty of Nothin'

If you fire up your Mac, only to have it sit there and stare at you with its one big eye (no startup sound, no monitor, no nothing), it's time to check the obvious again: is it plugged in, turned on (don't forget to check the switch on your power strip)? If that's not it, check the cables: make sure you connected everything properly (even your keyboard and mouse cables). If that doesn't get it, you have a serious dead-Mac situation on your hands. Call the para-Mac-ics.

Floppy Disk Icon with a Question Mark

An icon of a floppy with a question mark is your Mac's way of asking where the System Folder is. If you start up from an external hard drive, make sure it's plugged in, turned on, and connected to your Mac's SCSI port.

If you start from an internal hard drive, try turning your Mac off for, oh, about fifteen or twenty seconds, and try it again. If that doesn't do it, try it again, but zap your PRAM (look earlier in this chapter for details). If that doesn't get it, pop in your rescue disk (see Chapter 10) or the Disk Tools disk from your set of System disks or your System software CD. Both should have startup information so your Mac will run.

When your Mac starts from the disk, one of two things will happen: either your internal hard drive will finally mount, or it won't. If it mounts (its icon shows up on your desktop below your rescue disk), you need to install (or re-install) your System software. Something boogered it up so badly your Mac can't read it.

If it doesn't mount, your internal hard drive is boogered up in general. You can try taking a pass at it with Disk First Aid, but if a hard drive won't mount, most utilities can't touch it: call for help.

Ballad of the Sad Mac Café

Usually, when you start up, the first thing you see is a little smiling Mac: that's good. If you should ever see a sad Mac, that's bad. Your Mac puts itself through a series of self-tests at startup. It smiles when it passes and frowns when it doesn't. It also throws an arcane and oblique error message up on your screen. Write it down, just in case.

Try restarting from a rescue disk: it may be a problem with your System software. If it starts up and your hard drive icon mounts, it's your System software, and you need to re-install it (see Chapter 20). If it starts but your hard drive doesn't mount, there's something physically wrong with your hard drive. Call for help.

If it still gives you the sad Mac when you restart from the rescue disk, there's something wrong with your Mac itself. Call your Local Authorized Apple Dealer, and read off a copy of the error code: let them figure it out. You'll probably need to take your Mac in for repairs.

Not Your Usual Bong Sound

Every Mac makes some kind of **bong** sound when it starts up, even if you've turned down your Mac's volume with the Sound Control Panel (unless you have something plugged into the audio-out jack—oh, speakers come to mind—that isn't turned on).

If you hear any other sound (four notes or a horrified shriek—oh, wait, the shriek was *me*), there's something wrong. Usually, you'll get this four-note samba when you've just installed something: new RAM chips, a new SCSI device, or an expansion card. The notes mean that whatever you just installed is installed incorrectly— try again.

For SCSI problems, check the "General Scuzziness" section near the end of this chapter for more information. For any other kind of hardware, check your manual, and re-install it.

Problems in the Finder

Sometimes, your Mac will start up fine, only to give you grief when you try to do something. Here are some of the more common problems.

Disappearing Files

Usually, if a file disappears abruptly (say, while you're copying it onto a floppy, or moving it into another folder), it's because your finger slipped off the mouse button while dragging it, and it landed in that same place all of your odd socks go from the dryer.

Luckily, your Mac has a **Find** command (⌘-F) in the **File** menu, or under the menu. Tell your Mac to look for that puppy by name, or by other criteria (part of the name, kind of file, and so on) when you click on the **More Options** button. If you can't remember anything about the file, you'll have to dig around in folders manually to find it. Sorry.

Can't Empty Trash

The Trash isn't smart: it lets you throw away almost anything. The only things it won't let you throw away are the following:

➤ **Locked files** You have to unlock them first, in the file's **Get Info** window (⌘-I).

➤ **Files from locked disks** You have to unlock the disk. Eject the disk (⌘-E), flip the disk's locking tab, and reinsert it into your disk drive.

➤ **Files that are in use** For document files, use the appropriate application to close the documents. For extensions or control panels, simply drop them in the Trash and leave them there until the next time you start your Mac; they won't load from the Trash, and you can empty it then.

System Errors

System Errors are also known as **bombs** or **crashes**. Your Mac has a minor nervous breakdown and with its last breath before passing out, it throws a polite, but useless, **Sorry, a system error occurred** message on your screen. (Don't confuse a system error with a system **freeze**, where everything seizes up: you can't move the mouse, select a menu, nothing. I'll talk more about system freezes later.)

Throw your hands up in disgust, and restart your Mac. You can try to click on the **Restart** button in the message, but that almost never works. If you have one, use the power key (on your keyboard), or just turn your Mac's power off for a few seconds (15–20). There isn't much else you can do when it happens. Everything you were working on is gone except for what you already saved to disk.

You can do some things to prevent bombs and crashes, though. They usually happen for one of three reasons:

➤ **Memory** The application you were using ran out of memory (RAM); check out the "Digital Amnesia" section of this chapter for more help.

➤ **Software** The application may be badly written or may not be compatible with your version of the System software. (If this is the case, call the company. Follow the steps in the "Now You Can Panic" section). Or you may have an extension/INIT conflict (see the next section). Or something's screwy with your copy of the application or your System software (you may have to re-install it).

➤ **Hardware** If your Mac crashes when you tell it to do something with a piece of hardware (save to your hard drive, print, and so on), the hardware may be at fault. As always, check the obvious first. Try turning the peripheral off and then on again. If the problem involves your hard drive, it may need its driver repaired or to be reformatted (see Chapter 10).

Sibling Rivalry: Extension and Control Panel Conflicts

Extension and control panel conflicts cause most of the grief in the Macintosh universe—at least in my Macintosh universe. The main culprit is usually an extension (or INITs, as we fossils call them). Control panels only enter into it when they have an extension component (you may not actually see it). For a variety of reasons, not all extensions and control panels get along. Sometimes, they fight over the same scrap of memory. Sometimes, they try to fiddle with the same bit of your system (the menu bar, the desktop pattern, or such), and sometimes, they just crash.

When you have an extension conflict, you'll know it. Right after you load in a new extension, your system will start crashing on a regular basis. It will crash either right at startup when the two extensions collide (Coming Soon! *When Extensions Collide!* An SF masterpiece!), or as soon as they both try to fiddle with whatever they fiddle with. Here's how to fix it.

First, you have to isolate the two extensions that are causing the trouble. The first one is easy: it's the last one you installed. The other one is harder. Open your Extensions Manager control panel. Under the **Sets** pop-up menu, select the **All Off** option. In the listing of all your extensions and control panels, locate the last one you installed, and turn it on by clicking to the left of its name; a check mark will appear where you clicked. Restart your Mac.

If you aren't running System 7.5, you can probably turn up a copy of the Extensions Manager from your favorite online service or MUG. If you can't wait to get it, you can do all this manually: Don't flinch now. Pull all of your extensions (except the new one) out of your Extensions folder and out of your System Folder (leave them on the desktop, or drag them into an empty folder). Restart your Mac. Instead of turning them on with the Extensions Manager, you'll return them, one at a time, to the Extensions folder inside your System folder. It's tedious, but it works.

If your Mac starts up okay, turn on one more extension with the Extensions Manager, and restart again. (If your Mac crashes on startup, all by its lonesome, that new extension is bad, bad, bad: trash it and get on with your life). Add an extension, and restart. Add an extension, and restart. Repeat the process until your Mac crashes. The last extension you added before the crash is the other troublemaker.

Now you can do one of two things. Either throw out one of the troublesome extensions or learn to juggle extensions. Sometimes, changing the order of the conflicting extension load can resolve the

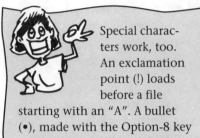

Special characters work, too. An exclamation point (!) loads before a file starting with an "A". A bullet (•), made with the Option-8 key combination, will load dead last. Blank spaces work as well: a file starting with three blanks at the front of its name loads before files with two, which load before files with one.

problem. Try getting one to load first, the other last. If that doesn't work, reverse the order. You can change your extension loading order by adding letters to the beginning of their names (they load alphabetically). Add an "A" to the beginning of the extension you want to go first, a "B" to the second, and so on. (Naming/renaming files is covered in Chapter 7.)

It's another case of trial and error. It's tedious and time consuming, but it's also effective. If all this sounds too involved, you can always try a third-party INIT/Extension manager (I like the aptly named INIT Manager, from Baseline), which lets you change the order your extensions load without fiddling with their names. It makes the whole process a lot simpler.

Problems within Applications

Yes, believe it or not, sometimes weird things happen, even in your favorite application. Even the most stubborn, un-Mac-like application will grace you with an occasional error message before it poops out. Here are a few of my favorites.

Application X Has Unexpectedly Quit

Well, that's bloody helpful. Unless you fell asleep at the keyboard, you probably saw your document zip into nothingness. The likely suspects: the application ran out of memory (skip to the "Digital Amnesia" section); got into a fight with another open application (you may want to close that one, if practical); or the application isn't compatible with your version of the System software (you need to upgrade whichever one of them is older).

Microsoft Word Prefers 6 Gigabytes of Memory, Only 28K Available

More memory difficulties. In this particular instance, you have too many applications open at the same time. Close some, preferably in the reverse order you opened them (last to open, first to close). That frees up enough RAM for the greedy application to open. Skip ahead to the "Digital Amnesia" section of this chapter for other memory tips. If you get that message with no other applications open, you need to buy yourself some RAM, or you're going to be very irritated. Check out Chapter 17 for details on buying RAM.

Absolute Zero: System Freezes

Absolute zero is the temperature at which matter comes unglued (*Thanks, Mr. Wizard!*). A system freeze is what happens before *you* come unglued. Your screen locks up, and you can't do diddly. Kiss your unsaved work good-bye. Like a System Error (discussed earlier), it's hard to recover from a freeze, but you can do something.

Press the ⌘-**Option-Esc** key combination. If it works (it doesn't always), you'll get a warning saying, **Do you want to force the application** *(Whatever it is)* **to Quit? All unsaved changes will be lost.** Like you have a choice. Click on the **Quit** button. The cranky application will (probably) quit, but any other open applications and documents will be spared.

Freezes usually happen with a build up of crud in your Mac's RAM. If it happened in one application, it may happen in any others you have open. Save yourself the heartache: save, quit, and restart.

The Bomb Party

Applications crash for pretty much the same reasons the Finder crashes. You may want to sneak back to the "Problems in the Finder" section and review. Before you do, let me say this: There are different error codes for application crashes vs. Finder crashes vs. any other Macintosh mishap. None of them makes any sense to human beings.

You can, if you enjoy that sort of punishment, get tables of error codes and figure out what they all mean. They don't mean squat to the likes of you and me—well, not to me. I wouldn't know an "unimplemented trap" if I got my foot caught in one. Do yourself a favor: write down the error code, and call the technical support line at the company that wrote the program. Let them figure it out.

Problems with Documents

Sometimes, your Mac can behave like a cranky three-year-old. It stamps its digital feet. It holds its digital breath. It whines: "I don't wanna, and you can't make me!" Don't you believe it. In most circumstances, you *can* make it.

Application Missing and Other Snotty Remarks

Sometimes, when you double-click on a document's icon to launch the application that created it, you'll get some variation on the **Application Missing** message. Your Mac either offers to open the document with SimpleText, or it sits there like a shlub.

If you know deep down in your heart that the application is hiding somewhere on your hard drive, find the application's name with the **Find** command in the **File** or menus. When your Mac uncovers it, launch the application by double-clicking on its icon and trying to open the document with its **Open** command. If that doesn't open it (or even if it does), I'd rebuild my Desktop File (as explained in the beginning of this chapter).

If you know you don't have the application in question, you can always launch the closest application you have (a word processor for a text file, a painting program for a paint file, and so on), and try to open the document with that. If all else fails, there's always SimpleText. It can open some truly ornery files (as long as they're small).

Document Cannot Be Opened

Occasionally, even if you have the right application, files can't be opened. They get damaged, somehow, and unreadable. This is when a set of disk utilities comes in handy. Many of the utilities packages come with a file repair utility that will try to fix a file with spit-and-bailing wire so you can open it one last time and save a new and improved copy. If the file is total garbage (it happens sometimes), the utility can at least try to salvage some of the data from the file so you won't have to recreate all of it.

Not Enough Memory to Open Document

Either you've run out of RAM overall, or your application needs to have its memory allocation changed to deal with this document.

Whichever, you'll need to take some of the steps outlined in the "Digital Amnesia" section of this chapter.

File Is Locked

You can't do much more than read a locked file. That's why you lock it, for protection. Sometimes, like hiding a valuable thingy in a very safe place, you forget that you did it. Don't be ashamed; it happens to all of us. Close the file; then unlock it with the **Get Info** command in the **File** menu in the Finder.

Problems with Floppies

So it doesn't catch you by surprise, the answer to most of these will involve one of the utilities on your Disk Tools disk from your System software set or a commercial disk utility.

Disk Unreadable... Initialize?

That could mean you grabbed an unformatted disk. If you're sure you did, simply initialize it. If you inserted a disk that you *know* has data on it and your Mac says it can't read it, **Eject** it. Your disk has been damaged and become unreadable. Take a whack at it with Disk First Aid (on the Disk Tools disk) or another disk utility, and see whether it can be saved.

Please Insert Disk X

This was more of a problem with the earlier releases of System 7. I haven't run into it much with 7.5. If you build up a couple of disk icons on your desktop by ejecting disks (⌘-E) rather than putting them away (⌘-Y), when you finally try to put one away, your Mac will keep asking you to insert one or all of the other disks. You can make it stop by pressing the universal Macintosh stop command: ⌘-. **(period).** Your Mac will probably get huffy and put the disk away anyhow.

Of course, you can avoid this problem by putting your disks away instead of ejecting them, unless you're copying between two disks.

Operation Could Not Be Completed Because of a Write Error

Your disk drive burped while writing a file to disk. Try to save it again. If it doesn't work the second time, the disk may be bad. Save the file to a different disk. Take a pass at the bad one with Disk First Aid to see if it is bad, and if it can be saved. If it can't, see if you can salvage any data with a file recovery utility and throw that bad boy away.

Disk Full

What time is it when an elephant sits on your fence? Time to get a new fence. What time is it when you can't fit any more on a floppy disk? Time for a new floppy. If you get this message when saving to your hard drive, you may want to read the section on compression utilities in Chapter 16, the section of Chapter 11 on System junk you can throw away, or the section on shopping for a hard drive in Chapter 15.

Disk Won't Eject

You've tried to put a disk away, either by using the **Put Away** command (⌘-Y) in the **Special** menu, or by dragging its icon into the Trash. The icon went away, but the disk didn't come out of the drive. Yikes!

Don't panic. If you don't need the disk (or the drive), leave it there until you shut off your Mac. The next time you restart, your Mac will eject it (unless it has a System file on it). This isn't especially good for the disk or the drive, but it works.

If you do need the disk or drive right away, here's what you do: straighten one end of a pretty sturdy paper clip, just to the first bend. Gently, but firmly, insert the straightened part in the little hole to the right of your disk drive and push firmly. It will spit out the disk.

Disk Is Locked

Like a locked file, you can't do much with a locked disk except read its contents. You can't save to it, and you can't delete anything from it. That's why you lock it. If you do have to do anything other than read a file from the disk, eject it from the drive, push open the locking tab on the back, and reinsert it in the drive. Voilá. Remember to lock it again when you're done because you probably locked it for a reason.

Problems with Hard Drives

Most of the problems that can happen to floppy disks, explained earlier, can also happen to your hard drive (after all, it's only a big floppy disk). Because of the complications added by the extra hardware and the nature of SCSI devices, some other problems may crop up.

Where's the Drive?

If an *external* hard drive's icon fails to appear on your desktop, there may be a couple of things wrong:

➤ Check the obvious: plugged in, turned on, cables connected (and to the right port).

➤ Check your SCSI savvy (for details flip back to "Talk Scuzzy to Me" in Chapter 17, or "General Scuzziness" in this chapter).

➤ Did you turn on your external hard drive before you turned on your Mac? If not, turn the drive on, leave it on, and restart your Mac. (Or if you have one, you can use a disk mounting utility to mount the drive. SCSIProbe is a great one—and it's free—get a copy from your favorite MUG or online service.)

➤ If that doesn't do it, try testing the drive with Disk First Aid (or another hard drive utility), or updating its driver software with Apple's SC HD Setup utility.

➤ If that doesn't get it, you may have to reformat your drive (explained in Chapter 10—I hope you've been backing up your data regularly), or there may be a mechanical problem you'll need to get serviced.

Sloooowly, I Turned

Sometimes, the files on your hard drive seem to take forever to load. The problem may be caused by file fragmentation, where bits of your files are split up all over your hard drive. To fix file fragmentation, you need a disk utility package that includes a *disk analyzer* (to see if your disk is fragmented) and an *optimizer/defragmenter* (to fix the problem). These utilities are discussed in Chapters 10 and 16.

Digital Amnesia: Memory Problems

Random-access memory (RAM), or the lack of it, can cause you all sorts of hassles, especially with memory-greedy System 7 (remember, we're talking about RAM, not disk space). If you have a Mac with System 7.5 and only 4 MB of RAM, do yourself a favor: buy more. Flip back to Chapter 17 for information on adding RAM. Even if you have more than 4 MB of RAM, you can still run into difficulties. Here are the most common.

Out of Memory Messages

When you try to run a big, fat application, you may get a message that says something like, **This big, fat application prefers 1024K of memory to run, only 768K available** or **Not enough memory to open document.** Depending on how cranky the application is, it may ask you to quit any applications you have open, or it may ask whether you want to try to run the application anyway. You can try, but you'll probably need to change the application's memory allocation.

Similarly, if you can't open a document because of memory, you'll definitely have to change the application's memory allocation. Here's how do to it:

1. Quit the application in question.

2. Click on its icon to select it.

3. Select **Get Info** from the **File** menu (or press ⌘-**I**).

4. You'll get the application's **Get Info** window. In the bottom right corner is the Memory Requirements box.

   ➤ The *suggested size* is what the company recommends as an optimum memory setting. You can't change it.

   ➤ *Minimum size* is the least amount of memory you want the application to have. Double-click in the text box, and enter your minimum memory allocation. Generally, it can be a little less than the suggested size. If you change it and the application won't run, increase the minimum size until it will.

   ➤ *Preferred size* is the amount of memory you would like the application to have (in the best of all possible worlds). You change the number the same as you did the minimum size. Don't set the Preferred size to more memory than you have. Leave your System a little elbow room. Check to see how much memory your System uses with the **About This Macintosh** command in the menu.

5. Re-open the application. Your Mac will try to assign it the amount of memory specified in your *preferred size* setting. If that much isn't available, it will get as close as it can to that setting, without going below the *minimum size* setting.

Check Your Cache

If you frequently get **Out of Memory** messages, you can pare down your memory usage by limiting the amount of RAM set aside as a cache with the Memory Control Panel (discussed in Chapter 11).

Even a minimum cache (32K is the smallest) will help your Mac work a little more quickly, but anything over 256K runs smack into the law of diminishing returns. The memory you assign to the cache (over 256K) won't noticeably increase your Mac's effectiveness. You can free up a little RAM by reducing the size of the cache while still maintaining your Mac's performance.

Virtual Memory

In a pinch, you can fake your Mac into thinking you have more RAM than you actually do by turning on virtual memory, also in the Memory Control Panel. If your Mac can't handle virtual memory (Mac Classic, SE, LC, or Mac Plus), you won't even see the option in the Memory Control Panel. Don't panic; you aren't missing much.

With Virtual Memory turned on, you can select a hard drive to use as your fake RAM. You can create as much fake RAM as you have empty room on the selected hard drive.

If you have 4 megabytes of real RAM and 8 megabytes of free hard drive space, you can fake your Mac into thinking you have 8 megabytes of Virtual Memory. Why only 8, why not 12? Here's why: When you turn on Virtual Memory, your Mac will read in as much information as your real RAM can hold (in this example 4 MB). When you want it to read in more stuff (say, from another application), first your Mac will write all of the information already in RAM to the space you assigned on your hard drive. Then it dumps that memory from RAM and reads in the new stuff. When you want to read in the old stuff again, it writes the new stuff to your hard drive, then reads the old stuff back into RAM. (Are you confused yet?)

So the total amount of RAM you have (your real RAM, plus your fake) can't total more than the amount of hard drive space you have to write it all in, because it has to be able to hold all of that information. That's also why it's a bad idea to use virtual memory to create more than double your real RAM: your Mac will spend all of its time reading and writing the data that won't fit in your real RAM. If you have 4 MB of RAM, don't set Virtual Memory to more than 8 MB, even if you have the hard disk real estate to spare.

In addition to being confusing, virtual memory will also slow down your Mac incredibly (all that reading and writing of data takes time—lots and lots of time). It's okay for infrequent, emergency use, but if you find yourself using Virtual Memory on a regular basis, you should bite the bullet and buy more real RAM.

Defragmenting RAM

Just as your hard drive's storage space can become fragmented, so can your RAM. Here's the scenario:

You have 6 MB of RAM (6144K). Your System takes 2 MB (2048K) of RAM (because of all those funky extensions you use). You open your word processor to write a blistering letter to the editor of your favorite Mac magazine. Your word processor (MondoHuge Words version 6.1.3x) uses 3 MB (3072K) of memory. When you finish, you send the letter to your laser printer, automatically opening Print Monitor, which uses another 64K of memory. While you wait for that letter to print, you decide to play a hand of Solitaire with a shareware game that uses 384K. While you're playing Solitaire, the printer finishes, and the Print Monitor goes away.

The phone rings. Someone wants to make an appointment with you, so you call up your planning calendar, which uses 640K of memory. Your Mac protests: **Not enough memory.**

If you do the math:

System RAM:	6144K
System:	–2048K
MondoHuge:	–3072K
Subtotal:	1024K
Print Monitor:	– 64K
Solitaire:	–384K
Total available:	576K

There's not enough memory left to open your 640K calendar program. Ah-ha! you say. The Print Monitor shut down, freeing up another 64K. You should be able to open the calendar. In theory, that's right, but memory isn't like a pool where all the bits of memory float around and can get sucked up by whatever application needs them. Instead it's like—oh, let's say a loaf of French bread.

Each application cuts off a chunk to make a sandwich of a particular size. Your System software cuts a chunk and keeps it. The word processor cuts a chunk and keeps it. Print Monitor cuts a small chunk, and Solitaire cuts a small chunk. When the Print Monitor finishes, it puts its chunk of bread back on the table, right where it took it from. There's a gap between it and the chunk left at the end. Instead of having one big chunk left to make a real sandwich, there's two little chunks left with the Solitaire program's missing chunk separating them. Neither chunk is big enough to make your calendar program's sandwich. In order to unite those two chunks, you'd have to quit the Solitaire program.

When Solitaire tosses its chunk back on the table, the three chunks come back together again to form one very big chunk (if only real bread did this). Then you can open the calendar program. (All this talk of sandwiches is making me hungry. You?) In other words, memory is only available in chunks. When you free up chunks that aren't concurrent (right beside each other), you can only open an application that's as big as the biggest chunk available. Your RAM is fragmented. In order to open a big application, you'd have to close an application between those chunks of memory.

Here's how to avoid fragmenting your memory: If you always use a certain application (or applications), open it (them) first. Then open the applications you use only briefly or occasionally. When you close them, then you'll free up bigger blocks of memory.

If you know anything about accounting, it's like the LIFO theory: *last in, first out.* When trying to free up RAM, close the applications in reverse order of how you opened them: *last opened, first closed.*

Adding More RAM

Your best defense against these and any other RAM-related difficulties is to add more RAM. You won't regret it. Here are the Top 10 Reasons to Add More RAM:

10. No matter what anyone tells you, it *is* the size of your RAM that counts.

9. It's cheaper than buying a new Mac.

8. You'll actually be able to use the spell and grammar checkers that came with your word processor.

7. Buy enough RAM, and you'll be able to keep all of your applications open all of the time.

6. Applications almost never get smaller.

5. Applications almost always get bigger.

4. You'll need lots of RAM to do all the weird and wonderful things you'll be able to do with freeware and shareware extensions and control panels.

3. You'll need it if you get into PostScript fonts and Adobe Type Manager, or if you want to try QuickDraw GX.

2. You'll need it if you want to add a CD-ROM drive, scanner, or other funky multimedia tools. Animation and other way-cool multimedia stuff (like big sound files) take oodles of RAM.

1. You can reduce your stress level when you eliminate most (if not all) of those annoying out-of-memory messages.

In order to use more than 8 MB of RAM in your Mac, you have to turn on the 32-bit addressing function in the Memory Control Panel (as discussed in Chapter 11). Otherwise, your Mac will ignore any memory over 8 MB. However, not all Macs can use 32-bit addressing, specifically: Mac II, IIx, IIcx, and SE/30 models. These particular Mac models can't handle it. Don't despair. You can get a hold of Mode-32, by Connectix, which will allow these older Mac models to use over 8 MB of memory. You can get it free (well, almost free) from Apple, by calling 1-800-776-2333. You also can download it from Apple's areas on eWorld and America Online. There is a System 7.5 compatible version available.

Peripheral Neuropathy

Sometimes, our Macs are working fine, but all of a sudden—bam! One of the bloody accessories decides it's time to blow some smoke up our shorts. There are easy ways to deal with many of the common problems that don't involve sending your peripherals out for repairs.

Eek! The Mouse!

Our mice can seem to get lazy: they don't want to move the pointer as far as we moved the mouse. There are a couple reasons that may be happening.

Don't ask me why this happens, but it does: if the mouse cable gets too snarled and tangled around itself like a phone cord, it gets cranky. Unplug it from the ADB port (while your Mac is turned off, naturally). Hold the plug-end at eye level while the mouse-end dangles, spins, and untangles itself. It can work wonders for a sluggish mouse.

The other thing you can do is clean it. Turn your mouse over on its back. There's a ring around the gray ball that locks it into place. Turn the ring (there is an arrow to show you which direction), and remove it. Remove the ball. Clean it with some rubbing alcohol, and set it aside. With a cotton swab (or one of those spongy, lint-free numbers), clean off the three rollers inside the mouse. They're usually white or a clear plastic color. They turn black when they're dirty: the black stuff is built-up dust, oils, and other ka-ka. Just clean them. Pop the ball back in, lock on the locking ring, and try it out. It should work much better.

Keyboard Acrobatics

Unless you cover your keyboard when it's not in use, it's a prime place for crud buildup. I find an occasional blast of compressed air (the kind without those nasty chlorofluorocarbons, thank you very much) right between the keys will go a long way towards keeping the keyboard crud-free. You can also unplug it from your Mac (while it's turned off, of course), turn it upside down, and give it a good shake. Big chunks of crud may come floating out.

If the keys begin to stick, you can *carefully* pry out the offending key and swab around it with an alcohol swab. That should ungunk it. Another shot of compressed air may help, too. (It is possible to open some keyboards and clean inside. I don't recommend it for anyone who's the least bit nervous about it.)

If your keyboard is giving you a whole lot of grief, it may be time for a new one, or a visit to your Local Authorized Apple Dealer for a checkup.

My Printer Won't Print

As always, check the obvious first: plugged in, turned on, connected properly to your Mac. If all that's okay, open the **Chooser** from the menu. Make sure that the correct driver is selected and configured for your printer.

If you fail to find the problem there (especially for laser printers), take a long look at the document you're printing: does it have four or five fonts or a complicated graphic; or is legal-sized paper selected? It may be overwhelming your laser's memory. There may be too many things for it to cope with. Try removing the graphic or changing the fonts to simplify the document, and print it again. Or print a basic text file of "Mary Had a Little Lamb" as a test. If it prints this time, the complicated document is to blame: remember the KISS rule (Keep It Simple, Stupid). You either have to learn to limit yourself to simpler documents, or you have to buy more memory for your printer.

My Printer Prints Badly

If the problem is jagged text from a laser printer (or any printer with ATM installed), you're probably using a font that isn't built into the printer and that you don't have a printer font for in your Font folder. Using the application you used to create the document, check to see which font is selected (Caslon Bold Italic, for example), and then look in your Font folder to make sure that the printer font is installed. If it isn't, scrounge up the disk it came on, and re-install it. (See Chapters 13 and 14 for more information on printers and fonts.) If you don't have the correct printer font, you'll have to live with jagged text, or switch to a font you do have a printer font for.

If it's a font used in a painting or drawing program, don't hurt yourself with all this looking. It stopped being a font when you put it in a picture. Now it's a picture of a font, and will look jagged regardless.

If the problem is icky, dark streaks across your laser printout, your printer is dirty. You can clean the rollers (after you let them cool down) with an alcohol wipe or swab, or print the Cleaning Page file that came with your printer driver disk.

Icky, light streaks, on the other hand, mean you're probably running out of toner. Remove the toner cartridge, and rock it gently (like you had to do when you installed it). This will redistribute the toner that's left so you'll get a little more mileage out of it. Meanwhile, buy another one.

Not just easy, cheap too! Plain isopropyl alcohol is perfect for many technoid cleaning jobs (if you haven't noticed). I always keep a bottle of it and a box of swabs nearby at all times. Call me the Heloise of Macintosh.

A streaky printout with a dot-matrix printer means either your ribbon is shot (it probably had a hole punched in it) or your print head is dirty. Remove the ribbon, and check it for holes; replace it if necessary. If that isn't it, try cleaning the print head with alcohol on a swab, and then print a test page without the ribbon. That should clear it up.

A streaky printout from an inkjet printer means the print head is probably clogged. Try cleaning it with an alcohol swab. You may also be running low on ink.

315

Print Monitor Errors

Print Monitor is good about letting you know when things go wrong. If your printer is out of paper, it will let you know. If it doesn't have enough memory, it will ask politely before it snatches some more. Depending on how you have Print Monitor configured, the messages will pop up on your screen and discretely signal you from the **Application** menu, or just beep. See Chapter 13 for your configuration options. Your best bet is to do what Print Monitor tells you to do; it usually knows best.

General Scuzziness

As I said earlier in Chapter 17, dealing with the requirements of building a functional SCSI chain is a weird and wonderful experience. The closer you come to the six SCSI device limit, the weirder it becomes. These are the rules (explained in more detail in Chapter 17, but worth repeating here):

➤ You can only add six SCSI devices to your Mac.

➤ You must set each one with a different SCSI ID number (1–6).

➤ The first (physically closest to your Mac, usually an internal hard drive) and last (the one furthest away from your Mac) items in the chain must be terminated.

➤ The total amount of SCSI cable connecting your chain cannot exceed more than 20–24 feet in length (unless you install a signal booster before the 20-foot mark).

➤ All of these rules are subject to change at any moment.

I know folks who followed these rules to the letter, and their SCSI chain didn't work. I've known others who didn't follow one of these rules, and their SCSI chains worked fine. Go figure. My best advice, when faced with a SCSI problem, is to try anything and everything possible with your combination of devices. Either that, or at the first sign of trouble, call the technical support line for your latest SCSI device, and ask them for help.

Pick a Card: When PDS and NuBus Cards Go Flaky

Short of using the hardware diagnostic tools (like Apple's Personal Diagnostics, seen in Chapter 16), the simplest thing to do when an expansion card starts to get flaky is this:

Pop the hood on your Mac (if you're comfortable doing it, and bearing in mind that it may void your Mac's warranty), and check to be sure that the card is still firmly seated in its slot. Sometimes, vibrations (you pounding on the keyboard, footsteps, or heavy traffic) may shake your cards loose. Look to see that the bottom of the card is fully in the slot (little golden prongs, like fingers, will be exposed if it isn't). If it's loose, gently but firmly push the card back in. Be careful: cards are fragile (not *that* fragile, but you can break them if you push too hard or in the wrong direction).

If the idea of doing that gives you the jimjams, don't do it. Call your Local Authorized Apple Service Center and let them check it out. It's not worth the gray hair.

When All Else Fails...

Read the manual.

Okay, Now You Can Panic

Just kidding; you really don't have to panic. If things still aren't working, pick up the phone and call technical support.

Before you pick up the phone, there are a few things you should have handy:

➤ A list of any error messages you received.

➤ A list of everything you tried to fix the problem.

➤ The make and model of the hardware in question, or the name and version number of the software.

Technical support, typically, means the part of a software or hardware company devoted to answering technical questions about their product. I expand the definition to include anyone I can call in a pinch—user group members, Mac friends, and so on—especially because many companies have added 900-numbers, pay-per-minute technical support lines.

317

➤ Your system configuration: Mac model, System software version, amount of RAM, any and all peripherals, and what port they are connected to.

➤ A list of the other software that was running at the time, including version numbers.

➤ A list of the contents of your System Folder: especially your extensions and control panels.

➤ A pen and paper for taking notes.

If you have all that together, take three deep breaths, and calm down. You're ready to dial.

Making the Call

First, try to call from a phone that's close to your Mac so you can try suggestions right then and there, without having to run back and forth or play telephone tag.

When you call technical support, the first thing you should write down is the name of the person helping you: if you have to call back about the same problem, ask for her by name so you won't have to explain everything all over again. The person you spoke to will probably remember you (with a little prompting—after all, they take a lot of phone calls). Remember: be nice. These people are there to help you. They didn't write the software; they didn't build the hardware. Be fair and give them a chance.

Also, be clear and precise: "I'm having trouble with the Mac so-and-so hardware/software, model/version number. I'm using it on a Mac LC 575 with 10 megs of RAM and an 80 meg hard drive running System 7.5. When I try to do this, this happens." She will ask questions: what applications were you running, what extensions? That's why you put all that system information together before you called.

You should write down all suggestions and the results. If it works, you have it on paper for future reference. If it doesn't, you have it on paper so you know what you've tried. This is pure sleuthing, a process of elimination. Nine times out of ten, you'll get a solution. Tech-support people answer many calls, see many of the same problems, and know what to do right away. Sometimes, it takes awhile—she may even have to chase down another technical-type and call you back.

I Can't Get No Satisfaction

Technical support people are people. Some are good at their job, some are bad, some are good but having a bad day. If you can't reach a satisfactory resolution with one, ask to speak to a supervisor. Keep taking names, keep on moving up the chain of command until you hit the CEO, if necessary (not that the CEO will know how to fix your problem—if she does, buy stock in the company). Chances are you'll never have to go that far, but… who knows?

You can always resort to letter-writing campaigns by the members of all the MUGs you've joined, and phone calls to the Better Business Bureau. Meanwhile, you should be working the network I talk about establishing in the next chapter, calling on your other resources.

The Least You Need to Know

Things go wrong for a reason. Once you've shot a few troubles on your own, you'll begin to get a handle on what kinds of things cause what kinds of problems. It only takes a little practice. Hopefully, this chapter will act as a primer, helping you along as you become a do-it-yourself kind of Mac troubleshooter. Whatever troubles you encounter, keep these four thoughts in mind:

➤ Don't panic.

➤ Check the obvious—more and more things will fall into the "obvious" category as your Mac skills increase.

➤ Solutions that don't work are not failures, they're the elimination of possibilities. Troubleshooting is a process of trial and error. It can be a trial and you will make errors.

➤ Call for help wherever you can, whenever you can, especially if you feel intimidated by a problem.

Getting a Grip

Right now, I'd be content to see you close this book and go on your merry Macintosh way. Not happy, mind you—just content. I think you've absorbed enough information (or at least remember where to find it) that you can cope with the day-to-day stuff, and even some of the more unusual problems that arise.

Nothing really bad or bizarre will ever happen. Your Mac will start up the first time, every time. You'll never hit a major snag in an application. Files will never get damaged. System software upgrades will be compatible with every piece of software you own.

However, cynic that I am (and I seem to get more cynical every day), I know that poop happens. This chapter is about preparing for it, and dealing with it. Since no book (or person) can anticipate every single thing that could go wrong with your Mac, you'll discover some resources in this chapter to help you out when poop happens—sort of a paperback pooper scooper.

Plan Ahead

Everyone knows how to deal with a crisis reactively: the poop hits the fan, and you freak out. You just react to the crisis. Right now, you may be primed for a major freak-out. You go chugging along, using your newly acquired Mac knowledge happy as a clam, and blam! Your Mac goes berserk, and you freak. I don't want you to freak. I want you to be *proactive*. You should try to anticipate the crises before they happen, either to avoid them or to be prepared when problems eventually happen.

Keeping a fire extinguisher in your kitchen is proactive. Marshaling your personal resources (saving for a rainy day) in the event of a crisis is also proactive. You may have already done a few proactive things without even knowing it. If you sent in the registration card on your Mac and any software you bought, that's proactive. You've let the companies know that you bought their product and you may come looking for help if something goes wrong. If you bought an AppleCare service contract to keep your Mac's warranty up and running for an extra couple of years, that's very proactive. However, there's more you can do.

Join the Mac Community

One thing's for sure: computer geeks love to talk shop. Most of us do, anyway. It makes us feel smart. When you're in your local computer store (buying disks or just cruising the new software racks), talk to folks. Ask their opinions on stuff.

Befriend a salesclerk, preferably one who knows her stuff about Macintosh. Introduce yourself. Learn her name and say hello when you walk in. Always ask for her help when you're ready to buy something; she'll really appreciate that if her paycheck's based on a percentage of her sales. If she knows you, she'll be more likely to help you in the future. Aside from the help aspect, clerks often get advance information on (and even demo versions of) new software and hardware. They may let you play undisturbed on the store's Mac so you can try stuff out before you buy it.

MUGs-head Revisited

Earlier, I talked briefly about the benefits of joining a Mac User Group (or MUG). Getting access to libraries of freeware and shareware is incentive enough to join, but there's more. Joining a MUG also puts you in touch with many people who are in touch with many people who are in touch—ad infinitum—with many other Mac users.

There probably isn't anything that can happen to your Mac that hasn't happened to at least a few other people in your MUG. Even if, by some outrageous twist of fate, something new and completely off-the-wall happens to your Mac, it will be reassuring to pick up the phone and hear a calm, rational voice say, "Hmm. That's bizarre, but don't panic. Let me see what I can find out." And you sigh with relief knowing that you're not alone with your problem.

MUGs also publish newsletters with news that's important to Macintosh users. Sometimes, the big, glossy magazines can be a little out-of-touch with the needs of us every day computer users who don't have $5,000–$10,000 to blow on the editor's idea of a must-have piece of hardware.

Magazines

Another way to anticipate difficulties is by subscribing to a Mac magazine. Right now, you can pick up three Mac-specific magazines at your local newsstand: *Macworld*, *MacUser*, and *Mac Home Journal*.

Getting a magazine (and reading it) can keep you abreast of the latest developments in the Mac community. You'll also get reviews of software and hardware, upgrade announcements, and columns devoted to various tips and tricks that could help you out of a jam.

The Life Online

If you have a modem, you can also make all kinds of contacts through electronic services and bulletin boards. I know I've talked about them before, but they're just so useful.

I've often solved big, big problems with the help of people I've never met, just by posting a note in an appropriate area of America Online (usually the Hardware and Mac Operating System Forums) and other services. Mostly, it has been application or peripheral specific, but that's because when your Mac itself takes a nose-dive, it's hard to connect to a computer service.

Additionally, there are electronic magazines online—call them e-zines, 'zines, or whatever—that can be far more current than any traditionally published fare (since there isn't the long printing process to slow down distribution). *TidBITS* and *Info-Mac Digest* are two, and there seem to be new ones every day.

The long and short of it is that online services and bulletin boards are an excellent resource for help, information, and moral support. I won't beat it into the ground, though. Well, maybe just a little.

Computer Shows

Computer shows are another great place to meet all kinds of computer users. They're the traveling sideshows of the '90s. If you live in or near a big metropolitan area, chances are one or two will pass your way each year. You'll see ads in your local paper or flyers in the computer store. They aren't always the best for Mac users (since many of them focus primarily on IBM-compatible machines and software), but there are some for us, like the traveling Mac show.

In addition to vendors getting you to buy junk, there are usually workshops and discussion groups about all kinds of uses for your Mac. At the good shows, some of the workshops are basic; some are very advanced and specialized. There's something for every level of Mac user.

If a traveling Mac show never hits your neck of the woods, but you can afford to travel, there's always Macworld. Macworld is a huge exposition that seems to be held almost daily somewhere in the world. There are also shows held in Canada, Japan, and other fun-filled locations around the world. The big two are held in Boston, MA in August and in San Francisco, CA in January. This exposition is put together by *Macworld* magazine, and it's the showplace where all the Macintosh-related companies try to unveil their new products. (I say *try* because in the rush of getting things ready, they often miss little details, such as getting their product to work—not that I'm bitter or anything.)

Working Your Network

Once you've surrounded yourself with as many Mac friends as you can muster, you're in a prime position to compare notes, receive advice and help, and grow into a Macintosh guru in your own right. It won't take long.

Your best troubleshooting tool when you hit a snag is your telephone. Call your Mac friends. Call the clerk you befriended at the store where you bought the troublesome product. Call technical support at the company that makes that pesky product. (For more on getting good technical support, see Chapter 21.)

I get plenty of calls from people I know wanting advice or help: Elizabeth was trying to decide between two Macs, which one would give her the most bang for her buck? Ted had a floppy disk stuck in his Mac Plus's drive (this was only yesterday, by the way) and couldn't get it out. While I was tinkering with it, he drilled me about a good, simple telecommunications program for hooking into the Internet.

Ask all the questions you can when possible (bribing with coffee, lunch, and/or a nice gift as necessary), and find your way. One day soon, you'll be asked to return the favor and help another Mac novice go along and get along. Won't that be nice?

The nature of Macintosh is such that once you master a concept, you can usually apply it across the range of Macintosh applications and hardware. The simple act of using a word processor, graphics application, or other program—and knowing what you like and don't like about it—gives you valuable experience. It's valuable to you because you never have to deal with the issue again. It's even more valuable to others who may not want to deal with the issue at all.

Fasten Your Seat Belts. It's Going to Be a Bumpy Ride

There's an old Chinese curse that goes, "May you live in interesting times." In terms of Macintosh, the times are interesting, indeed. There are some big, big changes lurking on just the other side of the horizon (there's more about them in Chapter 2).

Some of the changes have already started: consider Apple's devotion to the new line of Power Macs; new ventures with former rival IBM; the launching of their own online service, eWorld; and the next generation of Newton technology. Any or all of these changes and advances may pose some sticky puzzles for old-school Mac users. You may need all the help you can get just to keep up. Like the White Queen says in *Alice in Wonderland* (or is it *Through the Looking Glass?*), "Around here it takes a whole lot of running just to stay in the same place."

What does that mean to you now? Maybe nothing; maybe everything. Apple is preparing some major changes in the way Macs work. Along with change, there's always a period of awkward adjustment. Some new things don't quite work right; some old things that used to work don't on new machines or updated versions of the Mac OS; and some things that sounded good in theory are kind of wonky in practice. Change is good, but it can be, at times, traumatic and problematic.

The point is that in order for you to decide if you want to play along, you'll have to know what's up Apple's sleeve. Staying tied into the Mac community is one way to do that. If you decide to play the Power Mac game, then you'll need the help and support of others who may have a better handle on the rules of the game. If you decide not to play, you'll definitely need the support of your peers as applications and hardware stop being backward-compatible with older Macintosh models.

Besides, once you're hooked into the Mac community's grapevine, you can just sit back and watch the poop fly, all smug and self-satisfied because you saw what was coming and purchased a plastic slicker and a big umbrella.

The Least You Need to Know

I could boil down this little list even further: BE PREPARED. But that would rob me of my chance to tell you to join a user group again, so I won't do it.

➤ Every Mac user you meet is a potential resource for you. Learn how to win friends and influence people.

➤ I can't say this often enough: Join a Macintosh User Group (MUG).

➤ When you run into a problem you can't handle, pick up the phone or dash off some e-mail. There's no shame in admitting you need help.

➤ The computer times, they are a'changing. You have to stay connected to the Mac community if you want to keep up.

DUDE, WHAT'S ERGONOMICS?

I DON'T KNOW, DUDE... I THINK I FLUNKED IT...

Speak Like A Geek: The Complete Archive

68K Mac   Since the introduction of the Power Mac, Macs based on Motorola 68000 chips have become generically known as "68K Macs."

active   With windows (and applications), *active* and *inactive* mean pretty much what you'd expect. An active window is the one that is foremost on your screen. All of its details, such as the stripes in the title bar and the dot pattern in the scroll bars, are right where they should be. You can work in or with this window. All of the windows that are behind the active window will be stripeless and dotless. These windows are inactive. You can't do anything with them unless you click on them to bring them to the front.

ADB   Stands for Apple Desktop Bus (pronounced by saying each letter, "A-D-B"). The Apple Desktop Bus is the standard way of connecting mice, keyboards, and a few other peripherals to the Mac. The Desktop Bus has been standard since Apple introduced the Macintosh SE. (Before the SE, they used connectors that looked like the ones that connect your telephone cord to the wall jack—in case the question ever comes up in Trivial Pursuit or something.)

alert box   An *alert box* will warn you (alert you, even) that you're about to do something you may not want to do. If you close a file without saving any changes you made, you'll lose those changes. The alert box just wants to be sure you really, really want to do whatever you just told your Mac to do. You can tell it to carry out your order, or you can cancel the order. It's up to you, and your Mac won't give you any more lip about it.

backup   A spare or emergency copy of something. You can *back up* your hard drive, make a *backup* copy of a program or data disk, or even back up a single file. Although everybody should back up their data on a regular basis, the only folks who actually do it are the ones who have been traumatized by the loss of an important file.

capacity   How much something holds. In many Mac-related usages, it denotes how much stuff you can cram onto a diskette or hard drive.

clip art   A collection of graphic images meant to be copied and pasted into other documents.

compressed   A file that has been mashed down with a *file compression utility* to take up less disk space. *Compressed* files have to be *decompressed* (unmashed) before you can work with them.

cursor   There are a variety of *cursors* you will use on your Mac. One is the arrow. You control cursors with your mouse and use them to point at and select items on your Mac's screen.

DA   See *Desk Accessories*.

Desk Accessories   DAs are mini-applications that let you do a variety of things. Why call them *Desk Accessories* instead of little applications? Because you can call them up and use them no matter where you are or what you're doing on your Mac. Instead of being full-featured applications, most Desk Accessories will help you do one or two little things (jot a note, add a couple of numbers, and so on).

desktop publishing   Literally *publishing from the top of your desk*, as opposed to having to pack up all your text and woes and send them to a typesetter and printer.

dialog box   Sometimes, when you give your Mac a command (like to *open* or *save* a file), your Mac requests more information to complete the task. Macs get this information by using *dialog boxes*. They're called dialog boxes because the Mac asks you a question and you answer it. That's a dialog—short and sweet.

dip switches   Little teeny-tiny switches (like microscopic light switches) that you have to use a pencil-point or other teeny-tiny thing to flip because most fingers are too big to do it. They must have been invented by a dip. You generally find them on the backsides of SCSI devices.

disk(ette)   Storage media for computers. The first floppies were big, 8-inch monsters made of a soft plastic that sort of flopped—well, it moved anyhow. Then came those 5.25-inch disks, favorites by many DOS users. When 3.5-inch disks were introduced, they called them *diskettes* (because they're so small and cute). But you can call them disks if you want.

dither(ed)   If a person is in a dither, they're all confused. When a picture is *dithered*, the dots that make it up are all confused. The dots get jumbled and tinkered with so the eye is faked into seeing many more shades of gray than are really there. Dithering reduces the quality of an image by making it look blurry.

document   Just about any file you produce with an application is called a *document*. Your Mac calls these files "documents" to easily distinguish them from applications and folders.

dots   There are many words used in computing to distinguish one kind of dot from another. In a printout, dots are just called *dots* (as in *dots per inch*) when they make up letters and lines. On your monitor, each dot is called a *pixel*, borrowed from the terminology of television design. It's a contracted form of **picture element.** In drawing and in fonts, a dot that is part of a letter or line is called a *bit* because it takes one *bit* (the smallest unit of memory) to create and place that dot somewhere.

download(-able)   If you use a font in a document that isn't already in your laser printer's memory, the printer sends a message to your Mac asking it to send that font down. The process is called a *download*, or downloading, and also applies to file transfers between computers. A font that can be sent to a laser printer is called a *downloadable font.*

electronic bulletin board (BBS)   These are just plain folks who (when you have a *modem*) let you access a wide variety of files and information on their computer(s). *BBSs* are usually small, home-grown services that charge little or nothing for you to join them, unlike commercial online services.

environment   In computerese, the *environment* is much like the environment of the world at large or your "work environment." It's the atmosphere, surroundings, and even the decor of your computer. The Macintosh environment is graphical and sometimes called a graphical user interface or GUI, (pronounced "GOO-ey") because it uses pictures (icons) to represent functions and operations.

ergonomics   The science of designing things to accommodate the natural shape and motion of the human body. The bridge of the Starship Enterprise is very ergonomically designed. It's from the Greek word "erg" which denotes a unit of work. Or it's a cross between "ergo" and "economics" because any product that boasts "sleek, ergonomic styling" will cost 50% more than its nonergonomic competitor.

export   The capability of an application to save a file in a format easily imported by another application, usually with the **Save As** command.

fat binary   Software that's written to run on any Macintosh (including Power Macs) is written in what's called *fat binary* so that it can take full advantage of whatever Mac you own. For example, before System 7.5, Macs, Performas, and Power Macs each had their own versions of the Mac OS. Now they can all run System 7.5 because it's written *fat.* Unfortunately, that means the application itself is fat and takes up a lot of space on your hard drive.

format   See *initialize.*

FPU   *Floating Point Unit*, a chip that relieves the CPU of the burden of doing mathematical calculations, thereby giving the Mac some added speed. They're sometimes called math chips or math co-processors. Believe it or not, many spreadsheets and other applications that you think of as obviously math-related (calculators, and so on) don't make use of an FPU. Go figure.

fragment (-ation, -ing)   *Fragmenting* occurs when you save data to your hard drive, and your Mac has to stash it as quickly as possible. It writes it in whatever space it can find, which is not necessarily all together. You can wind up with files being *fragmented*: a bit-bit here, a bit-bit there. That's okay in terms of *writing* the file, but when you want to use that file later, your Mac has to search all over your disk to find all those bits, which can slow your Mac down.

freeware   A special kind of software that is free for your use. Its partner is *shareware.*

GUI   *Graphical user interface*, pronounced "GOO-ey." It's an interface (like Mac's) that uses pictures to represent functions, rather than all typed commands.

Hayes-compatible   A term that identifies a modem which conforms to the standard set of modem commands developed by the Hayes Corporation. *Hayes compatibility* is fairly standard among modems. I wouldn't mess with one that isn't—it will complicate your life unnecessarily.

highlight color/highlighted   Your Mac wants to show you when you've selected an item. Icons go dark. Text, including the names of files and folders, gets washed with a color.

import   The capability of an application to take a document created with one application and use it itself.

inactive   See *active*.

initialize   Initializing, or formatting, a floppy disk is like cutting up a pizza into easy-to-manage, easy-to-eat slices. A whole blank disk is just too hard for a Mac to eat in one quick sitting, so it cuts it up into smaller, easier-to-read sections. It then writes a map of the different areas so it can keep track of where it put things (this map is the *Desktop file*). That makes it easy for the Mac to find things quickly when you ask for them.

insertion point (or cursor)   The vertical line that moves ahead of your typing to show you where the next thing you type will land.

jaggies   The rough edges of letters and drawings that would be smooth if it weren't for the limitations of computer (and monitor) technology.

launch   To start an application. It can also be called *starting* or *opening* an application or program.

modem   An electronic device that allows your Mac to interact with a distant computer over phone lines.

multitasking   A geeky way of saying "doing more than one thing at a time." In computing, it generally means running more than one program simultaneously.

network   An assortment of computers and peripherals linked together. In its simplest terms, a *network* can be as small as one Mac hooked up with one laser printer via AppleTalk. At its most extreme, a network can be dozens of Macs hooked up to each other, as well as to several printers.

NuBus   A high-speed slot that accepts cards that work along with your Mac's central processor to supplement its functions. The information is fed along a data path called a *bus*, like your Mac's ADB (Apple Desktop *Bus*) that feeds your Mac information from your mouse and keyboard.

online service   These are companies and just plain folks who let you (if you have a *modem*) access a wide variety of files and information on their computer(s). *Online service* generally refers to corporate entities, and everything you do with the service costs you some money. CompuServe, America Online, and PRODIGY are online services.

PDS   *Processor Direct Slot.* A slot that feeds information directly into the central processor of your Mac, rather than through a bus.

parallel printers (and/or ports)   Receive bits of information in sets of eight. Most IBM-compatible computers come with two parallel ports, so parallel printers are popular for them.

partition   A *partition* on a hard drive is like a partition in a house. It's a wall that divides one section of your hard drive from another. Creating a partition is *destructive*: you'll erase everything from your hard drive. You need to copy *everything* onto floppies before you try this, so you can copy it all back when you're done. See Chapter 10 for details.

peripheral   An add-on piece of equipment, like a printer, that's not essential to operate the computer—like extra options on a car, you don't need air conditioning to use the car, but it makes it more comfortable. I think the term came about back in the days when you could only add things, like hard drives, as external options that sat on your desk in the periphery of your computer. Nowadays, the term is used vaguely. An internal hard drive can be considered a *peripheral*, as can a keyboard and a monitor, but try and run a computer without them.

point size   A font term borrowed from typesetters. One point is approximately 1/72 of an inch. Point is abbreviated pt. (as in 12-pt.).

propeller-head   An adjective used to describe someone fascinated by the technical minutiae of computing. From the famous propeller beanies kids used to wear. Also known as *toy brains*.

proprietary   The property of, or specific to, a particular computer or service.

SCSI   Pronounced scuzzy. It stands for *Small Computer Systems Interface*. It's another way of connecting peripherals to computers.

scan(ned, -ner)   A *scanner* is a piece of hardware that converts text, photographs, or line drawings into digital information that you can use on your computer. You *scan* a page. A *scanned* image is a *scan*.

screen name   Literally, the name that appears on the screen whenever you "speak" to someone else on an electronic service, such as America Online or CompuServe. Try to pick one that suits your personality.

serial (printers and/or ports)   *Serial ports* are standard on all Macs. The printer and modem ports are both serial ports. Serial ports send or receive bits of information *serially*, that is, one at a time.

shareware   To use this kind of software, you pay a fee (generally small) directly to the program's author. Always pay your *shareware* fees.

stationery pad   Behaves like its real-world counterpart. A document saved as stationery, when opened in an application, appears as a new, untitled document, so the original *stationery pad* is never altered. This format is ideal for letterheads, form letters, or any other kind of file or information you use frequently with only minor changes.

SYSOP(s)   Short for *System Operator*(s), pronounced "SIS-op." That's the propeller-head in charge of an electronic bulletin board.

technical support   Typically, it means the part of a software or hardware company devoted to answering technical questions about their product. I expand the definition to include anyone I can call in a pinch—user-group members, Mac-friends, and so on—especially because many companies have added 900-numbers, pay-per-minute technical support lines.

The Mac   Okay, okay, technically this isn't a definition *per se*, but it will help you to speak like an honest-to-goodness geek. While saying (or writing) something on the order of "the Macintosh is such-and-such" is *grammatically* correct, *real* Mac-heads omit the "the."

third party   Not the party you go to after the first two. *Third party* refers to a company that isn't you and isn't Apple. Most often, they're referred to as *third-party developers*.

utility   Generic name for computer software that does something "useful," without necessarily producing a finished product. Diagnostic, disk repair, and screensaver programs are all *utilities*.

version number   The (re)incarnation of the software. Version 1.0 is its debut. Version 1.2 will fix everything that should have been fixed before 1.0 was released. Version 2.0 will be its next incarnation.

Version 2.1 will fix the new incarnation, and so on. When the first number changes (1.0 to 2.0), it's called a *version upgrade*, a major overhaul. 2.0 to 2.1 means it's still essentially the same program, but now it works. Versions such as 2.1 are sometimes called *bug fixes*.

virtual memory *Virtual memory* uses part of your hard drive as a substitute for RAM. The information that normally gets stored in RAM gets written to an area on your hard disk. Virtual memory can fake applications into thinking you have more RAM than you really do.

virus A nasty bit of programming, usually hidden inside legitimate software, designed to mess with your computer. Some are harmless, flashing a message on your screen. Others are destructive, scrambling all of the data on your hard drive. All of them are a pain in the hindquarters. Many utility packages come with virus detection and deletion components.

Index

E

F

343